Alaska

Alaska

Promises to Keep

Robert B. Weeden

Houghton Mifflin Company
Boston 1978

Library of Congress Cataloging in Publication Data

Weeden, Robert B.
Alaska, promises to keep.

Includes bibliographical references and index.
1. Alaska—Economic conditions. 2. Alaska—
Social Conditions. Natural resources—Alaska.
I. Title.

HC107.A45W43   309.1'798'05   78-16121
ISBN 0-395-27123-1

Printed in the United States of America

v 10 9 8 7 6 5 4 3 2 1

To Judy
And Alaska,
With Love

Acknowledgments

The concepts and ideas in this book have come from the Alaskan woods and tundra, from colleagues and students, from readings, from friends. Perspectives of science came both from my own research and, much more importantly, from resident and visiting scientists at the University of Alaska. The viewpoints of resource managers from many state and federal agencies surely can be found at or just below the surface everywhere, for I have worked and talked with scores. The impatience of the activist, which likewise is not hard to find in the text, came naturally as a result of almost twenty years of involvement with the Alaska Conservation Society and other local and national groups.

The book got its start in 1972–73 when the Varian Foundation of San Francisco, the Sierra Club Foundation of that city, and the Western Pennsylvania Conservancy jointly funded the eight months of work leading to the first complete draft. Although the manuscript was rewritten several times thereafter, I owe a tremendous debt to the support of those patient people. Drs. Richard A. Cooley and Grant McConnell, of the University of California (Santa Cruz) paved the way for those grants and gave me continuing encouragement in the years that followed. Later drafts were written at odd times while I taught and did research at the University of Alaska (Fairbanks). Several university typists labored at the manuscript in 1976, 1977, and 1978; their help was crucial and greatly appreciated. Carol Henderson and Marian Tompkins, especially, deserve deepest thanks.

Much of the time and mental energy spent on the book was stolen from my wife and children. While I cannot really make amends, at least they can share with me the relief of knowing the job is done and perhaps with readers the hope that it won't happen again soon.

Contents

Introduction

Frontier Death, Future Dream

In a world where wind, water, and ice continually gnaw away the veneer of living things, it is no surprise to find opportunistic organisms like wild mustards and mosses that are quick to invade bare ground. With their far-flung seeds and spores and their ability to grow in full exposure to the elements, such plants soon cover the raw earth. But almost invariably their time of dominance is short. They specialize in being first but have little staying power in the more complex and competitive communities that follow.

Humans also obey nature's edict to fill vacuums. We call it pioneering. For thousands — possibly millions — of years there were frontiers, lands gravid with wealth, either uninhabited or occupied by people unable to exploit all of the countryside's resources. In the nineteenth century civilian armies from industrialized nations invaded the last frontiers: South Africa, Australia, and western North America. Only the North was left.

Alaska was one of the last frontiers. Several thousand Alaskans can remember when exploitive pioneering began in earnest in the 1890s. The memory of Alaska as a frontier is still with us: common among Americans who read Robert Service and Jack London, strong among Alaskan sourdoughs, adopted as a convenient surface sheen for economic development projects, repeatedly used as a gimmick by travel agents.

The blunt truth is that the geographic frontier is gone and that its lingering image in the public mind is often a dangerous delusion. Pioneers think boundless riches lie over the next mountain; in reality, the North's renewable resources are less productive than those available where the pioneers came from, the mineral resources small in relation to the nation's demand. The pioneer wants to conquer and subdue the land, and of all places on earth the North can least withstand such an extraordinarily destructive philosophy. Pioneer lives are molded and confined by utilitarianism, but what kind of future does unalloyed utility permit either Alaska or the United States as a whole?

However, if Alaska's frontierism is a dangerous anachronism, so are many of its other characteristics a fabulous opportunity. Most of Alaska is held in public trust, still not committed to an exclusive use. The objectives of Alaskan land stewardship can reflect the needs and intents of all Americans, which today are a far cry from nineteenth century Manifest Destiny and Benthamism. Alaska's communities have ample opportunity to achieve a special destiny, firmly Alaskan in character but reflecting the bitter experiences of sprawl and decay in older states. Even Alaska's expected affluence, frightening in its potential for wreaking mischief on Alaskan styles of living, holds its promise that if we can find the understanding to create a new kind of society, we won't lack the money to do it.

Alaska has tremendous significance for the whole nation. This significance does not stem from the oil, gas, minerals, timber, and fish that the nation can expect to flow out of the North, because at best that flow can postpone only slightly the reckoning our society must face for its own profligacy. Alaska's full meaning is not to be found in the wildlands that can — and should — become parks and wildlife refuges, because unless a new social context is created for them they will
xiv be little more than curiosities in the sad museum of mankind.

Nor is Alaska important as a last resort for the nation's would-
be pioneers; there just isn't room for many people in the
North. To me, Alaska's significance is the chance it gives the
nation to test today's new social and environmental under-
standings and, from that test, to develop new purposes and
practices for our nation's anxious cities and beleaguered coun-
trysides.

Every writer of social commentary, and in particular every
writer of an "environmental issues" book, sees his own time
as a turning point in history, his own region or discipline as a
critical pivot. Probably each is correct; history has as many
turning points as a snake's back. Only time will tell whether
the decade of the seventies brought more than its measure of
change to America's arctic state, but I am far from alone in
sensing a gathering of momentum, a poising of forces, and a
ferment of new perceptions in Alaska today.

Frontierism was a dream, and because people must dream,
we should speak without bitterness of yesterday's fantasies
whose flaws seem so clear in retrospect. With honest nostalgia
we can say good-bye to the best of it, which was the search: a
vigorously masculine, outrageously romantic search. What destroyed the frontier was the discovery of the bonanza. Ironically, it was discovered not by frontiersmen but by corporation
men. The Big Rock Candy Mountain was plumbed, and it was
full of oil, and the crude taste of money killed the dream.

Now we need another dream. The handiest comes right off
the shelf, mass produced in the United States for developing
countries all over the world. It is called Bigger Is Better.
Alaska is already trying it on for size — indeed, has one leg in
the trousers — and the sales pitch is intense. But somehow the
fit is poor because our shape is different. And we hear rumors
that the material doesn't wear well.

I know of no dream in humanity's stock that we can adopt
wholesale successfully. Humanity has never before faced the
kind of problems it has now created. Certainly the North has

had no past experience with material affluence. Also, futures have to be tailored out of pasts, and our past has unique threads and patterns too valuable and too strong to obliterate with patches.

We cannot freely pick and choose among these traditional patterns, selecting those we like and discarding those we don't. Nor can we manipulate events inside Alaska entirely to our own liking. As Aldo Leopold said of wild things, we are often herded about by the compelling orders of circumstance. Yet there is a margin of choice in any human situation. If we know our society's capacities and understand our land, if we are alert to changing relationships in Alaska and the larger world beyond, and if we have attainable visions and processes for reaching and improving them, we will be able to use that margin of choice for creative human development.

Scores of Alaskans, and many friends of Alaska, are conscious of Alaska's promise and are working to achieve it in their own ways. It is humbling to realize how many truths I will never find through my own limited senses. Yet an Alaskan biologist, environmental advocate, and dreamer of dreams should have something of value to contribute. The times demand that I try.

Alaska

CHAPTER I

From Land Bridge to Pipeline

Newsmen in Wenatchee, Washington, and Naples, Florida, must shake their heads at the strange assortment of stories about Alaska pouring in a staccato rush off the teletype every day.

Take a selection from an average week in mid-February 1978:

A famous Soviet writer, a Chukchi born within sight of Alaska in East Cape, Siberia, followed an unusual open-sesame visa through Eskimo-dominated western Alaska hoping to help re-establish communications between people on both shores of the Bering Straits.

More than a half million gallons of crude oil spilled into the forest near Fairbanks after the Trans-Alaska Pipeline was blasted open by a saboteur's bomb. The highly touted, very expensive leak detection system and shutoff valves supposedly protecting the countryside from such insults failed to work.

A group of disgruntled radio and television owners filed a massive brief with the Federal Communications Commission protesting the licensing of major broadcasting stations in Alaska. The commission promptly logged a record 900 letters from other Alaskans protesting the protest.

Alaska's Senator Ted Stevens, a staunch advocate of free enterprise, told state legislators in Juneau that they should appropriate several billion dollars to help build the natural-gas

I

pipeline from Prudhoe Bay to the Midwest, warning them that otherwise the business world might not touch the project.

The governor announced plans to break ground for the biggest agricultural venture yet north of 60°, a state-financed effort to grow barley in interior Alaska for sale to Japan.

An Environmental Protection Agency spokesman told Fairbanks it was starting its final probation period as a nonattainment area under air-quality regulations. ("Nonattainment" is bureaucratese for a hopeless situation unless drastic action is taken.) Meanwhile, municipal leaders were trying to convince the state administration that Fairbanks is just the spot for a major petrochemical industry.

The Alaska Department of Fish and Game killed seven wolves just south of the Tanana River so that more moose would be available for hunters.

What is behind the outlandish activities in America's wildest state? Are they part of a pattern? Do they mirror a past or foretell a future? How did the simple life on the northern frontier get to be so confusing?

Beginnings

Alaska's first frontier began a long time ago. Sometime between 30,000 and 50,000 years before Christ was born, archaeologists think, and certainly long before the final Wisconsin glaciation laid siege to the continent, people drifted into Alaska from the west. Hunters, they were, from Siberia and beyond; and they followed spears thrown eastward into Alaska, eastward into Yukon, and southward through Canada, establishing the ancestral roots of all of the Western Hemisphere's native people. For a long time during the height of continental glaciation, Alaska was really a part of Asia, connected by a thousand-mile-wide strip of land now flooded by the Bering Sea, and blocked off from the rest of North

2

America by ice. Blade-making people were scattered through much of Alaska and western Yukon throughout this time. By 4000 B.C. Alaska's northern Eskimo people had developed a very different culture from the Aleuts and Eskimos of the western Pacific Coast of Alaska; today the Eskimos of Alaska north of Norton Sound cannot understand the traditional language of Eskimos to the south. The Aleutian Islands, inhabited for at least 8000 years, harbored direct ancestors of today's Aleuts as long ago as 3000–4000 B.C.[1] And in still another ancient frontier invasion, Indian people moved into interior and southeastern Alaska from the east and south after the Wisconsin-era glaciers released their grip.

The first Alaskans and their descendants were able to use only a small part of the huge variety of natural resources we depend on today, and that limited set of resources defined how and where and in what kinds of groupings they could live. The basic economic unit was small because the countryside or seaside couldn't support very many people in any one place, when the people traveled by foot or hand-powered boat. The basic social unit often was mobile, even nomadic, because there are few places in the North where food is available consistently every season and year after year. And although trading could and did link people hundreds of miles apart, trade was much less of direct economic than of cultural importance.

Some favorable places on Alaska's coasts, especially around the Gulf of Alaska, supported settlements for long stretches at a time. Other sites were occupied repeatedly over the centuries by short-lived communities. In most of the vast Interior, people had to live in small, extended-family groups, always on the move, in order to survive.

Most Americans picture pre-white, aboriginal societies in some sort of stable, almost dead-ended cultural condition, "in balance" with the natural order. The problem with that concept, of course, is that the natural order itself is unstable (and nowhere more so than in the North) and forces human societies to change. If a child swinging between two ·swaying trees is "in balance" that balance is only a statistical average that ignores the uncertain and variable trajectories that define reality.

Furthermore, the bargain that early Alaskans struck with nature was a distinctly human one. It involved wresting from sea and land not merely an existence, but enough surplus energy to support art, music, conversation, religion, and politics. In places where that surplus was greatest, as among the Tlingits of southeastern Alaska, the intricacies of the aboriginal society were an eminently successful training for the transition to the industrial society that has taken place in a few swift lifetimes.

And so, when Captain Vitus Bering's Russian ship cast anchor just east of the Copper River Delta in 1741, there were about 75,000 people already living in Alaska. Nine out of every ten lived along the ocean shores: 40,000 Eskimos scattered from the Arctic to Bristol Bay; 16,000 Aleuts on the Alaskan Peninsula and Aleutian Islands, perhaps 1,200 Athapascan Indians around Cook Inlet and Prince William Sound; and 11,800 Tlingits and Haidas in southeastern Alaska. Some 6,000 Athapascans lived in the Interior, mostly along the Tanana and Yukon rivers.[2]

The Russians were the vanguard of Alaska's second and most recent frontier. Like the first North Americans, they came from Asia; but, unlike the earlier people, they were able to sail back and forth almost at will (the extreme dangers of the voyages notwithstanding). They probed for resources, largely furs, for a century, never thinking or acting like permanent settlers, always looking for riches to take back home. Russian fur traders enslaved Aleuts as hunters of sea otters; the effects of that enslavement still color the lives of the few thousand remaining people of Aleut descent. The Russians met more resistance eastward across the Gulf of Alaska, the Tlingits of southeastern Alaska forcing Russians to stay in fortified enclaves and to give fair value for furs and other goods. In fact, the outright warfare and massacres of the Aleutians were never repeated in the later period of white settlement.

There is still tangible evidence of Russia's century in Alaska. The Russian Orthodox church is locally strong in some south coastal settlements. Aleut names and Aleut genes bear testimony to that sorry chapter in Northland history. Scores of Russian names sprinkle Alaskan maps, though largely for places that do not and never did show any real Russian imprint. Steller's sea cow is gone forever and the sea otter still has not repopulated most of southeastern Alaska. Still, it was the Czar's last act — the sale of Alaska to the United States in 1867 — that held the most significance for our future.

The wave of frontiersmen from America and Europe actually overlapped broadly with Russia's period of spotty dominance in coastal Alaska. "Boston men" and southerners from a dozen nations sailed up to take part in the exploitation of furs and whales, while Hudson Bay Company traders followed the Yukon River into the heartland of Alaska. Competition for fur seal and sea otter pelts, spurred by fantastic prices brought in city markets in Europe and the eastern seaboard of the United States, led to bloody piracy among seamen and unthinking slaughter of the animals.

Native people suffered the most, as in all the world's frontiers. Largely a "peaceful" swamping of indigenous cultures, the taking of Alaska by whites nevertheless devastated Native families and settlements. Smallpox, influenza, and tuberculosis brought by the fur miners and later the whalers and gold seekers swept through Alaska in the nineteenth century, completely wiping out some Native communities and cutting the population in half by 1839. For a century afterward nearly every Native in Alaska was exposed to tuberculosis repeatedly; this and other fatal diseases held Aleut, Eskimo, and Indian populations below 40,000 until the 1950s.

Terrible though these diseases were, at least there was hope of a technical fix through medical science and public health programs. Tuberculosis deaths eventually were all but eliminated, in fact, after one of the most phenomenal medical campaigns ever waged. Some of the other diseases, like smallpox, are no longer widespread and rarely cause death. (This is not to say that the health gap between Native and non-Native is a thing of the past. Native Alaskans still have serious health problems, most of them a legacy of long social subjugation. Poor and crowded housing, impure water, and poor sanitation still lead to high rates of respiratory infection, deafness from ear infection, gastrointestinal diseases, and dental problems. Perhaps more significantly, certain mental disorders are more prevalent among Native people than among other Alaskans, and high suicide rates and alcoholism are tragic evidence of severe and chronic stress.) There is no technical fix for those other stresses, built up over decades of purposeful destruction and remodeling of Native cultures — monumental neglect and erosion or theft of subsistence resources.

The Alaska Organic Act of 1884, which set up civil government in the new District of Alaska, sanctioned systematic cultural destruction even while it admitted the validity of undefined aboriginal rights. A federal Commissioner of Indian Affairs described the policy prevailing in 1889 in embarrassingly blunt form. Indians must be absorbed into our national life, not as Indians but as American citizens, he said. The Indians must "conform to the White man's ways, peaceably if they will, forcibly if they must." The Indians must be prepared for the new order through a system of compulsory education. The traditional society of Indian groups must be broken up.[3] Missionaries from Moravian, Russian Orthodox, Presbyterian, and Roman Catholic churches undertook the same process.

Schools and churches caused a permanent change in the distribution of Natives, too, which as much as the teachings caused an upheaval of old ways. Instead of adopting the seminomadic life of the Athapascan people, or sending teachers and missionaries to each small Eskimo or Aleut village, the white system demanded that Native people stay in

larger and more permanent places where bigger and more satisfying school and church structures could be built. Seasonal
moves to fish camps or sealing camps or caribou hunting areas
were pinched out to allow church and school attendance. The
simple fact of clustering caused local wipeouts of game resources while leaving much of the hinterland untapped. Purchased food became necessary or was made to seem desirable;
hence, cash was needed, and, inevitably, jobs through which
cash could be earned. The alternatives? Welfare, or disobedi-
ence of the new order. On the one hand a topsy-turvy world
where unwed mothers and the elderly bring in more money
than able-bodied males; on the other a hopeless running battle
with the pleaders and police of a foreign government.

Some of the animals Natives relied on for food fell prey to
commercial hunting or fishing, further increasing the dependence on cash or welfare. Whalers almost extirpated the
bowhead whales of the Bering Straits and Arctic that were so
important to Eskimo people. By the turn of this century,
whales and walrus were eliminated as food sources. Overwintering whalers and Natives alike had to use caribou and musk
oxen in the Arctic, and shortly those species, too, declined.
The invention of fish canning techniques in the mid 1800s and
the subsequent spread of commercial fishing up the West
Coast pre-empted important subsistence salmon runs all the
way from the Columbia River in Oregon and Washington to
the Yukon River in southwestern Alaska. Commercial deer
hunting for hides and meat temporarily reduced populations of
the species in southeastern Alaska, just as market or campmeat
hunting drastically (but temporarily) depleted supplies of
moose and mountain sheep around mining camps in the Interior early in the twentieth century. Intensive herring fisheries
depleted the silvery clouds of this crucial link in Alaskan
marine food chains, affecting seals, salmon, halibut, whales,
and marine birds. The 1916 Migratory Bird Treaty between
Canada and the United States made traditional Native spring   7

and summer waterfowl hunting and egging illegal, though it did not prevent this activity from continuing in places like the huge Yukon-Kuskokwim Delta, where people depend on such subsistence practices even today.

It is true that industrial markets increased or "created" resources in the economic sense. For example, fur markets in Europe and the United States placed high monetary values on seal and walrus hides and land and freshwater furbearer pelts. A variety of minerals, petroleum, fish, timber, and shell-fish — even scenery — have commercial value now. The amount of food, clothing, and shelter purchasable with earnings from these resources is greater than a person would get in a subsistence economy. (A delightful story is told of an enterprising Delta Eskimo who discovered how profits are made. He would take whitefish he had netted to the store, turning them in for food stamps. In another store he traded stamps for the same number of fish plus extra "store food.") For too many Natives, however, that gain remained an abstraction. The individuals who lost access to subsistence resources often failed to benefit from the modern resources except indirectly (and questionably) through subsidy or welfare. Even the Native who would take advantage of new resource opportunities was thrust into a strange and often intolerably stressful way of life.

Accompanying social disruption, and largely caused by it, geographic dislocation of Native peoples added a fourth aspect to a dismaying situation. From the late 1800s through the present there has been a strong movement of Natives from small to larger settlements. Eskimo and Athapascan Indians traditionally were nomadic or prepared to move whenever necessary, but their wanderings were made as whole families and communities. No historic parallel prepared them for the estrangements of nineteenth and twentieth century migrations. Whites chose the places for churches, hospitals, defense outposts, canneries, sawmills, and stores: those places attracted

Aleut, Indian, and Eskimo people. Settlements like Barrow, Kotzebue, Bethel, Nome, and Tanana began to dominate their respective regions and now serve as way stations for young Natives on their way to Anchorage, Fairbanks, and Juneau. The moving of rural children to attend schools in successively larger Alaskan towns, and even to training centers in other states, added to the stream of urban migration.

Thus through some 200 years of contact with whites, Alaskan Natives seemed, from the perspective of most European-Americans, to fade further into the background. There was almost no person-to-person communication between the cultures, precious little understanding of Native problems, and no apparent reason why whites, in their own self-interest, should be much concerned.

Except for a few perceptive teachers and government administrators, white Alaskans scarcely have been aware of the cumulative agonies of Native peoples. Their energies have been thrown into economic activities and the politics of resident versus nonresident control of those activities. These were the central — almost exclusive — concerns of the southerners who became the active players in the colonization process we call the Last Frontier.

A Century of Americanization

The point is arguable, but I think of the Last Frontier as beginning around 1880. Before then — throughout the fur exploitation period of the early 1800s — whites saw themselves mainly as explorers and exploiters, not settlers. Even the purchase of Alaska in 1867 from self-proclaimed "owners" was almost thwarted by widespread doubt that the North was inhabitable. But in 1878 two salmon canneries began successful operation in southeastern Alaska. This new technology ushered in a revolution in Alaskan fishing, just as 9 the building of two pulp mills at Sitka and Ketchikan in the 1950s revolutionized logging in Alaska. And then, in 1880, Joe Juneau and Richard Harris discovered a mountain of low-grade gold ore on the steep slopes of a shallow side channel of Lynn Canal, and big-time mining came to the North. In 1884 Congress set up civil government in the District of Alaska so miners could legally claim land. Gold and salmon for the men-folks, the comfort of government for the families: Alaska might even be worth settling!

Salmon and gold dominated the economy of Alaska for sixty years, with high-grade copper from Kennecott's mines in the Wrangell Mountains shouldering a brief place for itself in the last quarter century of that period.

Alaska's salmon stocks are fragmented into thousands of distinct "runs" using streams and lakes scattered along tens of thousands of coastline miles. Because of the limited range of boats and the fast spoilage of fresh-caught fish, canneries had to be built at frequent intervals along the coast. By the time of peak salmon catches in the 1920s there were almost 150 canneries in Alaska. Many of them, though highly seasonal in operation, became the nucleus of a community. The disastrous salmon declines of the 1930–1960 period led to abandonment of scores of these wood-and-sheet-iron structures, whose rotting wharves and moss-eaten roofs haunt many a secluded inlet now perhaps destined for the clatter of a helicopter base for offshore oil exploration. Others still operate, the summertime center of a babel of young fish packers and chuffing of seiners, trollers, gill netters. The fisherman's style is the dominant style of coastal Alaska from Ketchikan to Dillingham, having outlasted the grubstaked prospector's life given its final fling in Alaska's gold rushes and converted to permanent legend by Jack London and Robert Service.

Gold discoveries did indeed help to settle whites throughout Alaska. Juneau and Douglas in 1880; Circle in 1893; Klondike in 1896–1898; Kobuk and Nome, 1898; Fairbanks, 1902; discovery, rush, boom, fade. These and dozens of other discoveries drew men to pan and dig.[4] Rarely, families followed. Only Juneau, Nome, and Fairbanks grew; and their growth long since has been nurtured by sources other than mines. The copper mines at McCarthy echoed the typical experience. Extraordinarily rich copper, including pure nuggets weighing as much as two or three tons, was discovered there in 1899. Major shipments began in 1911, when the Copper River and Northwestern Railroad (made famous by Rex Beach's *The Iron Trail*) was built between the mines and the coastal port of Cordova. In 1938 the mines closed and the railroad began to crumble under the onslaughts of water, earthquake, and landslides. Today a dozen people live year round in the former townsite.

In many ways, frontier Alaska belonged not so much to America as a whole as to the Northwest. Ties with Canada were important: the Cassiar gold rush in northern British Columbia led to later discoveries in southeastern Alaska, very much as the Klondike stampede in Yukon drew northward those who discovered the Nome, Fairbanks, Chandalar, and other Alaskan camps. Many Britishers and Canadians adopted Alaska as their home in mining's heyday. And of course San Francisco, Portland, and Seattle were financing centers, manpower pools, and transportation hubs for the fishing, mining, and logging activities that energized the Last Frontier.

The peculiarly colonial characteristics of Alaska's cash economy (to distinguish it from the simultaneous but separate subsistence economy) determined not only who would come north, who would stay, and what they would do, but also their basic social self-perception and hopes for the future. The economy was a hardscrabble, narrow-based affair for most residents. You worked in the fisheries or the mines, or you sold goods to the people who did. Employment and business were highly seasonal. Placer mining and most prospecting took place when water was available, from May to September. Fishing, especially where crabs and halibut were unimportant, 11 squeezed itself into a frantic two or three warm-weather months. Logging shut down with the coming of winter storms in November and December. Construction all but stopped when hands and feet numbed and cement froze. Snow used to be called "termination dust" by transient construction workers. Furthermore, nonresident banks and corporations controlled production, transport, and marketing. Paired with the long-distance government decisions coming from Washington, D.C., this "Outside" control did much to shape local attitudes. Every action has an equally atrocious reaction, to paraphrase a law of physics, and in this case the reaction was to demand self-government.

Alaska's non-Native population at the outbreak of World War II was as peculiarly impermanent as its economy. Men greatly outnumbered women. Single people, male and female, outnumbered families. Transients, seasonals, and boomers drifted in and out with the tides of fortune and rumor. The white population in coastal Alaska remained widely distributed in numerous small towns, but the rest of non-Native Alaska had gathered itself into two primary centers, Fairbanks and Anchorage.

The mood of Alaska in the 1940s and 1950s, then, was ripe for peaceful rebellion. The gold rushes had filled Fairbanks and Anchorage and a host of smaller towns with machismo and chip-on-the-shoulder independence; the careful, less romantic, stay-at-homes had waved good-bye to the ship at the dock in Seattle. The pioneers felt their isolation and drew together clannishly. Their constant search for the bonanza had somehow eluded them — or, worse, when a bonanza was found, it mysteriously disappeared south with the last September sailing. Life had frustrated their dreams, and somebody had to be blamed.

The obvious scapegoats were the Outside corporations who skimmed Alaska's cream and the federal bureaucrats who helped them. The obvious solution was an assertion of a self-sufficiency in political life that had been denied by a monopoly-dominated economic life; in other words, statehood. Considering that Alaskans had no local legislature and no congressional representation at all up to 1912, and had no vote in Congress, a weak legislature, and a presidentially appointed governor until 1959, the attitude wasn't surprising.

Statehood became the Holy Grail of most of Alaska's resident non-Native work force and business community, except in the Southeast where businessmen liked things the way they were. Countless speeches, editorials, and eastward pilgrimages were made on that crusade. Oddly enough, though, the final pressure needed to achieve statehood came from cheechakos — newcomers — not sourdoughs. The newcomers were the young professionals and businessmen who rode into Anchorage and Fairbanks on the back of cost-plus military contracts in the 1940s and early 1950s. (Military construction became one of Alaska's most important economic resources when military strategy required a distant warning and defense net in Alaska against bombers and missiles threatening from across the Bering Straits.) Economic and political power concentrated in Anchorage and Fairbanks. Simultaneously, throughout the 1940s, nonresident businesses rapidly lost interest in Alaska as salmon, gold mining, and copper mining hit rock bottom. They had opposed statehood earlier, but by the 1950s they didn't much care. To cut the fascinating story of the fight for statehood short, Congress finally passed the Alaska Statehood Act on July 7, 1958, and Alaska was admitted to the Union on January 3, 1959.[5] The Railbelt (Anchorage and Fairbanks, connected in 1924 by the Alaska Railroad) was elated, southeastern Alaska had divided feelings, and the rest of the state slept on.

The years since statehood span my own Alaskan experience. Sifting through the scores of noteworthy events for some hint of pattern (admittedly dangerous at close range), I think that the significant processes have little to do with statehood or its direct political or economic consequences. Rather, the nub of the past twenty years is the drawing together of two sets of historically distant groups: urban and rural Alaska on the one hand, and Alaska and the rest of the nation on the other. It once was entirely possible to be a national political leader and not care a whit about Alaska. Oil and wilderness — to over-simplify — have made that impossible. And once urban (largely non-Native) Alaska could and did ignore rural (mainly Native) Alaska except as a storehouse of resources; no more. Obviously by speaking of a drawing together I do not imply a convergence of values or objectives, but simply a recognition of roads traveled together.

What happened to cause the sudden turbulent mixing of long-separated streams of urban and rural change? One ele-ment, certainly, is that statehood failed to deliver the spectacu-lar economic growth old-time white Alaskans longed for. In fact, statehood initiated a slow but inexorable weaning of Alaska from uniquely generous federal grants, heightening the local tax burden. Frustrated to the point of screaming (which, not altogether figuratively, was a common editorial tone in major Alaskan newspapers in the 1960s), business-oriented urban Alaska found itself willing to do or promise anything to get construction started on the Trans-Alaska Oil Pipeline. And the second element: Rural Alaska grew restive about unful-filled promises of settlement of aboriginal claims, and in the late 1960s found itself with the means to force that settle-ment — the power to prevent or substantially delay that same pipeline project.

Dogs will neither mate nor fight if there is too great a dif-ference in their sizes. By analogy, there could be little interac-tion between Native and non-Native Alaska as long as the one was passive, isolated, and fragmented, the other the creator and controller of the power structure. Throughout the fur, fish, and mining booms, this fairly described the relationship of the two Alaskan societies. Then, in the 1960s, Native Alaska found a cause that would unite them and make the rest of the state take notice.

The cause that pushed aside age-old hostilities among various Native cultures was the battle for settlement of aboriginal rights. The leverage to force this overdue settlement came with the discovery of oil in arctic Alaska and the need for a pipeline right of way.

Long before statehood, Native leaders knew that their people had land rights. Congress had acknowledged the existence of such rights in the Alaska Organic Act of 1884. A few Natives also knew that those rights were being rendered meaningless by the inexorable transfer of land title to homesteaders, miners, businessmen, and recreationists, and by the withdrawal from public domain of land masses ranging from small military bases to the vast 23-million–acre Naval Petroleum Reserve No. 4 in arctic Alaska. These threats were too sporadic and disjointed to create really deep and widespread concern among rural leaders until they were struck with the full implications of the Alaska Statehood Act and its promised 104-million–acre grant of public-domain lands to the state. Concern grew by leaps and bounds. Protests of state selections spread. In 1963 Native people of the central Tanana Valley successfully stopped a state proposal to select a large marsh area and develop recreation there for the benefit of Fairbanks residents. The normal processes of land transfer among federal, state, and private entities soon were so beclouded by the question of aboriginal rights that between 1966 and 1968 a succession of "land freeze" orders was issued by Interior Secretary Stewart Udall. By 1969 all disposals of public domain lands and rights-of-way were halted. This in itself gave the state a reason to wish that Native claims could be settled. The threat of long delays in building a pipeline to carry oil from Prudhoe Bay turned that wish to active lobbying in Congress. In December 1971, after a remarkable interplay of civil rights, environmental, industrial, state, federal, and Native interests, the Alaska Native Claims Settlement Act established the basis for the co-evolution of Native and non-Native societies in the new state.

It is worth commenting that the rising unity and strength of Natives alone might not have been enough to force the issue. If the state had uncovered in the 1960s a number of different and highly valuable resources which could have paid off the promises of the statehood movement, urban Alaska might not have been so eager to settle aboriginal land claims. But no such discoveries, except for petroleum at Prudhoe Bay, were made. Instead, the state faced mounting costs with diminishing or stagnant resources: fish stocks stubbornly refused to respond to the "new regime" in management, mining and agriculture disappeared almost totally, military expenditures wavered, and the growth in logging in southeastern Alaska produced no palpable revenue surplus to flow into state coffers.

Oil discoveries and the Alaska Native Claims Settlement Act not only melded the political lives and economies of rural and urban Alaska, they also turned the nation's eyes northwestward.

Most Americans seem to have viewed Prudhoe Bay as a fine (if somewhat distant and drawn-out) side show — something for page-two news stories when a particularly flamboyant spokesman for a conservation group, oil company, Native association, or government agency caught the ear of a reporter. Only conservationists and oil companies, among the citizenry, were in earnest about the stakes. Even the ephemeral 1973 oil shortage and the more serious natural-gas shortages in the frigid winter of 1976–77 failed to give Americans much sense of the significance attached to the discoveries in the Arctic.

In a totally different and even conflicting way, the nation was reminded of its stake in Alaska by a brief "sleeper" provision of the Alaska Native Claims Settlement Act. This provision, section 17 (d) (2), gave the Secretary of the Interior two years to develop, and five more years for Congress to act on, recommendations for new national wildlife refuges, forests, parks, and wild and scenic rivers selected after a thorough canvassing of all public-domain lands in Alaska. Knowing the extremely rapid growth of the state's population and economy and the finality of ongoing transfers of federal holdings to Native corporations and the state, the conservation community in "the Lower 48" rightly proclaimed this the last chance to save the northern wilderness.

In the 1940s and the early 1950s, Alaska played a minor role in national affairs as a defense outpost — a place colonels would call from if the Pentagon needed to be told of rumored violations of our airspace. The state gained statehood amidst skepticism and benign amusement. Americans heard about the Good Friday earthquake in 1964 and the Fairbanks flood in 1967, but it wasn't until the Prudhoe petroleum discoveries and the pipeline debate that curiosity changed to interest. And now we play a dual role on the American stage, a last refuge of that long-lost wild America so wistfully remembered, and a last storehouse of oil and gas, secure from the mavericking and blackmailing of fickle foreign suppliers.

CHAPTER II

Today

Turbulent times.

Clattering cats blade new subdivisions. Clean fingers flip stock sheets. Like huge mechanical dragonflies, helicopters dip to set claim stakes on desolate ridges. Gold-rush photos decorate Petroleum Club walls. Boot points grinding butts, young Eskimos in black watch the street crowds. Game guides wrangle over territory. Capital, capital, who wants the capital?

Turbulent times. Chip-on-the-shoulder, greedy, wary, ambiguous times. Watch out for the union bosses, the environmentalists, the Feds, the Natives, the Birchers, the corporation men, the Seven-Day Opportunists. Watch out for Anchorage.

In 1975 there were 405,000 of us, fewer than in the city of San Jose in a space three times as big as California. How could we feel so crowded?

On the move. Half of us here in 1970 (not counting children under five) were not here in 1965, and half the 1970 population was gone again in 1975. In Fairbanks in 1976, one person in four planned to leave within two years — and the survey excluded obvious transients.[1] Touch and go in Anchorage, Valdez, Glennallen, Bethel, Juneau. Twenty dollars an hour for straight time: little wonder they left Seattle, Los Angeles, Tulsa, New York, Little Rock.

And the swift streams of change in urban Alaska set eddies swirling in the bush. From the far Aleutians, the Alaska Peninsula, and Kodiak young people moved north to Anchorage, draining the region of 15 to 20 percent of its population between 1970 and 1975. Barrow became the bureaucratic hub of the North Slope and a stopover for petroleum crews and their agency watchdogs, and doubled its population in five years. Valdez tripled in size. Anchorage's bedroom communities along upper Cook Inlet doubled, while the town itself grew 30 percent, to reach 178,000 in 1975. Bethel, Kotzebue, Togiak, and other settlements far off the road system became centers of Native corporate activity and way stations for young Natives going . . . somewhere.

There has been a lot of speculation on how the settlement of Native land claims will affect Native population shifts in the state. The main short-term effect has been to increase (and finance) Native involvement in politics and cash economies. In this sense, the Alaska Native Claims Settlement Act has paid for airfares between two cultures, dramatically shifting Native leadership to regional centers and, of course, Anchorage. In the long run, the demands of land ownership, created by the act, may well set a countercurrent toward the villages. When "our land" (the old way) becomes "my land" (the white way), the scales may tip for many in favor of staying home.

Obviously the geographic pattern of job opportunities has a massive effect on internal migration as well as the influx of Outsiders to the State. Alaska has always had a high unemployment rate — from two to five times the national average — in both rural and urban places. Native joblessness is chronically high, even discounting those able to make their way in a twilight economy of wildlife and welfare who are not really members of the work force. The pipeline boom put many young Natives on payrolls, but participation in the activity varied greatly from village to village.

In the state as a whole, the work force climbed dramatically in the mid 1970s. On the average, there were 171,000 people employed in 1976 each month, not counting military personnel. The trade, service, construction, finance, and related industries employed 64 percent of the civilian work force. Another 8 percent were in mining, fishing, logging, or other aspects of natural-resource industries; and the rest worked for state (8 percent), federal (10 percent), or local government. Unemployment stayed high through the whole pipeline project because so many came north looking for work. In 1977, unemployment rose, reaching 20 percent in Fairbanks in midwinter.

Railbelt to Whalebelt

There are still many Alaskas. The homogenizing forces of coke and satellite TV and oil money so far have eroded the fantastic diversity of Alaska only superficially.

The *Southeast Panhandle* is fish and chips and a Thousand Island green salad. It is an elongated but distinctive region bound together by shared seas and salt water and storms, shared mossy green forests, gleaming eagles and leaping salmon. There are no big towns. Even in Juneau, a government town and the most populous in Southeast, you can meet the same friend three times in a lunch hour around the shopping district. There are only 50,000 people, after all, in this 450-mile–long region. Most of them are fishermen or loggers, or people who sell to fishermen and loggers, or process fish or timber. Between the half dozen well-spaced towns, tiny settlements nestle in unexpected bays, harboring Tlingit fishermen, part-time loggers, retired people, and young kids from California. In Juneau, they worry about the seat of government moving to a non-place called — whoever heard of it? — Willow, north of Anchorage; but the rest of the Panhandle talks about salmon and weather forecasts and rumors of mineral strikes.

When you wait for a cab at 5th and C in *Anchorage* you don't often lift your senses above the traffic to search for a view of the mountains between gaps in buildings. You are in

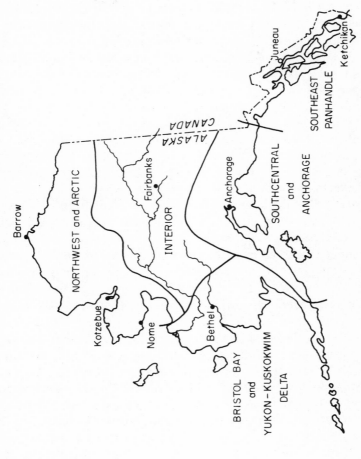

FIGURE 1. The regions of Alaska

the Fifth Avenue of the Tundra or in the Great American Nightmare — take your choice. Whatever your reaction, you are at the center of gravity for people, politics, and dollars in Alaska. Steel-floored discotheques, subsidized buses, broken bottles in back alleys, Cadillacs in multilevel parking garages: all the trappings of Everytown, America.

Economically the Anchorage mini-megalopolis is a region unto itself, but with fine disregard for such things, the geographers make the city a one-liner on a far-stretching map of a region defined by mountains and the sea. The *southcentral* region is spectacular. It is encircled east, north, and west by an unbelievable series of mountain ranges running solid from the coast to the Interior from one hundred to three hundred miles away. The Coast Range, Wrangells, Chugach, Kenai, and Talkeetna mountains are impressive in themselves; and all are embraced in the long arc of the Alaska Range from the Canadian border to western Cook Inlet. From there the Aleutian Range sends its volcanic thrusts 1500 miles down the Alaska Peninsula and out in endlessly lonely steps into the Aleutians, marching toward Japan. In this great jumble of rock nestle tiny towns like English Bay (population 60) and Kaguyak (population 60), facing the sea, and Copper Center (250) in the intermountain valleys.

West of the Aleutian Range is still another face of Alaska, the *southwest* region. (You could argue that there are two regions here, because salmon-dominated Bristol Bay is very different from the Yukon-Kuskokwim Delta's subsistence style.) The land itself is harsh, swept by gales out of the Bering Sea. It is a doubtful land for trees, and except for the sea it would be beyond doubt for people. But out of the sea flow the silvery streams of salmon every summer, a signal for the region's 18,000 Eskimos and Aleuts and 10,000 whites to shift from kitchen to galley. The catching of salmon — whether for fun, profit, or belly — is an annual affirmation of belonging. Time enough in the fall to pick up your individuality as teacher or roustabout. It is hard to remember that for forty years after the first salmon cannery began operation in the bay, in 1884, residents ignored the commercial salmon fishery. Chinese from San Francisco came up to clean and pack the fish, and Italians and Scandinavians caught them.

Salmon are caught commercially in the Kuskokwim and Yukon Delta area too, but the industry is much newer and less important economically to the Yupik Eskimos that comprise over 90 percent of the district's population. The delta's people live as close to a pure subsistence lifestyle as it is possible to find in Alaska today; except for salmon, nothing exploitable by commerce has been uncovered there yet. The people live in some 50 villages concentrated along the coast and major rivers. They speak Yupik proudly. Still able to travel the vast unbroken marshy tundras and snaking sloughs without seeing a stranger from the city, nevertheless they cannot escape the looming bulk of the other world just beyond the eastern horizon.

"Please try to fathom our great desire to survive in a way somewhat different from yours," the elders of Nightmute said in 1973 at hearings on the Marine Mammals Protection Act, "and thus see why our hunters will continue to go out." And a young man working away from his Chevak home said, "The only time I really feel I am myself is when I am hunting. Every year I must return to the tundra if only for a few days. I have to do this." [2]

Up the coast, through the Bering Straits and around the long corner into the Beaufort Sea basin, is another Eskimo region where subsistence economics prevail. The people are mostly Inuit, closely related to arctic coastal people in Canada. They are whalers and sealers and walrus hunters, and they know the seasons for arctic char and whitefish, caribou and ducks. Three towns are regional centers for *northwestern* Alaska: Barrow, Kotzebue, and Nome. Only Nome, once a gold camp, has more than a scattering of non-Natives. The region's economy is that peculiarly northern mixture of subsistence, disjointed and somewhat obscure government activity, and retailing and transportation services. Commercial whaling and reindeer herding waxed and waned a lifetime ago, and except on the North Slope, Alaska's petroleum era is still beyond the horizon.

These four regions — the Panhandle, Southcentral, the Bay and Delta, and the Northwest — are seaside regions. In the middle lies the sprawling *Interior,* fondly if somewhat extravagantly called The Golden Heart of the North by Fairbanksans. Fairbanks, like its rival city on Cook Inlet, has unaccountably achieved that critical mass that attracts the lion's share of regional growth. (I say "unaccountably" because accident created the community, stubbornness made it last, and inertia keeps it from moving to a better place.) Fairbanks now has some 56,000 of the Interior's 80,000 people. Quiet under awesomely cold skies in winter and lazy under the massive white clouds of summer, the other villages of the Interior are either Indian communities, or, at the sparse road junctions, polyglot conglomerations of minor commerce.

Fairbanks itself is sprawling northward into the hills surrounding the flood-plain city core and filling in the flatlands with warehouses and shopping malls in response to a three-year surge of pipeline construction money. Unlike Valdez, which can rely on tanker-terminal operations to pick up construction slack, or Anchorage, where oil and pipeline management people live, Fairbanks may fade a bit unless there is an encore. Still, money attracts money, and bulls outweigh bears in Interior Alaska's economy today.

Urbanites, Villagers, and Other Alaskans

Are Alaskans really more involved in argument about the present and future than other Americans, or are we just noisier? It certainly seems that we are highly susceptible to forming organizations, and that more of us are immersed in the business of persuasion and politics. We are not bashful about battling for a public future that validates our personal past and fits our personal plans. That in itself is not remarkable. Perhaps what sets us apart is the startling distance that separates points of view.

For example, what shared experiences, what legends and lullabies, what common language, can bind urbanite and Yupik villager?

Urbanites — and I use the term for those people who are not only in the city but of the city — come from an Eastern, Far Western, or Middle American metropolis. They go to Honolulu or Mexico City for vacations. They leave, eventually, for higher salaries or more status in Washington, D.C., Houston, or Seattle. To them the vast reaches of rural Alaska are places where Natives meet tours in costume and where field men are when they radio for supplies.

Urbanites are employed by government, biggish corporations, law firms, and the University of Alaska. They are highly educated and well off. In their workday they measure progress by agency size or corporate earnings, and it is hard for them to use other yardsticks for social progress. Many are professionally trained and are strongly motivated by the values and perspectives of law, medicine, public health, management, and other professions.

These people of the city are a high-energy group, accustomed to organizing and leading. They are largely responsible for municipal, state, and national government, for concerts, art councils, and glass-and-stressed-concrete buildings in half a dozen Alaskan towns. They may enjoy (or feel compelled to enjoy) certain kinds of outdoor recreation like skiing at the Alyeska resort near Anchorage, the sun gleaming from bright plasticized goggles, clothes, boots, skis. Some of them campaign for city parks and better zoning decisions.

25

To most urbanites the North is an assignment. Many leave again in months or a few years, having found nothing in Alaska to compensate for the discomforts of the climate or the smalltown atmosphere of even the biggest Alaskan cities. Some stay out of strong attachment to the Alaskan environment, and they can be a powerful constituency in local and statewide environmental issues. Politically, the group is growing in both size and influence. Well over half of Alaska's legislators represent urban constituencies in Anchorage and Fairbanks.

A handful of Alaska Natives are true urbanites, at least in terms of lifestyle and verbalized values. A far larger group, however, is totally estranged both physically and mentally from city life. About 20 percent of all Alaska Natives live in communities with fewer than 200 people, and an additional 50 percent live in places with 200 to 300 people.

I have a mental image of a middle-aged Eskimo or Indian villager: going to the store, the church, the airstrip; to the boats on the beach, to the river for water, to the hills for caribou, to the fish camp, to the weekly movie at the schoolhouse, to visit the neighbor; sensing the fog, the wind-flung snow, the sun, the mosquitoes; the smoothness of ivory, the pain of aging joints, the frozen ear, the scouring gut; pride for the year's first whale, bewilderment for the first child in school, hurt for the daughter gone to Anchorage, the father drunk; love for the scrambling babies; thinking of leaving for Anchorage, of starting a fish cooperative, of hunting, of the torn gill net and broken snowmobile; of the next government check, of the old potlatches, of the overdue Sears order, of the oddness and menace of the news.

The statistics say the village Native has less income, worse health, poorer education, and less opportunity than the Native who lives in town. But though suffering when friends and family members leave, and confronting many painful social problems, the villagers at least have roots in a familiar place and the comfort of the recurring seasons and their routines.

Urban Natives have lost or set aside the stabilizing influence of familiar country in favor of the expected excitements and economic improvements of the cities. They are often barred from jobs by their lack of formal education or by outright discrimination and prejudice. The excitements they see usually are those of the undersides of cities in the bars, alleys, old hotels, and jails.

Some Natives "make it" in the town, where they may lead quiet, unobtrusive lives as store clerks, heavy-equipment operators, artists. Others, more aggressively ambitious, may become leaders of Native organizations. These are the Eskimos and Indians who led the drive for recognition of aboriginal land claims, and who are in position to control the use of the cash and acreage settlement.

Many Alaskan townspeople are not urbanites but pioneers whom the countryside can no longer support, or whose business or advancing years brings them into town to live. They are sourdoughs, the old-timers among the newcomers. They have lived in Alaska longer than the urbanites, and many came from rural or smalltown environments in the South 48, rather than cities. Sourdoughs show the influence of a deeply ingrained paranoia about "the Feds" and "Outsiders" in their We–They view of Alaska with respect to the rest of the world. They have a strong belief in the great Alaskan cornucopia, a belief easily turned to bitterness if they have missed a share.

Sourdoughs may be bankers, local politicians, roadhouse keepers, prospectors, bush pilots, truckers, highway engineers, or newspaper editors. They or their parents came north in boom times, and when the tide went out, they stayed to await its return. They are not born anymore because the times are not right, and probably never will be again. They work hard, or used to work hard when young, sometimes with a Calvinist's religious dedication but often in hopes of getting something for nothing from the land: a big strike, a bonanza, a mother lode. They think of statewide economic development in terms of windfall oil finds and copper strikes, and commit 27 themselves eagerly to new highways, massive hydroelectric dams, and other projects that will catalyze development. Their self-imagery as pioneers is easily mobilized by politicians using a few well-known slogans: "Open up the country!" "Federal bureaucrats are trying to run Alaska." "Let the Outside preservationists clean up their own back yard!" In short, they are romantics masquerading as hard-bitten pragmatists.

Sourdough attitudes toward the land are curiously ambivalent. They know the land intimately but not intellectually, tending to scoff at the seemingly mysterious concerns of ecologists and wilderness enthusiasts. They love the country and treat it with mixed gentleness and roughness.

A fourth group of people who live in towns is less interested in corporate expansion than urbanites and less steeped in economic romanticism than sourdoughs. They are professionals, a rather large grouping of natural and social scientists, technicians, teachers, engineers, medical and dental practitioners, magistrates, law enforcement personnel, social case workers, and others. Highly educated and trained, they think of their work as more than a job; many are dedicated crusaders in behalf of the goals of their profession.

Alaska has an exceptionally high proportion of professional people, especially scientists, managers, and program administrators. They comprise the backbone of many civic organizations, including environmental organizations, where their skills, knowledge, or intellectual approach often propels them into committee chairmanships and offices. They rarely seek public office, which would jeopardize their professional work standing. A few professions support lobbies, but most look upon lobbying and unionizing with distrust. The scientists among the group, in particular, tend to avoid the risks of political activism.

In terms of Alaskan residence, the professional group stands midway between urbanites and sourdoughs. The professional has nationwide — even worldwide — mobility, and may leave Alaska for a bigger university, a federal regional head-quarters, or Washington, D.C. However, a surprisingly large number of professionals have lived in Alaska for ten years or more. Strong attachments to the wild country of Alaska are common, often leading to deep conflicts of personal goals, especially among geologists, engineers, and others whose work can lead to a loss of the values of wild Alaska. Alaska also has the attractions of a small society, offering professionals a more open field, more varied responsibilities, more chances for advancement and recognition.

Living cryptically in odd places throughout the whole state there are people who by choice keep their lives apart from the main run of society — the loners. They may work, and if they do, it is a seasonal job like fishing, logging, trapping, or re-porting local weather conditions to commercial bush airlines. They may simply subsist off the land or have some kind of remittance from government or past savings or parents. Many are college graduates or college dropouts who have turned from mainstream society out of anger, frustration, or philo-sophical disagreement. They build cabins, yurts, and geodesic domes. They bury themselves in the chores of wilderness sur-vival and sometimes unearth their selves in the process. Most are asocial and apolitical, though once in a while a few will surface as leaders in an attempt to capture a political party by overthrowing "the establishment." In turn, they are usually ignored by society and pressure-group politics. Loners live more like pioneers than the sourdoughs do, but without the lat-ter's ambition to conquer the wilderness and fill it with people.

Periodically throughout recent Alaskan history, boomers have been a highly visible part of northern society. The recent pipeline construction boom was no exception. The hotels, bars, stores, and trailer courts of Anchorage, Fairbanks, Val-dez, and small towns along the Trans-Alaska Pipeline route teem with boomers with pointy-toed boots, big hats, and Texan drawls. Organized labor, including the Alaska Team- 29 sters Union Local 959 which received national publicity in 1975 and 1976, became an exceptionally potent economic and political (and social) force in Alaska in mid-decade, based on the swelling number of highly paid skilled and semi-skilled people moving north to get in on the action. The majority of these boomers left their families "in the States," consider themselves transients, and have little understanding of the North or interest in its long-term welfare. Some — often to their own considerable surprise — will stay, captured by any one of the melodies of the northern Lorelei.

One of the questions I am asked most often by people who don't live in Alaska, but who are intensely interested in it, is how these varied constellations of Alaskans feel about conservation and economic development? The question is a crucial one for the whole subject of this book.

Judging from the words and actions of most political administrators and legislators and from the flavor of newspaper editorials written for Alaska's urban papers, there seems little doubt that the political tide is still set toward traditional economic development. The first popular test of a program or law is whether implementing it will increase or decrease the conversion of natural resources to goods and dollars, expand or shrink job opportunities, raise or lower state revenues, promote or dampen commercial enterprises. Dominant political views see environmental protection as a nice thing in itself, but a harassment or outright danger when it becomes an issue in a particular development program. As one prominent state senator put it in 1970, there are two different kinds of legislators, both concerned with saving the environment: one would protect the environment no matter what it cost, the other would protect the environment as long as it didn't cost anything. The balance is certainly skewed toward the latter. During the great debate in 1977–78 over proposals for new national parks and refuges in Alaska, only one legislator out of sixty was willing to testify in behalf of the conservationist position as expressed in Congressman Morris Udall's bill.

A closer look at Alaskan politics suggests that political leaders are likely to show a stronger pro-development attitude than their average constituent. In town after town — Cordova, Homer, Kenai, Anchorage, Kodiak, Fairbanks, and others — municipal leaders and a tight following of businessmen urge a faster growth and less discriminating support of new industry than the townspeople approve in professional surveys. The community leaders often move on to the state legislature, where they join rural people whose activities in Native corporations have been their springboard into politics.

The stridence of pro-development voices is related to how much of a budgetary pinch Alaska is feeling at the moment and to whether some major industry or development project is frustrated by unexpected delay. An excellent example is the sequence of changes in political attitude from September 1969 to 1974 as the fortunes of North Slope petroleum development waxed and waned. In the fall of 1969, when a billion-dollar windfall was in the state's pocket, euphoria swept Alaska. The days of scrimping and saving seemed over. There was a good deal of half-embarrassed but sincere discussion of the quality of life and social wrongs that needed to be set right. A news article written by a young state senator from Fairbanks was typical:

The quality of living in Alaska will become a major issue confronting Alaskans within the next few years. No longer living a hand-to-mouth existence, our people will be able to look at the larger issues before them. Our state can decide what sort of quality environment it desires, what sort of social structure it wants, and what kind of society it will create.[3]

Early in 1970 the legislature passed a budget amounting to twice that of the preceding year. It repealed a long-standing industrial tax-incentive law, passed oil-spill control legislation, and established the first major units in the state park system. In 1971, the legislature established a new cabinet-level Department of Environmental Conservation.

31

Then lawsuits and sudden federal concern over pipeline construction technology stalled the Trans-Atlantic Pipeline project, the means by which the windfall was to be extended into a long-term source of revenue. Budget worries grew severe. Fiscal conservatism asserted itself, and a definite environmental backlash set in. The 1972 legislature did almost nothing in the environmental field. "Sierra Go Home" bumper stickers blossomed, and editorials shrilled about the excesses of the environmentalists. But still another change in attitude occurred in 1974 after construction began on the Prudhoe–Valdez project. Relieved of the need to worry about whether the line would be built, Alaskans began to look around at some of the personal costs of boom-time growth. Apprehension and disgruntlement with price gouging, crime-rate increases, crowded streets, and sudden subdivisions surfaced in the August primaries when gubernatorial candidate Jay Hammond, running on a controlled-growth platform, won a surprisingly easy victory over Wally Hickel, widely known to Alaskans as a pro-development businessman. Mr. Hammond won narrowly over former Governor William Egan and settled down to the task of redirecting the thoughts and energies of the massive state bureaucracy. Then another fiscal crisis arose, spawned of public spending that for years had exceeded public income. Once again, environment took a back seat.

Without question, most Alaskans love the wildness and beauty of the state. This feeling is expressed in countless ways: local art, devotion of leisure time to outdoor experiences, articles in the popular press, political speeches — in every way, in fact, except in the majority of state and local government actions. Polls consistently show that most non-Native Alaskans came north because of the uncrowded and beautiful land they expected to find, and that they want Alaska's back country to remain wild. During a unique eight-day seminar in November–December 1969, over 100 Alaskan opinion leaders selected by the legislature to debate Alaska's future as a rich oil state spent much of their time on questions of environmental quality. They sensed that the special feel of Alaska emanated from nature and from human experiences in nature. Relieved (they thought) of the burden of figuring out how Alaskans could earn a living, they defined Alaskan living largely in terms of the state's wildness and beauty in terms of the freedom of lifestyle that is part of Alaska's tradition.

Conflicts between economic growth and environmental protection often bring out a distrust of Outside interest in Alaskan affairs, a legacy persisting from pre-statehood colonialism. Excited as Alaskans were about the 1969 lease sale, many could not help wondering what sort of bargain the state had struck with the huge, powerful, international oil industry. Had a friendly genie been let out of the bottle, or had all the ills that could plague mankind escaped from Pandora's box? Similarly, when conservation groups promoted federal withdrawals to preserve wild country and when they sued to halt pipeline construction and to set aside a major timber sale in southeastern Alaska, the dominant Alaskan response was not to examine the merits of the actions but to rebel against Outside interference.

In many ways Alaska's official government voice has had the sound of sourdoughs. The sound is partly genuine: many Alaskan leaders, in and out of office, are sourdoughs. But more and more, the litany of the frontier and the colonial Alaska has the mustiness of patriotic fervor brought out of closets for special occasions. The simple answers, like opening up the country with roads, postponing environmental safeguards until Alaska catches up, and belaboring the nonresident scapegoats, seem less useful today to Native Alaskans, professional administrators and scientists, and urbanites. The real political power of those ideas probably lies in their convenience for commercial interests.

There is very little direct evidence about how Native Alas- 33 kans feel about conservation issues. My impression is that Natives do not consider "environment" (in the sense used by more affluent Americans) to be of very high priority. Maintaining fish and game and their habitat is of great interest to Natives as a practical step necessary to allow continued hunting and fishing. However, land withdrawals to preserve wildlife are opposed by Natives if their harvest opportunities seem to be in jeopardy. When Native groups oppose economic development projects, it is usually because the projects threaten subsistence resources and homes (as in the case of the Rampart Dam proposal, many road construction projects, and the several early Atomic Energy Commission projects in Alaska), or because the Natives want to assure their share in the benefits of the project. Few Natives have much interest in pollution in the abstract, but vigorously work for pure water supplies, sewage treatment, and solid-waste disposal in the villages. Land is home to some Natives in a much more intensely personal and even mystical way than for most non-Natives, but only time will tell how this feeling will affect their actions as private owners of huge tracts of land.

Issues

You can tell a lot about a place by the problems its people talk about. In Alaska much of the talk that reaches news media is couched in the traditional phrases of economic development, vintage 1950. (Perhaps that is the language of the business community which underwrites the media, or perhaps society at large tends to define problems so they can be understood by its oldest administrators.) Beneath the highly visible debate over economic growth, however, is a strong current of concern over change as it affects individuals. We talk about the effects of economic and population growth on life itself; though vulgarized and made superficial by constant

34

repetition, the terms "impact" and "lifestyle" stand as frequent code words for that deeper and more personalized set of issues.

Rural Change, Rural Choices

Not so long ago, rural Alaska was space, isolation, wildness, independence, innocence; a backwater; an unwitting hermitage; a storied utopia happily left to Natives and adventurers. Now there is change in every dimension. The land's secrets, once guarded by remoteness, are daily laid bare on seismic and magnetometer charts and the dull red mottled images of infrared satellite cameras. All resources are coveted. The countryside, once merely (and lightly) used, now must be owned, and every vested interest eagerly paints its designated color on the newest map. Since 1971, Natives themselves have become a vested interest, operating formally through business corporations, searching for local or distant investment opportunities while dogging the federal government to complete the conveyance of land assured by the Alaska Native Claims Settlement Act.

Rural villages are tossed in crosscurrents. Their citizens are constantly moving away and returning, and newcomers flow in and out. Precisely when there are strong pressures for communities to organize to accept new school-management responsibilities, to run utility cooperatives, to cope with microcosmic urban sprawl, and to influence the regional Native corporation, the skills for modern leadership, always scarce, are often drained away from the village.

And where should rural leadership lead? Toward complete capitulation to the economic life and institutions designed in New York and Washington, D.C.? Into a heartbreaking guerrilla war with change itself? Toward some idealized hybrid culture, hoping — like the crossbreeder of porcupines and jackrabbits — for the best?

35

Writers are fond of alluding to the choices open to rural people, as though they were somehow given a free pass to a cultural supermarket. But choosing and achieving require clear vision, unequivocal decisions, a means of sending the message, and a responsive larger society. So often we blindly send warped arrows at armored and moving targets. Little wonder that rural Alaska is a broth of ephemeral alliances and schisms. While one regional business corporation is bolting from the Alaska Federation of Natives, its own ranks are split by rebellion of village councils. While one Native corporation makes a pact with an oil company on a joint exploration venture, another allies with conservation groups to establish a new wildlife refuge. There is no consistency, in rural Alaska, either of problem perception or response — a fact as true for the ancient tribe as for the newest Native corporation.

Anchorage 3, Alaska 2

For several decades, growth has gravitated to Anchorage and the satellite communities it controls. The Alaska Railroad began the process, military expenditures and Cook Inlet petroleum discoveries continued it, and the Trans-Alaska Pipeline experience proved that major projects anywhere in the state would confirm Anchorage's pre-eminence.

This sort of centripetal growth is an economic truism, especially in developing regions. People, firms, and government gravitate to the action, and the action goes where people, firms, and government are. The Alaska case isn't unique. Yukon has its Whitehorse, British Columbia has its Vancouver, Massachusetts has Boston, Georgia has Atlanta. There may be a difference of degree, however, because in Alaska there are no serious within-region competitors for the economic pie, whereas there is keen competition among cities in the Northeast, South, and other regions of the United States.

The size of Anchorage is an obvious political issue in Alaska. For example, Anchorage leaders have long wanted the capital to be in or close to their town, but for years the very strength of that desire united the rest of the state in opposition. On the third (and successful) try, in 1974, proponents of the capital move split the opposition by assuring that Anchorage itself would not become the capital city. If the move is consummated (there is still some doubt), the new site will be in the Anchorage ambit of influence; the political power of Anchorage cannot help but increase. Even more emphatically, southeastern Alaska will lose a major source of economic stimulation and cultural diversity. It is not too outrageous to predict a withdrawal into provincialism as the Southeast drifts farther from the economic and political center of the state.

Anchorage's dominance means a dominance of urban perspectives in Alaska's populace, a fact with both hopeful and doubtful implications. If urban Alaska sees its destiny as growth, if that growth is ultimately fed by the extraction of resources from rural Alaska, then the city can be expected to run roughshod over the country whenever village Alaska's "Slow Down!" clashes with urban Alaska's "Hurry Up!"

The Last Scramble

Alaska was purchased in 1867. Its land lay in passive federal trusteeship for the next ninety years, with only a few scattered blocks given any permanent agency ownership, and with only the scantiest peppering of private land disposals. By early 1958, 99 percent of the land was still federal. By late that year a new state had formed and 28 percent of the land had been promised to it as a patrimony, though it remained to be seen where that state acreage would be located. In late 1971 the Alaska Native Claims Settlement Act promised 44 million acres (about 11 percent of the state) to Native corporations and required a later Congress to consider a final major series of land withdrawals from the public domain for national parks and other conservation areas.

Throughout this entire two decades, the ownership of land   37 was a prominent issue in Alaska. There were — and still are — five well-defined parties to the struggle: federal park and refuge agencies, federal multiple-use land agencies, the state, Native corporations, and non-Native private citizens. By the mid-1970s the scramble reached a peak. The end was in sight (by 1980 the game will be won or lost), but no group had achieved much more than a measure of chips to let it sit in on the last hand. Natives knew how much land they would have, and general locations were firm, but they were not sure when the land title would be conveyed or what easements or other liens would be attached. The state faced huge uncertainties about what lands would still be open for selection when Congress finally disposed of the national-interest lands question. The two blocs of federal agencies fought for the biggest and choicest pieces of public domain. And the diverse, poorly organized, would-be private landowners fought nearly everybody to get in on the last chance for an American to get free land from the government. They opposed parks and refuges to keep as much land as possible in public domain, hoping the state could gain control of good land which, in turn, it would sell or lease.

Ownership, of course, is really only a way to control land use, which is in itself only a means of reaching more fundamental goals like gaining wealth or protecting living opportunities and qualities. Thus the issue of land ownership is an expression of the differing views held about economic growth, cultural qualities, and lifestyles.

Oil Money

Prudhoe Bay petroleum has twice presented Alaskans with a windfall of disposable income. The first time was, in a sense, a practice session. In September 1969, oil companies paid the state $900 million for leases in the area around the new discovery wells, and state leaders wondered what to do with an amount of money exceeding by sixfold the current year's budget. To make a long story short, they spent it. Over the next six fiscal years, government services and revenue sharing grew enormously, dipping into the 1969 windfall to compensate for annual deficits. By early 1976 the $900 million windfall was gone, and the state had to borrow money from Prudhoe Bay leaseholders (through a tax on oil reserves with a credit against future production taxes) to see it through until the oil began to flow.

The second and much more severe test begins in 1979 when, with Prudhoe production reaching 1.2 million barrels a day and the borrowed reserves tax paid back, Alaska probably will receive some $2 million each day from North Slope oil taxes. Though not all of this daily income is surplus to current operating needs, some of it is. What to do with these and other petroleum revenues in the future is a major issue among Alaska's leaders today.

Some generally accepted views are common in these discussions. First, there is an assumption that the state should get as much money as it can from its oil and gas; that is, we should not forgo some income by taxing petroleum more lightly. Second, there is recognition that oil and gas revenues are relatively short lived, being tied to a nonrenewing resource which national politics demand be extracted at a high rate. A corollary is that future Alaskans should not be deprived of all of the monetary benefits from oil and gas; hence that a share of current revenues should be set aside for them. Third, there is a widespread feeling, only vaguely thought through in practical terms, that oil and gas revenues should support intensified use and management of renewable resources like fisheries, agriculture, timber, and renewable energy sources.

Few people realize how fundamental an issue, in social and environmental terms, petroleum revenue management truly is. The full implications of wealth to a small northern society won't be revealed except through long and probably painful 39 experience. But for wealth to come so suddenly to a rough-and-ready frontier, itself fractured by cultural conflict and harassed by change and in an arctic and subarctic landscape where technological societies have little experience, conjures even for the most optimistic citizen a web of entangling problems. How can money be spent locally without being translated into more jobs, new immigration, bigger population, more demands for government services, more pressures on land and environment, more spending, and so on? Can investment managers be expected to favor more lucrative investments Outside given the political unpopularity of that idea? And even if investments are made Outside, how will interest be spent when it, in turn, adds significantly to annual revenues? Surplus revenue management, or at least the careful writing of policies that instruct that management, is going to be Alaska's most meaningful test of its own self-understanding in the next several decades.

Industrialization

The land ownership and revenue issues basically translate into the question: What kind of Alaska? So does a closely related problem widely discussed in the mid 1970s, the issue of industrialization. The reason for the debate is the fact that state leaders had to decide, very quickly, what to do with royalty oil and gas soon to be received in kind or in dollars. In 1975 and 1976 it seemed that if the state had not committed its royalty gas from Prudhoe through a contract with a purchaser, the federal government would assume that the gas had been "abandoned" (as far as determining ultimate consumption is concerned) to interstate commerce and would commit the gas irrevocably to a non-Alaskan market. This idea was extremely unpopular with business leaders. Soon it became an unquestioned state goal to prevent abandonment. But what kind of contract to write, when, practically speaking, Alaska could find little in-state use for Prudhoe gas for years after it came on stream, regardless of what domestic uses might be found for it in the more distant future?

Some Alaskans believe and hope that Alaskan natural gas and oil will be used as energy sources and basic chemical building blocks, in combination with local coal, to create a major petrochemical industry in the state. Of those Alaskans, some would permit the marketplace to decide whether such industries would develop here, others would subsidize petrochemical plants to assure that they would locate in Alaska. Other people question that industries based on exhaustible resources are good for the state in the long run, or that heavy industry is desirable at all. In 1977 Governor Hammond suggested a third policy: to support refineries that could supply local needs at favorable prices in an unsubsidized market, but to oppose large export-based refineries and petrochemical plants.

The debate looks not only forward into the state's future, but back into its past. A major root of the pro-industry argument is a determination not to be high-graded (today we say "ripped off") by Outside firms extracting and shipping raw materials without building permanence into the social and economic fabric of the North, as had happened too often in our history. At least one argument on the other side, however, is a rejection of bigness — big labor, big business — which would inevitably come with such industrialization (and had already come with Prudhoe discoveries and the oil pipeline).

Alaskans and the Feds

Crosscutting many of the issues of the 1970s is a familiar and persistent psychological tension, the local fear of dominance by the federal government.

The problem is partly a legacy from territorial days, an undying rebellion against distant authority which statehood failed to pinch out. In part, it is a symbolic presentation of a scape-goat for all ills of the day (too much economic activity or too little, inflation, and so on), inflamed by the obvious growth of federal involvement in such things as environmental quality control, wildlife management, public land management, and oil and gas development.

Alaskan politicians who wax oratorical about "the Feds" must surely have a hidden twinkle when they look at some of the contradictions in the popular argument. We are vehement in our disgust at federal bureaucracies that always get bigger; yet the outcry against any small dismantling of that bureaucracy in Alaska is swift and shrill. We ask for special consider-ations in federal laws and programs, but insist on anonymous equality when the other side of the coin — regulation and con-trol — turns up. The parallel with the behavior of adolescents is too clear to be comfortable.

Regulation and Freedom

Last, in this quick catalogue of contemporary issues, is a re-curring conflict between individual freedom and governmental regulation. It is hard to judge whether Alaskans feel this con-flict any more deeply than most Americans, but we do seem to express it very forcibly. Many — or at least some highly vo-cal — Alaskans object to nearly every aspect of modern gov-ernance at every level. Planning and zoning are anathema. Any abridgment of "traditional rights" (many of which never existed) of landowners is decried. Any restriction on the turn-of-the-century relationship between the private citizen and public land is viewed as a blasphemy against the American Way of Life. When Congress considered establishing new ref-uge and park areas in Alaska, the most outspoken of these po-litical fundamentalists seriously investigated a suit to declare the purchase of Alaska illegal.

42   All of this is just the spectacular (or bizarre) tip of a per-

vasive uncertainty and distrust of government. Whether we as citizens have innocently underestimated the inevitable consequences of a crowded world, or whether the momentum of government growth has powered it beyond clear need, is a matter for political scholars to debate and historians to judge. Meanwhile, the dogfights between private citizen and government official continue on a thousand fronts.

CHAPTER III

Realities

Southerners roared into Alaska on ironbound whalers, gold dredges, D-8 Cats, Winnebago Chieftains, and Lear jets. In the cacophony of exploitation, no one has taken pains to learn anything about the real nature of the North. Now we are paying the penalty of ignorance in damaged landscapes, inconvenient and costly technology, wasted resources, and an ulcerating self-revulsion. Do we, as a culture, intend to stay? Or will we duck and dodge and build up bad debts until the cornucopia shakes out hoar frost, and then pack up and head south?

If we do plan to stay, we have some things to learn (and unlearn). Southerners, after all, haven't been around ice floes or centuries-old black spruce toothpick trees or sixty below zero very long — and most of our time in the North we have been taking, not looking.

Looking is worthwhile. For too long, urban Alaskans, impatient for even more dramatic growth, have blamed administrative bungling or political obstruction when widely expected development ventures failed to materialize. Every rumored oil strike, every newfound fish stock, every big timber sale, thrums the chords of booming expectations that are so much a part of the pioneer. The only restraining forces understood and occasionally admitted are economic: too little local capital, high wages, scarce management talent, high freight rates, seasonal unemployment, flimsy support structures, low economic multipliers. In Alaska's towns of commerce the conventional wisdom is that small and soon-to-come changes in world demand for copper (or pulp or iron ore or fish sticks), or the next new highway, or cheap power, will release the economy into an endless climb.

It is true that Alaska's young economy responds to easing cost constraints or massive recource price surges. Few people realize, however, the hidden dimension of environmental characteristics which so greatly affect both the quality and quantity of long-term growth. The cost of piping water through frozen soil forces suburban Fairbanks homeowners to drill individual wells into sparse aquifers. This limits densities and increases commuting distance, which in turn requires the burning of more gasoline, thus increasing carbon monoxide pollution and ice fog which, on cold winter days, forces schools to close . . . and on and on.

Every American has a stake in "doing it right" in Alaska. Ignoring environmental realities will raise costs and reduce quality everywhere we turn, a physical and social circumstance more likely to stimulate rip-and-run than stay-and-build. Unless public and private policies are informed by these realities and imaginatively respond to them, we will continue to diminish priceless national treasures and degrade Alaskan living.

The Sparse Mantle of Life

Johnny Frasca prospected and mined around interior Alaska for years. When I knew him he was still mining, a vigorous, ruddy-faced, stocky man in his 70s, living on a creek at timberline 100 miles east of Fairbanks. On September evenings we would watch the maroon and amber hills for moose or caribou to put away for the winter, and often he would shake his head and say, uncomplainingly, "It's a hungry country."

45

A lot of expensive biological studies have proved the truth of that simple comment. Reaching far back into prehistory, the record of middens and village sites and the bones of young children tells us how thoroughly the human history of Alaska was controlled by hunger and speaks of the attempts, clever and desperate, of societies to evade it. Unless our industrial or post-industrial society collapses catastrophically, human existence will never again be so completely dominated by the patterns of natural biologic productivity. Nevertheless, as long as some people must or want to live partly off the land, as long as we hunt and fish for recreation and commerce, as long as we grow home gardens or entertain notions of commercial agriculture, as long as we want tourists to visit us, and as long as we care about soil erosion and sensible landscape maintenance, we must respect and respond to the stark facts of northern biology.

Northern Seas

The ice-covered Bering Sea and the cold gray scud of the stormy Gulf of Alaska aren't places you would look for animal life in abundance, but the surprising fact is that the far North Pacific is one of the richest places in the ocean world. Here deep ocean currents rise to the surface with their load of nutrients and spread across a vast continental shelf. Sunlight provides the energy for unimaginable numbers of single-celled, drifting phytoplankton to fix these nutrients into living tissue. Successively bigger creatures feed on plankton and each other. Somewhere along the chain, five to ten links from the origin of the process, people dip their nets and take their harvest.

The potential yearly catch of fish from the entire Pacific north of Oregon is awesome: over 2 million metric tons of herring, close to 2 million tons of pollock and other bottom fish, close to 1½ million metric tons of crab, shrimp, squid, and clams.[1] The actual catch, however, is much smaller because markets do not yet exist for some species, or because stocks are too scattered to be caught profitably. Today, even after Congress has extended the nation's legal jurisdiction over fisheries out to 200 miles or more, most of the fish and shellfish caught in the North Pacific go into the huge holds of foreign ships.

Fish farming and aquaculture have for decades held out their tantalizing promise of greatly expanding ocean harvests. Certainly farming the sea — growing a thick soup of plankton in oceanic "cages," enticing shellfish to settle thickly in artificial beds, enriching and controlling passage of fish into secluded bays — would break the bonds of fundamental inefficiency of traditional fishing. No longer would we have to travel miles to fishing grounds or trawl blindly along an unseen bottom. We would, if we harvested plankton, by-pass the inevitable energy losses that subtract up to 90 percent of the energy in every move from link to link along the predation chain.

However, this kind of aquaculture on a grand scale is no more than a dream. Practical demonstrations in northern waters are rare. Furthermore, it is not hard to guess at some potential problems. Who would eat plankton, for example, and would they pay enough to provide an incentive? If we harvest small fish, krill (small shrimplike animals), or plankton, what would happen to the bigger fish, whales, seals, and sea birds that now feed on them? Would cutting a kelp forest pose problems like those of cutting a spruce forest?

The traditional fisheries of the North Pacific are already under heavy pressure. Salmon are being caught right up to the limit of sustained yield and need to be rebuilt back to the much higher levels of stocks that once amazed travelers to Alaska. Halibut stocks have been badly overfished. So have Bering Sea pollock, flounders, and sole. Herring runs are locally depleted and under pressure from roe buyers. King crab catches boomed, busted, and have now recovered at least partly. A

47

few stocks apparently could sustain a higher catch: tanner or snow crabs are an example, as are ocean perch. In general, the total fishing effort on North Pacific stocks is close to the upper safe limit for the larger and most salable fish. The only major increase in catches by U.S. fishermen would occur if we displaced foreign fleets.

Fresh Waters

Hardly an angler in the United States doesn't dream of a fishing trip to Alaska where — according to the travel brochures and most sporting magazines — schools of trophy-sized salmon, trout, grayling, pike, and sheefish are lining up for a chance at a lure. There is good sport fishing in Alaska, if you pick and choose and get there first. But the cold fact is that Alaska's streams, lakes, and ponds, acre for acre, are less productive than those in any other state. The scientific standard for measuring productivity is the amount of carbon converted to plant tissue in a square meter of area each year. By that standard, Alaska lakes average far less than 100 grams of carbon per meter per year, much less than Bering Sea production.[2]

The sources of the problem aren't hard to find. Many streams and lakes are turbid with suspended clay and silt from glacier-ground rocks or riverbank erosion, limiting light penetration. In northern and central Alaska, shallow lakes and streams freeze to the bottom, eliminating fish as year-round residents. Other lakes and streams that do not freeze to the bottom nevertheless are covered with snow and ice for so long each year that oxygen levels drop below the tolerance threshold of fish.

What explains the fabled fishing in Alaska? Discounting the propaganda and tall tales, there are two reasons behind the beaming faces and strings of gleaming fish. One is that all of the salmon and many of the trout caught in fresh water gain their size in salt water; the productivity is in the sea, not the stream. The other is that when angling pressure is very light resident freshwater fish have a chance to live a long time, slowly growing to respectable size.

Subsistence catches can occur only in exceptionally productive lakes or in places where migrant freshwater fish (grayling, whitefish, trout) concentrate seasonally. There is no commercial freshwater fishery in Alaska at present with the exception of isolated small salmon fisheries. The slow growth rates of resident fish, coupled with the large catches demanded by commercial operations, would force such fisheries to alternately overfish and abandon each lake. Worse, such commercial operations would destroy important sport fisheries, which undoubtedly are more valuable even from a strict economic standpoint.

The restricted productivity of Alaskan fresh waters also has important consequences to the management of recreational fisheries. As the Alaska Division of Sport Fish wrote in its 1970 report to the Board of Fish and Game:

Our relatively unproductive streams will not tolerate a heavy harvest of trout and steelhead and the fragile stream-banks will not tolerate a good deal of human traffic. It will be biologically necessary to reduce bag limits, shorten fishing seasons, and close areas to fishing in the interest of sustaining a fish population.[3]

In the Talachulitna River north of Anchorage, for example, where growth of rainbow trout is good in comparison with most stream populations of this latitude, sport fishing by 1970 had reduced the average length of surviving trout. Apparently big fish were the first to take anglers' lures. The first signs of excessive harvest were visible even though the cost of getting to the stream (about $200 per party) greatly reduced fishing pressure.

Even the milder regions of the Panhandle are too sterile to   49 put flesh fast on freshwater fish. Sea-run cutthroat trout in southeastern Alaska mature sexually at six or seven years, when 10 to 13 inches long. Populations are small even in the better streams, numbering only about 2000 fish, of which only one in four will spawn. Hence, only very limited fishing can be allowed on any given stream. The world-famous trophy-trout and grayling fisheries of the Iliamna Lake region at the base of the Alaska Peninsula may be at the brink of serious trouble from overfishing, even though sportsmen can reach the area only by air, and must pay over $100 per night to stay at a fishing lodge.

Mammals and birds feeding in fresh water likewise reflect the biologic productivity of the water they live in. Solid estimates of aquatic mammal densities in Alaska are rare. Qualitatively, biologists and trappers know that mink and otter of interior and northern Alaska are much scarcer, in proportion to water area and shoreline available, than the same species along the beaches of southeastern Alaska, or in temperate zone waters. Similarly, muskrats of the relatively rich ponds (by Alaska standards) in the Yukon Flats never achieve the year-to-year abundance of muskrats in Iowa or Louisiana marshes.

Alaska wetlands harbor millions of summering waterfowl, but except in the most fertile marshes duck densities are lower than in the continent's top waterfowl production areas, like the prairie pothole region. The highest densities of ducks in Alaska are on the Yukon Flats, an area of floodplain ponds and sloughs whose fertility is enriched periodically with new deposits of silt, and the Copper River Delta. Breeding populations of ducks in those areas average 99 to 86 adults per square mile, respectively. The next highest densities in the state are far lower: 67 per square mile in the Tanana-Kuskokwim River marshes, 60 per square mile in the shoreline wetlands of the treeless Seward Peninsula. Despite an abundance of water, the Arctic Slope area has an average of only 15 ducks per square mile, a result of late ice-out dates and the lack of aquatic vegetation. Most rivers, streams, forest ponds (thaw lakes), and large, cold lakes in Alaska have extremely few waterfowl.[4]

Uplands

Alaska's uplands vary immensely in their productivity. Local variations often are great, and there is also a general trend toward reduced productivity from wet coastal forests of the south through the subarctic woodlands of the Interior to arctic and alpine tundras.

From Dixon Entrance at Alaska's southern extremity to the west side of lower Cook Inlet is a narrow rim of seaward-facing mountains whose slopes intercept moist air sweeping across the ice-free waters of the Gulf of Alaska. Here grow Alaska's biggest trees — Sitka spruce, western hemlock, western red cedar, Alaska cedar, and mountain hemlock — in a forest community much like the great evergreen coniferous forests of the Pacific Northwest. Trees extend from the beach upward to 2000 to 3000 feet, becoming shorter and wind-shaped at higher elevations. Mosses are constant companions of the trees, carpeting the ground, rocks, and logs, clinging to tree trunks and lower limbs. Where the soil is fine-textured and water-soaked the forest gives way to muskegs of sedges, grasses, mosses, and low shrubs.

Information about the real productivity of Alaskan coastal forests is shockingly sparse considering the millions of trees cut in the region. Forest scientists have occasionally measured the amount of wood added to tree trunks each year, giving us at least a rough way of comparing growth in the Southeast to other logging areas.[5] The best growth seems to occur when the trees are 50 to 90 years old. On comparatively fertile sites in coastal Alaska, these "young adult" Sitka spruce and hemlock put on slightly less wood than Douglas fir stands in Oregon and Washington and about a third of the annual increment in young California redwood groves.

51

Starting with these figures on tree-trunk growth, I tried to calculate total basic production of all plants in the Southeast forests. My estimate of 200–300 grams of carbon per meter per year, which ignores extremely poor and extremely rich sites, implies that forests of the Alaska Panhandle make green plant material available at about the same rate as southern New England hardwood forests, at half the rate of good pine stands in the South, and at one third the rate of tropical forests. Forested parts of Interior Alaska convert sunlight to vegetation at rates quite close to those in the Southeast, though on the average Interior stands are a little less productive. As is true everywhere, local variation in productivity is great. The cold, frost-filled, or boggy soils of northern muskegs and northfacing hillsides are more sterile than south slopes on well-drained soil.

The fundamental and inescapable fact is that loggers in Alaska have to have a good deal more patience than loggers in other states.

Tundra

Over half of Alaska is treeless. The entire North Slope, the western coastal areas cooled by the Chukchi and Bering seas, the Alaska Peninsula, Aleutians, most of Kodiak Island, and all mountain areas above 2000–3000 feet support a low and highly variable form of vegetation called "tundra." Individual plants are short or prostrate. They are adapted to short growing seasons with long cool days or meager light, the latter due to persistent coastal cloud cover and the slanting sun of high latitudes. Tundra plants are almost all perennial; they usually die back to the ground surface in autumn and depend on nutrients stored in buds and roots for quick starts in spring. They must cope with drying and cooling winds, sudden summer frosts and snowstorms, snow-blasting in winter, and ground-churning cycles of thaw and frost.

Not surprisingly, tundras are the least productive of Alaska's major biotic subdivisions. Tundra vegetation also is slowest to recover from trampling, breakage, or uprooting. Primary production is limited mostly by the shortness of the growing season (45 to 90 days) and the scarcity of available nitrogen and phosphorus in tundra soils. Many other factors are important, too, and result in local variations in biological production: depth of thaw in summer, amount of soil moisture, amount of soil-churning action, depth of snow cover, exposure to sun, and so on. Dry ridges in the Canadian Arctic are almost totally barren, producing tiny growths equivalent to about 20 cabbages per acre per year.[6] Alaska's poorest tundras are only slightly more generous than that. The average Alaskan tundra area is from one fifth to one third as productive as the Interior forest.

During the few weeks tundra plants can grow, their growth may be quite fast. Using stored nutrients to thrust stems, leaves, and flowers into the light, sedges, grasses, and perennial herbs may grow as rapidly as similar species in temperate regions. When roots and other underground parts are not harmed, recovery from certain disturbances like moderate grazing and light fires may occur within one growing season. Some shrubs like the larger willows will grow new branches rapidly after ice damage or browsing. At the other end of the scale are lichens, a group of rootless plants critical for caribou survival and notoriously slow growing. A scientist found that three important forage lichens on the Seward Peninsula added slightly over 5 mm of new growth each year, or one inch in 5 years.[7] In comparison with other parts of Alaska and Canada even this is a relatively rapid growth for lichens. In an area badly overgrazed by reindeer in the 1930s the remaining lichen fragments had not recovered fully after more than 30 years of protection.[8]

Particular kinds of disturbances can keep tundra from recovering as fast as individual plant growth capabilities indicate. 53

Severe fires in relative lush tundras (where fuel for hot fires is available) can eliminate most plants, especially mosses, lichens, and shrubs, for years. These sites may be taken over by grasses that can take advantage of nutrients released from burned organic material.

It is widely known that when tundra vegetation is scuffed up, compressed, broken, or burned, there is a high risk that a prolonged sequence of thawing, subsidence, and erosion will prevent revegetation for years or decades. The risks are greatest on moist slopes normally supporting the best-developed vegetation. The danger is proportional to severity of disturbance. When the vegetation is removed or damaged, the dark soils absorb heat from the sun and thaw to unusual depths. Pools of water form at the surface and increase average soil temperatures. When the subsoil is largely ice, as is so often the case in arctic tundras, thawing leads to slumping and, on sloping ground, to erosion. Plants cannot gain a foothold to heal the site. The thawing and erosion may spread to areas not disturbed originally. When healing finally occurs, the new plant community is almost sure to be different from the original one, hence highly visible. In what may have been an unconscious attempt at immortality, a member of a geophysical survey crew "wrote" his company's initials in the North Slope tundra to guide supply planes to camp. The bold initials GSI will remain an arctic graffito for centuries.

Push the sparse tundra growth through the guts of insects and birds and mammals, take a loss of 90 percent of the original plant energy in the process, and you have entered the second layer of tundra life, the grazers. Among these the insects are by far the most important to the system itself, but the life and times of the birds and mammals are of greater immediate human interest.

Lemmings are the most abundant warm-blooded grazers in arctic tundras in terms of total biomass. Their densities are hard to calculate because three- to four-year cycles in numbers are common, and populations vary widely in mean density from place to place. Lemmings illustrate very well the close relationship among physical, plant, and animal components of tundra systems. When lemmings are at peak population levels, they eat a high proportion of the green material, hastening decomposition. Removal of the dense vegetation allows the ground to thaw deeper the following summer, releasing nutrients locked up in the uppermost layers of frozen subsoil. Meanwhile, lemming populations decline from food shortage and high predation and are kept at low levels for one or two years by continued winter predation. The sedges and grasses grow rapidly in response to low grazing pressure and high nitrogen and phosphorus availability, the insulation effect of plants increases, frost levels rise, and the cycle is repeated.[9]

The peculiarities of that thin and vulnerable skein of life in the North are not just academic curiosities. They mean something to would-be fishermen, farmers, loggers, recreationists, businessmen, builders, land managers — and they'll mean more in our crowded future. True enough, it isn't easy to separate environmental pressures and constraints from economic and social ones, any more than a man shut up inside an iron maiden can tell which spike hurts the most. That doesn't make them less real.

Take farming, for example. There may be 20 million acres of arable land in Alaska, but only one acre in a thousand is actually being farmed. In this sense the biological limits to Alaskan agriculture may seem so distant as to be meaningless in comparison with the numerous present economic and social constraints. A second and deeper look, however, shows that environmental forces are always in the background, operating through the more palpable economic, historic, and social factors. The short growing season, long day length, and the cool evening temperatures narrow the range of growable crops. Every one of the North's environmental features challenges agricultural research and development, raising research and development costs far above those in temperate regions. With such a short season, the crop grower has almost no choice in when to plant or harvest. A week of bad weather in spring can raise havoc with crops that even in good years mature at the brink of frost; a week of poor weather at harvest time can easily scuttle a year's work. And every environmental risk is doubly hazardous in a region strung far at the end of an economic line of transportation, labor, capital, and management skills.

Livestock production in Alaska is in a similar situation. Natural vegetation can't be used any more effectively — usually less — by livestock than by wildlife, and fertilizing or other intensive management to raise productivity is economically out of the question. Often, places that would support livestock in summer are a long way from good wintering places. Furthermore, raising market-quality livestock for finicky American palates is impossible on natural forage, but raising or importing finishing feeds is highly expensive. Even ignoring the obvious fact that livestock would compete with wildlife, it is hard to imagine large-scale meat growing in Alaska. Small operations taking advantage of locally grown grains and waste industrial heat may be viable, but would only be the exception proving the rule.

We try to harvest forests on a sustained yield basis, which means that in the long term what is cut cannot exceed what is grown. Biological productivity determines how much a forest grows. In southeastern Alaska present timber harvests by no means use up the entire annual increment of potential growth, but the demands of competing land uses such as wilderness, community growth, fish and wildlife habitat, power development, and mining will never permit this full potential to be reached. This means that on land that is available to the logger, timber needs will constantly thrust outward against ecological limitations. Forest managers will try to push those limits back and undoubtedly will succeed — but at ever-increasing cost. Every technique for speeding up regeneration of tree stands after logging, fertilizing young forests, thinning too-dense stands, or killing insect pests increases investments and must be balanced against the value they add to the eventual harvest in 60 to 100 years. In the Southeast today the current harvest of trees is about half of the theoretical allowable cut but is at least three-fourths of the allowable cut on forest land legally available for logging.

In the interior current tree harvests are minute in comparison with theoretical yields. Again, a complex of ecological, economic, and social factors weighs heavily against any near-term major expansion of the timber industry. For example, natural wildfires keep millions of acres of "commercial forest" in immature stages. The obvious response is to suppress fires, but given the slow growth rate of Interior forests, the cost of sustained, year-after-year fire suppression over a hundred million acres of wildland is enormous. Sawtimber takes 100 to 150 years to grow in central Alaska, and stands on some sites may well begin to degenerate toward the end of this period because of rising frost levels in soils heavily insulated by mosses. Another ecological problem has become obvious with the limited experience on logged areas near Fairbanks: restocking in many places is very poor, apparently because seed production from remaining or neighboring trees is unreliable. Good seed years occur only one year in four or five; by the time seeds fall thickly on a logged area the ground may be in poor condition to allow germination. If logging is to be more than a one-time mining operation in such places, investments in restocking are necessary.

Biological constraints affect recreation and tourism management, too; but here the problems are related to quality and quantity equally. To the individual recreationist or sightseer the success or failure of a trip (barring accidents, airline strikes, or other logistic catastrophes) is largely a matter of the quality of the experience, which in turn is influenced by the 57 esthetic qualities of surroundings, crowdedness, and other related aspects. Many of the favorite settings for recreation in Alaska have little inherent ability to conceal people or their litter, and so a sense of crowding can occur at low levels of use. Beaches, tundras, mountain meadows, rivers, lakes, and shrublands are like that. Furthermore, northern environments show the effects of recreation usage very early. Alpine areas around the world are really vulnerable to trampling, grazing by packhorses and saddle stock, campsite preparation, and firewood gathering. No one has yet quantified limits of use, and obviously the question of carrying capacity is as much a matter of personal and society-wide standards of expectation as it is a function of ecologic response to disturbance. But intuitively we can feel the messages of caution flowing from a sensitive landscape.

Alaska's special vulnerability to damage from all-terrain vehicles is well known. Many other human activities create similar problems: evidence is abundant around new homes, road construction projects, military sites, and other construction jobs all over Alaska. Knowing the North's vulnerability and slow recovery, builders nonetheless often have chosen to accept the soil and vegetation damage (and force others to accept it) rather than bear the costs of prevention. Anyone flying into Fairbanks or Anchorage can see the evidence in raw new trailer parks and industrial warehouse areas.

Prevention and restoration are possible even under Alaskan conditions. Perhaps the best demonstration is within the Swanson River oil field on the Kenai Peninsula. This oil field has been developed on the half of the Kenai National Moose Range classified in 1958 as available for oil and gas exploration. The oil-field operator, Standard Oil of California, was required to develop management plans meeting wildlife and other environmental requirements requested by the refuge manager. These requirements have become more stringent with passing years. Seismic exploration restrictions held ter-

rain and vegetation damage to the minimum possible with trac-
tor, truck, and "weasel" operations, mainly by prohibiting
unnecessary tree cutting and other plant disturbance. Main oil-
field roadsides, oil-well pads, and campsites were seeded and
fertilized as part of the construction process. As a result, very
little soil erosion has taken place and the sites are more pleas-
ing than if left in a raw state.

There are signs that more construction jobs now include
similar measures to protect land surfaces. Some new road projects by the Alaska Department of Transportation have included successful seeding of cuts and fills. Oil companies
operating at Prudhoe Bay began experiments in 1970 to test
revegetation techniques under tundra conditions, largely using
non-native grasses. Similar research is being done on Am-
chitka Island, site of several underground atomic tests.

The implications of high vulnerability and slow recovery of
vegetation are especially important in wild areas. Wildness is a
valuable land characteristic, and it is becoming more valuable
yearly. The cost of destroying or damaging wildness, however
hard it may be to calculate, is increasing. It is highest where
the degree of change is greatest and where recovery times are
longest. Public-land-use policies have not yet reflected the values of wildness fully even in designated wilderness areas, and
scarcely at all in undesignated areas that are wild simply because they have been left alone.

The attitudes of the frontier rasp against Alaska's sensitive
landscape. Not only does the frontier orientation encourage
rough treatment of the land and an exploitive attitude toward
resources whose limits aren't recognized, it cloaks the fron-
tierist in a prickly, touch-me-not shield of spurious independence. "Let me alone," he growls, "and I'll tame this wilderness."

The tourist and immigrant, too, need to adopt new restraints
and new sets of values in the North, because so much of the
land and water has low capacity to produce and heal. One of 59

the main educational and land-stewardship challenges in Alaska is to make our social strategies fit our sunshine.

The Physical Environment

An Eskimo taking part in a conference on housing in rural Alaska once made a wry comment on southerners in the North. "Before the white man came," he said, "my people lived below ground and buried their dead above ground. When the white man came he taught us to live above ground and bury our dead below ground — and we haven't been warm since."

Southern people don't understand the North, and northerners don't understand southern technologic hardware. We have imported temperate-zone attitudes ("forests should not burn") and expectations ("breezes will disperse air pollution"). When these ideas led to trouble, we imported temperate-zone technologies to overcome the problems. In some cases the technology simply failed — which, by forcing innovation, may have been a blessing in disguise. More often the technology did work — but at enormous costs. Neither individuals nor governments have fully appreciated these costs; both have shown a preference for deferring the costs rather than paying for them out of current development.

Cold Country Wastes

No Alaska community meets statutory water-quality standards in its waste-disposal systems. Few can hope to do so in the near future.

Why? One reason is that the sudden firming of national attitudes toward water pollution in the past decade caught Alaska, long accustomed to a laissez-faire attitude toward pollution, without plans or finances to meet standards. More fundamentally, conventional ideas about waste disposal are unworkable in arctic and subarctic regions. The main reason is cold temperature, which affects waste disposal in several ways.

For one thing, disease organisms in wastes buried in frozen soils or permanent ice, or discharged into cold water, are often preserved in a state of suspended virulence. For example, garbage and excrement from parties of arctic explorers often contain organisms that, decades later, only need to be thawed out to be "as good as life." Fecal bacteria in wastes dumped into the Tanana River system at Fairbanks survive five times as long as they would live in temperate streams. As a result, sewage discharged in Fairbanks raises bacteria counts above federal standards for the entire 210 miles of the Tanana River to its juncture with the Yukon River.[10] In economic terms, this means that one small city has already "used up" the available waste-dilution capacity of the lower Tanana River Valley.

Another source of waste-disposal problems is permanently frozen soil, which can prevent use of septic tank or cesspool systems, and freeze-thaw cycles that can destroy the retaining walls of sewage treatment lagoons. Alaska's cold climate slows biodegradation in natural waterways, too, not only by slowing chemical processes but by reducing oxygen levels.

And finally, many conventional techniques rely on algae to produce the oxygen supply for organisms that decompose sewage. Because algal activity is less at low temperatures, much more waste-storage space is needed than in a comparable community farther south. Mechanical aeration techniques are subject to icing and subsequent breakdown.

A rough idea of the importance of coldness in treating wastes in Alaska can be gained from the fact that Alaskan towns exceed normal heating loads for the United States (6000 degree days to maintain an indoor temperature of 50° F) by 133 percent (Juneau), 172 percent (Anchorage), 236 percent (Fairbanks), and 332 percent (Barrow). To bring waste treatment facilities up to equivalent temperatures would require three times the heat input at Fairbanks as at St. Louis, Missouri.

Incineration, though expensive, is a solution to sewage disposal problems where frozen ground, high water tables, or waterway characteristics prevent use of other techniques. Unfortunately, much of Alaska is vulnerable to build-up of airborne pollutants. To incinerate wastes in those places merely transfers the problem from water to atmosphere.

Many social problems contribute to waste-disposal issues, adding importantly to the physical problems just mentioned. Scarcely any Alaskan community or local government has enough authority — or willingness to use its authority — to strike at the heart of water pollution problems through land-use control. Other problems are unique to the scores of tiny settlements in rural Alaska. These settlements are completely incapable of supporting a normal community share of waste-treatment expenses. Often they have no organization that can establish and operate utilities or obtain government grants. Government bureaus with specialized interests and compartmentalized views have filled this hiatus, though inefficiently. However, no agency among the several able to construct village utility systems has had any interest in making sure the systems are maintained. The villages usually cannot provide the technically trained people for this job, and agencies cannot station operators permanently in the communities. The North is studded with useless or grossly inefficient monuments to this build-and-leave system.

A combination of ecological, social, and economic factors also makes solid-waste disposal a special problem in the North. Natural oxidation and degradation processes are slow in the cold and often dry climate of Alaska, especially the Interior and Arctic. Burial is expensive in frozen soils, and in any case amounts to storage, not disposal. Wastes that accumulate along beaches, in tundra areas, or open forests are highly visible. Incineration is often both expensive and environmentally undesirable. Recycling or large-scale disposal is nearly impossible because of the exceptionally high cost of gathering wastes from distant points of use, and because of the small volumes of most recyclable wastes that are available.

People depend on the sweep and turbulence of air masses to carry away and dilute airborne wastes. Today in densely settled temperate and subtropical areas there is no "away." The Arctic is not at that point yet but suffers from another problem: in many parts of the North the air close to the ground is too stable to disperse air pollutants.

One of the chief reasons is the frequency of air inversions. Inversions occur when air movements are slight and when the air is colder close to the ground than higher up, preventing vertical mixing. Los Angeles is infamous for its inversions, which bottle up pollutants until the whole basin threatens to vanish into thick air. Not so well known is the fact that many northern communities have inversions that are as bad or worse and usually much more persistent.

Fairbanks is a characteristic if somewhat extreme case. The town lies in a valley opening to the south into the broad flatlands of the Tanana River. To the west, north, and east are hills. There is little atmospheric circulation in this pocket in winter. Clear skies are the rule in the region, so that in winter there is a daily net loss of heat at the surface through radiation. Air temperatures near the surface drop very low, commonly below $-40°$ C and sometimes to $-55°$ C, while at elevations a few hundred feet higher the air is breezy and considerably warmer. The resultant air inversions are steeper than in Los Angeles (from $10°$ C to $30°$ C rise in 100 meters of altitude in Fairbanks, compared with less than $10°$ C rise per 100 meters in Los Angeles). The inversions often last for weeks.

Conditions are perfect for high air pollution; only a source is needed. The community provides the source. The two most abundant additives are water vapor (from power-plant cooling waters, automobiles, heating-fuel combustion) and carbon dioxide. The water vapor becomes a pollutant at low temperatures, especially below $-35°$ C when all water in the air   63 freezes into tiny crystals, forming ice fog. The dome of ice fog covering Fairbanks during winter inversion episodes is getting bigger each year as the population of people, homes, automobiles, and other sources of water vapor increases. Air traffic frequently comes to a halt, driving becomes extremely hazardous, and the well-known ''cabin fever'' malaise of the North intensifies. In December 1975, after eight days of unprecedented ice fog, Fairbanks' mayor issued the borough's first ice-fog alert, calling for citizens to eliminate all but essential travel.

Other pollutants accumulate during inversions, too, regardless of whether there is ice fog as well. Fairbanks is classed among the top problem cities in the country in terms of carbon monoxide and ''particulate'' (dust) pollution. Ever since serious attempts to measure air pollution have been carried out in Fairbanks, downtown areas of the city often have had daily average CO and dust levels exceeding national legal limits. In the first quarter of 1972 CO levels in Fairbanks were higher than allowed by relatively lenient interim state standards 15 percent of the time. If the tougher standards scheduled for 1975 had been in effect, CO levels would have exceeded them more than half the time. In August 1975, three Fairbanks scientists announced that their studies had revealed CO levels in the blood of local citizens which were among the highest in the nation. Singled out by the federal Environmental Protection Agency as one of the most severely polluted cities in the nation, Fairbanks now faces the prospect of a complete re-evaluation of traffic and growth patterns, plus costly air-quality–control measures. Some downtown merchants still deny the problem, which may be good evidence in itself that high CO levels already have affected brain function.

Most valley lands of interior Alaska, as well as vast sections of central and northern Canada, are highly vulnerable to air pollution. Air inversions cover most boreal forest and tundra areas during much of the winter and occur commonly in summer. Even some coastal areas have seasonally quiet air, posing serious development problems. Valdez, for example, may find that the operation of incoming tankers and the TAP oil terminal uses up (perhaps even exceeds) the legal limits of polluting air discharges for the whole area. Air-pollution potential is therefore an important but often underrated factor in northern community and regional planning.

Permafrost

Permafrost is ground that stays frozen for at least two years in succession. The ground can be any sort of soil, gravel, bedrock, or pure ice, and it might have been frozen for thousands of years or for only a few. Northern Alaska is entirely underlain by permafrost and central Alaska has permafrost in large and small patches. Altogether about 85 percent of the state is in the arctic circumpolar permafrost zone.

It is hard to imagine what Alaska would be like without permafrost, because the landscape and its ecosystems are so adapted to and molded by its presence. If permafrost were to melt on the Arctic Coastal Plain, for example, the Prudhoe Bay oil fields, Barrow, and Wainwright would be flooded as the Beaufort Sea invaded subsiding tundra flatlands. The effect of melting would be quite the opposite in the hilly Interior; without permafrost as the subfloor keeping meltwater and rain at the surface, much of the area would become a cold parched desert.

Plants and animals have adapted to live in a permafrost region, the evolutionary process of adaptation being a very long and very costly one if we were to reckon the death of individuals and the extinction of species in the accounting. Man's adjustment has had a shorter history (thinking of modern society's invasion of the North), but here, too, a price is being paid. The costs of failure to understand and to work with permafrost are evident all over central and northern Alaska in 65 camel-humped roads, collapsed basements, abandoned wells, tilted houses, and upthrust bridge pilings. To cite but one case among hundreds, sections of a highway (Rex to Lignite) north of the Alaska Range cost 84 percent more to build where there was permafrost than where there was none. Even this added investment did not solve permafrost-related problems, as maintenance costs are also much higher for permafrost sections.[11]

Permafrost spells trouble in different ways. Disturbing permafrost areas often causes the upper layers of permafrost to thaw, especially in the southern permafrost zone where the frozen ground is already near 32° F. If the thawed layer has a high water content and fine-grained soil, the ground will slump, erode, or form pits (thermokarst). When pilings or foundations are dug into permafrost, differential forces in the frozen and active (seasonally thawing) layers heave the object upward. Permafrost also can cause local scarcities of drinking water by locking up moisture, leaving only a thin water-bearing layer available seasonally at the surface. As I mentioned already, permafrost can make most familiar methods of waste disposal difficult or impossible. And finally, permafrost increases the tendency for soil to slide downslope, causing intense pressures on any object in its way.

The Trans-Alaska Pipeline is a famous example of the special treatment engineers have to give to permafrost terrain. The key feature of this pipeline is that it carries oil at nearly the temperature at which it comes out of the ground (170° F) for 800 miles across areas both with and without permafrost. No insulation around the pipe could do more than briefly delay the thawing of soil around buried parts of the pipe. Thus, whenever the frozen soil has high water (or ice) content and would slump and flow downhill if melted, the pipe had to be built aboveground. This raised another engineering problem: preventing alternate thawing and freezing around the pilings needed to support the elevated pipe. The problem was technically easy to solve, because "thermopiles" or special pilings designed to prevent downward conduction of heat in summer, had already been tested in other arctic construction. The price, however, was very high. The need to build the pipeline above-ground in ice-rich permafrost led to the well-publicized argument — still unsolved — about the line as a barrier to caribou migrations.

Experience and research have resulted in a wealth of technical literature on how human activities are affected by permafrost and how to prevent or (much harder) correct the problems. Yet private developers and public agencies alike persist in making mistakes. In some cases the high initial cost of building to prevent later damage seems more important than increased maintenance and replacement costs incurred later on. The result is increased economic costs of development and increased social costs in terms of inadequate water supply, unhealthy sewage-disposal practices, and scarred landscapes.

There are other fragile or sensitive soil types in Alaska besides permafrost soils. Shallow, water-soaked soils on southeastern Alaska mountainsides are landslide prone. The dark volcanic soils of the Alaska Peninsula are easily churned up and eroded. And windblown (loess) soils covering slopes adjacent to the Tanana Valley are quick to wash away once laid bare by land clearing or road building. A common sight in Fairbanks in May is a line of stranded vehicles at the brink of a washout in a new subdivision, where eroding soil has plugged culverts.

Water Supply

At first sight, Alaska seems far too wet to have a significant problem of water supply. In fact, there are outright shortages of water in parts of the state, as well as widespread problems of getting enough drinkable water.

The rainy Panhandle occasionally has droughts in summer,   67 which, even when relatively brief, can cause communities to run short of water. The thin gravelly soils of the region overlie impervious country rock: underground water strata are uncommon. Communities depend on frequent rain to keep streams running or to fill small reservoirs. After a few weeks without rain, these communities are forced to import water by ship or use emergency sources of low quality or high cost.

In northern and western Alaska, some coastal communities have had unusual water-supply problems. The sea intrudes the beach gravels on which villages were built, eliminating wells as a source of water. Tundra ponds are usually very shallow, easily polluted, and contain high quantities of suspended organic material; they are poor sources of drinking water. Many communities rely on water or ice carried from free-running streams, often many miles away. Even the modest convenience of a community water tank requires capital subsidies, a source of electricity, a heated storage tank, and trained maintenance personnel. Settlements along the major rivers of Interior Alaska often face similar problems, with a turbid river in the front yard and permafrost at one-shovel depths in the back.

Urban Alaska is not without water-supply problems either. Most people in the Fairbanks area have individual wells. If these penetrate gravelly strata, water usually is plentiful but is easily polluted by nearby cesspools. The water also tends to be very high in iron, arsenic, and organic content. Many families cannot get water below their property because of deep permafrost or peat deposits, so they have to buy water to fill storage tanks in their homes. The Mendenhall Valley subdivisions of Juneau are perched on glacial outwash where the water table is within a few inches of the surface, preventing use of shallow wells due to the risk of contamination.

The root of these problems is in the Topsy-like growth of Alaskan communities. Urban Alaska sprang up where there were mines, fish, or military bases, not where modern planners would choose. As it turned out, many of the town-sites are places where water is scarce, floods and earthquakes occur, and air pollution hazards are great. Full realization of the present and continuing cost of these early non-decisions is just now dawning. Today's rural villages may or may not be in the same places that Eskimos, Indians, or Aleuts had settlements; but in any case they are often poorly suited for either the number of people now living there or the changing lifestyle of modern Alaska.

Among the most critical water shortages occur in the North Slope's soggy coastal plain. Here, in the months from October through May, fresh water is extremely scarce, being found only in a few lakes and in the aquifers of the biggest rivers. Petroleum exploration, development, and production, even in these days of infancy, have encountered serious water shortages. To make matters worse, the scarce sources of winter-season fresh water are critical to overwintering whitefish, grayling, and other fish. By 1975, fisheries management people had clashed with oil-field operators over the question of water for camp use and drilling. Today the conflict is still unresolved.

Fire

In the warm, dry summer months the northern forest and adjacent tundra ranges are highly susceptible to wildfire, much like California's chaparral region and the evergreen forests of the Rocky Mountains. Over the millennia natural (and probably some man-caused) fires destroyed and created plant and animal communities throughout central Alaska. Since 1900, fires have become much more frequent with the spread of people and machinery. Little was done until two decades ago to prevent or suppress these wildfires because no agency had the money to do so. In the past twenty years, the "Smokey Bear" ethic has influenced the public mind and purse to the point 69 where millions of dollars are spent annually by the Bureau of Land Management to suppress fires on the public domain.

The rationale for fire suppression is that wildfires endanger people and structures, prevent trees from growing big enough to harvest, and destroy wildlife and the beauty of the countryside. Although true in specific situations, these statements do not justify an all-out fire suppression policy. In a region as sparsely settled as Interior Alaska, many fires pose no danger at all to human life or settlements. Many fires occur on sites that will never support commercial timber regardless of how long they are kept unburned. Granting that most people don't like newly burned landscapes, the force of that argument is very low in the seldom-visited hinterland. And just as it is true that fires kill some animals and make the area less habitable for some species for decades, it is also true that many species depend on vegetation types that follow fire. As mentioned earlier, fire can also lower the soil permafrost line and release locked-up nutrients for recycling through plant and animal communities.

Recognition that it may be undesirable as well as economically impractical to put out all wildfires is taking root among land and resource managers. Fire-control administrators themselves have developed priority systems incorporating resource values, fire danger, and control costs. However, the present policy is to control all fires whenever possible. When fires are left alone it is from necessity, not a judgment that the fire's benefits outweigh its costs.

Ecologists and biologists in resource agencies are promoting development of land-use plans and a case-by-case analysis of wildfires as a substitute for the "put-it-out-if-we-can" policy. One reason is the knowledge that ecological benefits can result from forest fires in some situations. Another is the recognition that fire-suppression activities can sometimes be more damaging than the fire itself. For example, erosion from bulldozer trails and fire lines may be greater than in undisturbed burns;

also, heavy applications of phosphate-base fire retardants may cause early eutrophication of lakes.

The environmental problems people encounter when trying to build a permanent industrial society in Alaska are, in one sense, technical and economic in nature. Their solution can be seen merely as a matter of good engineering. But the engineer's ideal solution is rarely the least costly solution in a short-term sense, and the momentum of traditional "southern" solutions often prevents the widespread adoption of even the simplest and cheapest of the designs created by knowledgeable northern engineers. Coupled with the historic impatience of pioneers with modern environmental standards, the result is that the North is getting shoddier, dirtier, and less civilized by the day. We are, in our stinginess and haste, piling up tremendous cleanup debts that our children will have to pay. The strategy of industrialization forces northern residents to pay an unusually high cost to meet accepted standards of the rest of the nation. Failure to pay this cost has made us inhabitants of a second-rate manmade environment amidst the most exquisite natural environments in the world.

CHAPTER IV

A Time, a Place, a Future

Darkness, fire, frost, and cold are the internal environmental realities of Alaska. They affect the future of the North as much as the clash of cultures, the surge or retreat of immigrants, the warring of novelty and tradition, and the cherished prejudices of northern people. But behind this stage and those players is a looming external reality. We are in and of a larger world. If the ecologists' truth is that everything is linked to everything else, the bonds must ensnare Alaska no less than Abu Dhabi and Calcutta. To describe these links in detail is far too awesome a task for me. But some problems we all can see.

Population Pressures

Demographers quibble about how long it will be before the world's human population doubles, and indeed for many good reasons it matters a lot whether the doubling occurs in fifteen years or thirty or fifty. However, it is hard to find a demographer who doesn't believe that someday there will be eight billion humans where there are now four billion. One of the broad questions about Alaska's future relates to this seemingly inexorable fact: When and how will Alaska feel the effects of a world population in search of space and resources?

The world's crowded places are getting more crowded, but

simultaneously they are exporting people to less crowded regions. The North is one of these. Today about 85 percent of the people who live in the circumpolar North — Siberia, Scandinavia, northern Canada, Alaska — are recent arrivals from the South. No one can say when the North will become crowded, too, though intuitively we might guess that "crowding" will become onerous at lower densities here than in temperate areas.

Why has the North been invaded (or settled) by southerners? One obvious reason is simple economic incentive. When resources needed in the South were discovered in the North, people moved north to get them out and sometimes to stay. Fur, fish, minerals, petroleum, timber: All have motivated settlement of the North.

Economics is not the only force, however. Southern nations who claimed a part of the North have sometimes promoted immigration and settlement to affirm sovereignty. Certainly this was a dominant motive, up to the 1960s, in the sovietization of Siberia. Neither Canada nor the United States have undertaken massive settlement projects as the Soviet Union has. Still, the territorial imperative was a reason behind some programs such as the very expensive Matanuska Valley farm settlement projects of 1927 and 1935, in southcentral Alaska.

Oddly enough, both economic and noneconomic arguments have brought some southern-based circumpolar governments to a policy of *not* settling in the North. Greenland is an obvious example of the decision — made, in this case, in Denmark — that resident people in the North ought to be left alone or at least strongly buffered from drastic change; only in Greenland and Lappish Scandinavia, however, has this policy dominated events over a long period of time.

Recently southerners have started to realize both the variety and extent of costs associated with settlement in arctic and subarctic zones. In Russia, major mineral resource projects in the North are now seen as short-term activities, with temporary communities peopled with workers doing a two- to five-year stint at a mine and returning south.[1] The Atlantic-Richfield Company and British Petroleum (Alaska), Ltd., followed the same strategy in developing the Prudhoe Bay field; in this case "south" included Anchorage, Tulsa, Houston, and even London. In Norway, the operators of an iron mine in Kirkenes, at the latitude of the crest of Alaska's Brooks Range, own a resort complex in Sicily where they send mineworkers for rest and recuperation.

Although world population pressures will influence Alaska's future, that influence most likely will be felt indirectly. For instance, rising internal demands for minerals in a developing country in South America could eliminate exports to the United States, which might (though far from certainly) open a profit-making opportunity for mining in Alaska and result in further immigration from the other states.

It does seem that national economic forces will be the major factor affecting Alaska's growth for a long time. The United States has never really done much as a matter of public policy to settle Alaska, and it would seem to have little reason to do so in the future. Furthermore, living space is comparatively abundant in the 48 contiguous states, and our nation has a relatively low net annual growth rate; people will not be squeezed out to move to Alaska. Job opportunities, and to some extent the call of the wilderness, will for many years continue to provide the incentives for people to come to Alaska.

Alaska as Storehouse

Although Secretary Seward, in arguing the case for Alaska's purchase, sometimes alluded to the store of resources that surely must exist in the vast *terra incognita*, there was very little support for the notion that these resources were a valuable asset to the nation. Except for a few select fur species, all of Alaska's known or suspected resources already were in abundant and seemingly inexhaustible supply in other parts of the nation. The value of Alaska's resources then and for the next hundred years was thought to lie with the opportunity they gave to individuals and corporations to get rich. Alaska was a place where treasure was buried, and the fun was in the looking. If, by chance or skill or competitive ruthlessness you could find some of this trove, or wrest it from a discoverer, good for you. Alaska expanded the field for the great American dream of "making it."

In contrast, the view that Alaska's resources are valuable to the nation as a whole, enhancing or protecting its position among competing nations, or significantly nurturing the American industrial sector had few adherents until events of 1973 and 1974 made the nation look at its oil gauge. It would be hard to find any real evidence that northland resources meant anything at all to the nation, up to this decade. The only things that Alaskans sent south in any quantity were salmon and crabs, hardly in the category of public necessities and, anyhow, products of the North Pacific, not Alaska itself, capable of being exploited through Seattle. The minerals we shipped south were almost negligible in quantity, and our timber all went to Japan.

While Americans thought themselves in possession of ample supplies of natural resources in the Lower 48 or were confident of politically secure supplies from other countries, it was impossible for the storehouse perception of Alaska to gain a toehold. Today everything is different. Some former foreign suppliers of resources have become political adversaries. Others are still friendly but haven't let friendship stand in the way of reducing U.S. profits in favor of their own. On top of that, the decline of our own domestic petroleum reserves (rather accurately predicted by geologists for almost twenty years) has shaken America's deep faith in its resource self-sufficiency. Sensitized by the dramatic results of OPEC (Organization of Petroleum Exporting Countries) decisions, Americans are willing to accept the fact or threat of scarcities of other resources. Given that mood, the perception of Alaska as national resource storehouse has inevitable appeal.

Such a shift of broad perspectives can turn investors' heads in Alaska's direction. Reasonably good resource exploitation opportunities in Alaska are unlikely to go ignored. Nevertheless, the fact remains that the rules of the marketplace still prevail, and Alaskan resources of average grade and modest quantity still cannot compete with similar resources in better locations. Prudhoe Bay oil and gas obviously passed the test; petroleum deposits found in the first 42 years of exploration in the neighboring National Petroleum Reserve (Alaska) just as obviously do not.

Oil and gas are by themselves at the top of the list of nationally needed material resources found in Alaska. Metallic minerals arrange themselves at varying levels much lower on the scale of priorities. Coal is somewhere on the scale, and so is water. None of Alaska's exportable renewable resources — fish, wood, or farm produce — has a place on a scale headed "needs," nor is it likely that they will have in the near future except as exports making a minor contribution to balancing trade. They may or may not present business people with chances for profit, but the nation as a whole can take them or leave them.

Right now the sharply perceived national need for oil and gas puts Alaska on center stage. Among all of the external realities impinging today on the North, none can approach this felt need as a determinant of Alaskan development.

A research program conducted at the University of Alaska's Institute of Social and Economic Research (ISER) in the first half of this decade provided insights into the magnitude and pathways through which the impacts of petroleum development would be felt.[2] What they found is that Alaskan population growth is dominated by immigrant job seekers and their families. Because oil- and gas-related activities provide the only major source of new job opportunities in Alaska now and in the foreseeable future, the rates of oil and gas development naturally pervade the population growth picture. Furthermore, because oil and gas revenues are and will be such a huge proportion of total state revenues, and because state spending so greatly influences the whole Alaskan economy and job situation, petroleum tax revenues tremendously enhance the overall impact of this resource. If oil prices are low and oil and gas leasing is done slowly, Alaska's growth will be very healthy but relatively modest, the state's population reaching a projected 574,000 by 1990. If, in contrast, oil prices are high ($7 per barrel at wellheads was the figure used, which is less than the actual figure as events later determined) and federal and state lands are leased rapidly, our population by 1990 is projected to be 1,014,000. Beyond question, federal oil-pricing policies and federal leasing policies are powerful external forces shaping Alaska's future.

The University of Alaska research team assumed — with good justification — that the effect of varying petroleum policies and activity levels greatly outweighed the combined effects of any likely increase or decrease in other resource sectors. They assumed that fisheries' output (in real — not inflated — dollars) was close to its ceiling and would grow at only one percent per year through 1990. They credited the forest-products industry with considerably more growth potential, estimating that it would double its output before reaching a resource limit about 1990. In contrast, they assumed that neither nonpetroleum mining nor agriculture would change very much in the next fifteen years.

Anyone could criticize these assumptions about future growth, or simply make other assumptions on the basis of another view into the crystal ball. What is of interest here, though, is the degree to which events and decisions in the outside world might change conditions of life in Alaska, through 77

changes in the fortunes of resource industries. The Alaskan
fisheries already have seen a major national policy decision,
the congressional declaration of a 200-mile territorial sea and
exclusive fishing zone, which makes it possible for Alaskan
fishermen to displace foreign fishermen from many offshore
areas. Whether this will really occur is another matter. Considering the investments necessary to develop fleets capable of
exploiting offshore and bottomfish stocks, it may be well
beyond 1990 before the 200-mile extended-jurisdiction zone
results in greatly expanded Alaskan fisheries.

Several external forces control Alaskan timber output, too.
One is the Japanese pulp demand and housing market. Another
is the politics of preservation: the national decision to put federal timberlands into "Wilderness" or some other reserved
category. Still another is federal stumpage-fee policy, which
can be decisive in making Alaskan timber investments attractive or unattractive to nationwide firms.

It seems to me that the metallic mineral resource sector is
the one where wild cards are scattered so thickly through the
deck that any prediction is layered with uncertainty. First of all,
mineral markets are highly variable, being sensitive to changes
in U.S. foreign relations with countries supplying us with
ores, to technological innovation and obsolescence, to unexpected discoveries, and to many other factors quite beyond
Alaskan control. In addition, whether, when, or where major
discoveries might be made (especially in frontier areas) is almost completely unpredictable. However, the university
doubtlessly made a defensible (if conservative) judgment in
assuming only slight real growth in mining in Alaska by 1990.
Probably several major discoveries will be made well within
that time, but production could lag five or ten or even twenty
or thirty years behind.

Coal is something of a special case. We know there is a lot
of coal in Alaska, and we know where most of it is. The big
uncertainty is when any particular deposit might become a

resource — that is, become valuable enough to dig up. Here again, numerous external realities enter the equation. Federal air-quality standards help determine national coal demand, as does the price of competing fuels like gas and oil. New methods for dissolving or gasifying and enriching coal are constantly creating new possibilities for mining coal and marketing it as a synthetic fuel and chemical feedstock material. Another complicating factor is that as coal derivatives become more valuable per unit of volume or weight, shipment anywhere in the world becomes more feasible. Coal markets then will become worldwide in scale, as oil markets now are. How Alaska's coal will compete with other known massive deposits in other countries is an imponderable at the moment.

Water is a resource, plentiful in Alaska, that may become valuable enough someday to provide economic justification for transcontinental relocation. For at least fifteen years an engineering firm in Los Angeles has promoted the idea of transferring Yukon River water to the St. Lawrence Seaway, the Southwest, and other parts of the continent.[3] Predictably, the idea is dusted off during dry years in the West and Midwest. How many years away from economic feasibility this project is, I couldn't even guess. But obviously the broader question is, how much growth in the South will be permitted, and at what cost to the North? In many ways this is exactly the question the nation faces in deciding how fast to lease offshore and federal onshore lands for petroleum development in Alaska.

Conservation and Preservation

There is danger in emphasizing too much the influence of world and national economic forces on the rate and kind of change in Alaska's future. One danger is that economic analyses naturally emphasize matters of quantity, leaving to others the problem of quality. Another danger is that the effect of

79

other forces, more attitudinal and social than economic (though of course closely tied both fore and aft to economic moorings), will be neglected.

For example who can predict how strongly the American people will embrace the cautious and restrained use of energy and materials, that is, the conservation ethic? America will come to that ethic someday, either because certain resources run out, or costs go up, or because political pressures from poor countries force us to. Will we cling to our materialistic world view to the bitter end, or somehow respond to an unexpected attack of altruism? Will our government rely on volunteerism and incentives, or risk the use of stern and unpopular regulations? Can conservation successfully be married to solutions for age-old problems of wealth distribution? The answers to these questions can affect the rates and locations of growth and change in Alaska as profoundly as shifts in Japanese pulp markets or OPEC pricing policies. (As just one illustration, a gasoline pricing or rationing program which would reduce national automobile usage as much as rationing did in World War II could change the entire outlook for the tourist industry in Alaska and essentially eliminate some proposed highways from consideration as elements in a statewide transportation system.)

Congress's current struggles with the Alaska National Interest Lands legislation express yet another non-economic (some would even say anti-economic) force, prominent in our nation, capable of changing the entire future course of events in Alaska. This is the preservation ethic, the expression of a deeply ingrained national penchant for wild country. The question being posed is whether the majority of some 215 million acres of federally owned land in Alaska should be preserved in near-natural condition, off limits to most commercial resource activities. Cynics suggest that congressional interest in new parks in Alaska stems from the fact that this is a painless way to win the environmental vote at home. While this may be partly true, it ignores and denigrates the basic nationwide interest in wildland preservation which explains why the issue is even before Congress in the first place.

Perspectives

History is littered with the carcasses of inevitabilities that never happened and studded with surprises no one could foretell. Today's global energy crisis that furrows the brows of savants the world over may be "solved" by a rather trivial bit of technological tinkering — only to make us aware of the frightening extent to which our society is shaped in response to a casually accepted set of hardware.

In looking at some of the world forces that affect Alaskan events today, or might in the future, it is easy to think of the process as a one-way street, with Alaska the destination of all the hurtling machinery unleashed by a headlong, uncaring world. Certainly the traffic is heavy in our direction, but the flow in the opposite direction will not be zero. In fact, to the extent that Alaska is seen by the rest of the industrial world as a prime place to plunder (or preserve), by that same measure we gain a basis for a share in the destiny of that world. We cannot realistically expect to force other states to adopt energy conservation measures as a condition of assisting in outer continental shelf petroleum development, for example, but in concert with other coastal states faced with the same problem we can give a strong nudge in that direction. By successful example Alaska could set new trends in several significant fields: in the guided coevolution of widely different cultures, one post-industrial, the other partially subsistence; in progressive energy conservation and management; in cooperative management of public and private wildlands; in petroleum-resource and petroleum-revenue management based on concern for later generations; in the development of better ways to evaluate the 81 long-term meaning of alternative government programs and policies.

Certainly it is easy these days to be pessimistic or fatalistic. How can an Alaskan village maintain its own style when oil company executives will fly their own jets direct from Houston to speak at a town meeting on a zoning issue? How can an ordinary Alaskan exercise citizenship effectively when a few powerful unions and industries invest millions in a calculated attempt to become even more powerful? Aren't growth and the carving-up of the wilderness and capture by multinational corporations and pre-emption by federal decisions realities we must face? Perhaps. But it seems to me that the wise course, while comprehending the world as well as we can, is to search constantly for every possible bit of leverage available to create a more favorable reality.

Building Futures: A Dream

Grant me that choice is possible: Where can Alaska go, and how can it get there?

Since statehood, scores of articles have been written about Alaskan problems and policy choices, especially about popularly recognized topics like petroleum development and wilderness. Rarely, a more wide-ranging treatise has come along like Hugh A. Johnson and Harold T. Jorgenson, *The Land Resources of Alaska* (written in 1959 but published in 1963), George Rogers, *Alaska in Transition: The Southeast Region,* and Richard A. Cooley, *Alaska: A Challenge in Conservation.*[4] But while a few scholars have tried to describe and evaluate governmental policies, political leaders and officials either have been vague and noncommital or have so tightly circumscribed and subdivided their views that their cross connections and long-term meanings are invisible.

82   Problems are at places where paths diverge. When we

choose a path because it is smoothest for the next few steps, it is a matter of sheer chance whether the trail will be worse or better around the next bend. Yet expedience is our only guide unless we dare to try to create a specific and preferred future. Alaskans today, nagged intolerably by the pressures of change and buffeted by conflicting values, are like caribou galloping wildly, pursued by unseen flies. We have no sense of purpose and — except in the negative, an us-against-them residual colonialism — little sense of community.

This book deals with problems and solutions across a broad environmental and resource field. In fairness I should say something about the shape of that future Alaska which is my own guide through the maze of current events. It is not a specific nirvana, so brittle it would shatter with the first contrary turn. But it is a durable, feasible set of broad preferences about the interweaving of humanity and nature that might be accepted by a majority of Alaskans.

The first and most general idea is to strive to remain different. Alaska is an American place and will always move through time in general concert with the rest of the nation, but within the American spectrum Alaska can be a distinctive hue. The North has been different because of its history as a final frontier, protected by remoteness from thorough homogenization with mainstream America. Now the barrier of distance is breached and the threat of homogenization is immediate. The agents of uniformity are the flood of newcomers, big business and big labor, attracted by Alaska's new wealth, and (to a lesser extent) the coming of network satellite television to rural Alaska. The evidence of their impact is everywhere: in the absolute conformity of new shopping malls in Anchorage and Fairbanks, in the popularity of the *Bionic Woman* in western Alaska villages, in the instantaneous appearance of Adidas T-shirts throughout Alaska in 1976, and in the way the thought patterns of national and multinational unions and corporations have permeated urban areas.

If being different is important — and I argue that it is — obviously the problem is to sort out the meaningful differences from those that are just a put-on for the tourists. A bushy-bearded prospector adorning the tail of an Alaska Airlines jet is at best a faint whiff of something long dead if, in reality, the mining industry is totally dominated by the capital of huge multinational firms. If ancient Eskimo dance patterns are seen only by tourists given a forty-five–minute interlude in Kotzebue, when no young Eskimo learns those patterns and is respected for creating new ones, our difference is a total sham. No, the differences to cherish are those that are a matter of deeply ingrained style naturally flowing from the ways we develop and distribute wealth, shape our educational processes, plan our communities and interconnections, and relate to our natural environment. This kind of difference lives and evolves, while the frontier symbols are fading snapshots.

One of Alaska's most obvious distinctions is the breadth and scope and wildness of the landscape. It is a rare person — resident or visitor — who doesn't catch his breath at the vast sweep of our countryside. Range upon range of mountains glisten white and black under the wing of a jetliner. Bay after countless bay, walled by a near backdrop of dark green forests, are guarded by farther thrusts of rugged bedrock or ice. Mile after mile of subdued Interior woods and muskegs, scrawled with meandering creeks and rivers. Unfathomable stretches of flat tundra, cool and soggy prairies founded on a thousand feet of frozen ground. It will be hard to destroy this vastness except through total and prolonged thoughtlessness, through a wildly accelerated exploitation of energy and mineral resources. It would be easy, nevertheless, to lose the strong but subtly fragile flavor of wildness that makes Alaska's distances so special. A whole new field encompassing architecture, the design of resource-industry operations, the siting and design of roads and other transportation facilities, and land-healing techniques needs to be developed to sustain this flavor of wildness in countryside we use to produce goods and services. The entire field of recreation management, as well, needs to respond to this uniquely Alaskan challenge to emphasize natural and wild settings for outdoor experiences.

Just as the North is vast and wild, it is also diverse; and just as Alaska can remain distinctive among the states, so the regions of Alaska can be encouraged to cherish their special character. Our natural diversity is important in itself, perhaps, but it is a gift given by geographic happenstance, unearned and almost impossible to take away. Of much more significance is the human diversity that, in large part, follows from the basic facts of ecological and resource diversity. The dispersed communities of southeastern Alaska, bound together by shared seas, rains, and salmon, comprise a geographic and cultural neighborhood unlike any other part of the state. So is Bristol Bay a different kind of place, and the communities at the brink of the frozen northwesterly seas, and the Railbelt. Variety is more than spice: it is a source of understanding, perspective, and tolerance; a cornerstone of economic health; the source of choice.

For all its breathtaking sweep and its exciting variety, Alaska is still a place of comfortable human scale. A person's individual space is roomier. One feels capable of comprehending the whole of Alaskan society, of making personal connections throughout it, of being known within it. Without having to become either politicians or disc jockeys, hundreds of Alaskans are known by nearly everyone for their art, their public service, their piquant eccentricities.

Perhaps the enjoyable scale of Alaskan society is due to the fact that the North is, in the parlance of psychologists, an undermanned society. That is, there are no ''surplus'' people to become unwanted extras hanging around on the lot. We are pressured by stronger forces in more varied directions. We are called on to play more roles; we can scarcely avoid more challenges, more responsibility. We experience more failures and successes because we are tested more often, and even though we can distinguish the two more readily because of

85

this, we are less critical of others who, like ourselves, win some and lose some. In Alaska, an ambitious individual can make a mark earlier than in more crowded societies. The legislator in his or her twenties and cabinet member in his or her thirties is a common thing in the North.

All this is extremely important in defining a critical difference in Alaskan living, both in terms of individual satisfaction and in the making of public policy. Alaskan politics have been "smalltown" in flavor — in openness, in the rapid general diffusion of knowledge about people and events, in the sense of awareness and personal participation. If openness, simplicity, and knowledge are replaced during our years of "coming of age" by complexity, concealment, and apathy in politics, something very crucial and very special will have disappeared from Alaska. It is to the advantage of the power hungry to have this happen, and so we are in real peril today now that the stakes are big enough to bring out these hungers.

Does smallness have a numerical limit? Is there some upper limit beyond which a community or a region becomes crowded? So far, I have found it unprofitable to try to find such a numerical threshold. Smallness is a condition where human opportunity to achieve satisfaction is relatively abundant, where aggravating or debasing human frictions are relatively uncommon, and where environments are pleasant. Crowdedness is the opposite. With a population of 50,000, Fairbanks is crowded because traffic is too dense, the air is too thick with pollution, the Chena River is dirty, planning is nearly absent, nearby lakes are overused, and so on. But each of these is a correctable nuisance; presumably Fairbanks at 100,000 population could be made to seem less crowded. The heart of the matter is style and quality, not demographic statistics.

A final aspect of what I mean by a different kind of society has to do with the relationships between people and their physical surroundings: land, environment — call it what you will.

The heart of the difference lies in the directness, frequency, and visibility of these relationships in Alaska. Urban America, in reality more closely dependent on nature than any other society in history, can mask this dependence from its citizens. It is commonplace in the Lower 48 to grow up never seeing real soil, never being challenged by cold or heat, never comprehending the commitment of world space and resources required to keep your city alive. In Alaska, by contrast, everyone is involved with nature, and knows it. Nothing protects the homebuilder from the realities of permafrost and chinooks and ice jams and sixty below zero except his own knowledge and experience. We find our recreation within the wildlands, and many of us have been captured by rivers and tides, faced by angry moose and bears, or "misplaced" in a trackless hinterland. We know what can happen when a nail in a tire turns a winter evening on the town into a question of survival. The seasons strike robustly on us; the sun's return is an annual experience in renewal that affects us all. Even our business world is visibly dependent on nature, rising and falling with the fortunes of fish stocks, forests, petroleum, and minerals.

The danger, of course, is that the urbanizing of Alaska will draw the same veils over the realities of our oneness with nature, as now distort the views of so many millions farther south. The challenge is to use relationships with nature as a springboard to a heightened and permanent sensitivity. We should begin to think of our total surroundings as an extension of our house, and all living things as members of the household. Nowhere is an environmental ethic so urgently needed, nor so potentially rewarding, as in the North.

This, then, is the way I describe the goals or boundary conditions for Alaska's future: to be different, to be diverse, to be uncrowded, to admit our oneness with nature. The next question is whether we can sustain or achieve those conditions, and, if so, how?

CHAPTER V

To Earn a Living, To Fashion a Life

The American economy is an upside-down pyramid resting on a narrow base of farming, mining, energy production, logging, and tourism. An extraordinarily small number of people working at those activities generate the materials and profits from which the huge mass of the economy is nurtured. Alaska is no different, with two exceptions: to the list you must add subsistence activities, and the pyramid's base is comparatively broad. From a strictly economic viewpoint, the hundreds of choices made by government and individuals about rates and types of natural-resource uses are absolutely crucial to our collective material well-being.

On that score alone I would want to look at the set (or is it a mishmash?) of policies now determining the use of Alaskan resources. But the choices we make have consequences far beyond those usually discussed by the dismal science. Adlai Stevenson put it beautifully:

But a free society cannot be content with a goal of mere life without want. It has always had within it a visionary spark, a dream that man, liberated from crushing work, aching hunger and constant insecurity, would discover wider interests and nobler aims. If quantity comes first so that men may eat, quality comes next so that they may not live by bread alone. Free society in the West has brought most of its citizens to that great divide. The next frontier is the quality, the moral, intellectual and aesthetic standards of the free way of life.[1]

If style and quality are central to individual happiness and social progress in the post-industrial world, resource policies have to be consistent with the styles and qualities of living we want. In Alaska, questions of style are imbedded in every decision about renewable resources, the fishing, lumbering, farming, tourist service, and subsistence-gathering activities we intuitively feel are the permanent basis for Alaskan living. When limited-entry regulations grope toward economic efficiency in the salmon-catching business, what impact do they have on the life of fishermen? Can subsistence hunting be restricted to the use of traditional weapons — and if there are no restrictions, will subsistence living survive at all? What balance must be struck between big, energy-intensive agribusiness in Alaskan grain farming, and the kitchen garden, subsistence-gathering style of the homesteader? Would preserving wilderness in the Southeast spell doom to the timber industry?

Those are just a sample of the puzzles that wrinkle the brows and raise the temperatures of high federal and state resource officials in contemporary Alaska.

Fishing

Commercial fishing is one of those things that quite a few Alaskans do in summer, and many more dream of doing. Fishing, like prospecting and mining, has a place in America's image of Alaska. Ironically, some of the very characteristics that economists see as the drawbacks of the traditional commercial fisheries — high risk, ease of entry, low capital requirements for the individual, inefficient gear, high seasonality — are part of the attraction of the occupation. The catch is uncertain: so what? We like to gamble. Boats and gear are small and inefficient: but that is why a young person can hope to be an independent owner. Fishing is very seasonal: which is great for schoolteachers, bartenders, and others who like a change of job (or no job at all) in the winter.

Fishing is an odd industry. It employs more people than any other Alaskan resource industry; in a typical July, when fishing is at its annual peak, one out of every five or six working Alaskans is employed in the fisheries. Only petroleum exceeds fisheries in gross product value. And fishing is the lifeblood of scores of communities along the southern two-thirds of Alaska's vast coastline. On the other hand, commercial fishing profits cannot support many fishing families all year, and some years profits are zero or negative. In recent years, with relatively low total catches in the salmon fisheries and large numbers of fishermen and boats in the fleets, the taxable or spendable surplus — when you subtract costs from income for the whole endeavor — sometimes has been small to the vanishing point. Some argue that unemployment checks or other transfer payments are all that keeps the industry going in bad years.

Alaska has four major commercial fisheries. The most important one, the salmon "fishery," is really a complex of fisheries varying with the character of the waters where the fish are to be caught, the behavior of different runs of the five species of salmon, and the type of product to be marketed. Salmon are caught in nearly all inshore waters from Ketchikan to Bristol Bay and the Aleutians. There are isolated salmon fisheries as far north as Kotzebue on the Arctic Circle. Fleets from Japan and other nations seek salmon well offshore and west of the "abstention line" of 175° W, a source of frustration for Alaskans. Salmon management is centered in the Alaska Division of Commercial Fisheries and in the regulatory Board of Fisheries appointed by the governor. The yearly cycle of management is simple in outline but complex in practice, involving predictions of how many adult salmon are likely to return to inshore waters in a given year; deciding how many mature fish can be caught and how many must be allowed to escape the nets to spawn; adopting regulations setting fishing periods and limiting gear efficiency; enforcing the regulations; and checking actual escapement and spawning success. Simultaneously, other facets of management are active, such as running hatcheries, improving lake and stream environments, and negotiating fishing agreements with foreign nations. The total salmon catch from the northeast Pacific Ocean has averaged around 400,000 metric tons annually for all nations since 1961.[2] Alaska has harvested about 30 percent of the total. Salmon catches dropped sharply in the second quarter of the twentieth century due to overfishing. Improved regulation of catches has allowed some recovery after statehood, but high-seas fishing by foreign fleets as well as heavy nearshore pressure by U.S. fishermen sporadically pushed some stocks toward the brink of disaster.

Halibut support a second venerable and important Alaskan fishery. A deep-water fishery carried out with trawls and longlines, the halibut fishery is concentrated in southern Alaska and the Gulf of Alaska. It is a relatively prolonged activity, in comparison with the hectic compression of salmon fishing. The International Pacific Halibut Commission (Canadian and U.S. membership) is the principal instrument of halibut management through its decisions on harvest quotas and other regulations. Annual halibut catches averaged about 40,000 metric tons in the 1960s of which Alaskans caught roughly one fourth. In recent years, quotas for member nations in the commission have been forced downward in recognition of increased catches by Japanese offshore bottom fisheries, posing another problem in high-seas–resource diplomacy and management.

Sole, cod, pollock, ocean perch, and other kinds of ground fish comprise a third major fisheries complex. Canada, Japan, and the United States have been active in continental shelf areas of the Gulf of Alaska. Russia and Japan, and to some extent the Republic of Korea, found and exploited stocks of sablefish, flounder, and other species in the Bering Sea early in the 1960s. Catch statistics suggest serious overfishing of some

of these stocks. Scientists are concerned that excessive re-
movals of groundfish and shrimp from the southern Bering Sea
may have had (or may soon have) an effect on food supplies of
the millions of sea birds and marine mammals in those waters.
If true — and much more research will have to be done — the
consequences could be serious to Eskimos and Aleuts harvesting sea mammals and birds for food.

Shellfish harvests began over half a century ago in southeast
Alaska. The center of shellfishing activity shifted westward to
the Gulf of Alaska and Aleutian area after World War II when
new stocks of shrimps, scallops, and king, tanner, and
Dungeness crabs were discovered. Japan and Russia pioneered
several of these fisheries and have competed intensely with
U.S. boats. King crabs, by far the most important, were overfished in the mid-1960s when landings totaled 130,000 to
150,000 metric tons each year. Increasing shrimp and scallop
harvests took up some of the slack, but some stocks of these
species, too, have been exploited excessively.

Many of the problems of the Alaska fisheries are illustrated
by the expansion, decline, and beginning recovery of king-
crab fishing. King crab are harvested commercially along
more than 21,000 miles of coast from Juneau to Adak. The
fishery began about 1930 in the Bering Sea and spread eastward rapidly after World War II. At first, tangle nets and
trawls were used to catch the crabs, but these caused the loss
of too many undersized crabs and females; crab pots were developed to alleviate these problems. Discrete populations of
king crabs were progressively discovered by exploratory fishing; often a stock was overharvested within a few years and
crab fishermen moved on. Since only male crabs (which mature sexually at 5 to 7 years) at least 7 years old could be harvested legally, "overfishing" occurred when nearly all of the
males 8 to 14 years old had been caught, leaving a population
of young crabs dependent on one or two age classes of males
for breeding. Biologically the stock was in little danger at that

point, although a bad year for reproduction could leave a gap in recruitment of young breeding males. In economic terms, however, overfishing had occurred because not enough legal-sized males were being produced yearly to make fishing profitable.

Crab fishing was regulated by area, season, and gear limitations. Such regulation might have limited crab harvests to sustainable levels, but did not; neither research, management, nor enforcement efforts could keep up with the burgeoning fishery. In addition, these regulations clearly could not limit the number of fishermen setting pots. The fishery expanded almost exponentially in the period from 1959 to 1966; then catches dropped precipitously within two years to about one-tenth of peak levels. Regulations tightened and many boats left the fishery. Management biologists knew, however, that the boats would be back when enough of the overfished stocks recovered, permitting another boom-bust cycle unless entry-limitation systems or quota systems (or both) could be implemented. By 1973, quotas had been introduced and measurable recovery of some overfished populations had taken place. Formerly serious competition between Japanese, Russian, and American crab fishermen in the Bering Sea and Aleutian Islands is being alleviated through international agreements under which both Japan and Russia accept significantly lower king-crab quotas.[3]

Habitats, Stocks, and Fisheries

Fishermen and fisheries managers have their jobs cut out for them. They have to convince other Alaskans to set and enforce high standards of water quality for spawning, nursery, and maturation of fish. They have to make sure that enough fresh water is allocated to fish production regardless of how many other demands are made on the water. Together they have to regulate harvests to protect stocks and rehabilitate and enhance depleted stocks. They have to work out a sharing plan that

93

gives subsistence, commercial, and recreational interests in Alaska a satisfactory chance to fish. They have to protect Alaska's share of the North Pacific fisheries and enlarge it if possible. Finally, they have to test every potential action against its immediate or future effect on fishing itself, in all of its forms, as a set of Alaskan lifeways.

The commercial fisheries of Alaska all occur in salt water, and most subsistence fisheries depend on sea-run species even if the catching is done in fresh water. However, continued fish production depends on maintaining both marine and freshwater environments. The fresh waters are important mostly because salmon spawn and grow there, but also because gross pollution of major streams could affect the adjoining sea as well.

Salmon eggs and fry are extraordinarily sensitive to the quality (especially oxygen content) of the water percolating through the gravel where they live. Pollutants using up oxygen supplies or fine particles choking off the flow of water among the gravel can kill salmon spawn quickly. Streams carrying heavy natural silt loads are devoid of spawning fish, although adult salmon can migrate through turbid water to reach clear spawning areas. Silt from gravel washing and placer mining can be very harmful to salmon. For example, salmon and grayling declined in the Chena River drainage near Fairbanks in the heyday of placer gold operations in clear tributaries. Fish populations rebounded when mining became unprofitable and summer silt loads declined, despite severe organic pollution of the lower Chena River from Fairbanks's sewage.

Whether logging harms salmon streams in southeast Alaska is a matter of continuing controversy. Lacking firm evidence to the contrary — and with a few studies in hand in which no harmful effects were found [4] — the Forest Service believes that careful logging will not affect fish. On the other hand, there is general agreement that logging on unstable soils, poor construction of timber access roads, dragging logs across streambeds, and dumping slash and other debris in streams has hurt fish stocks. The Forest Service obviously does not condone poor logging practice. Unfortunately, economic incentives to cut operation costs and inconsistent surveillance of logging shows have allowed such abuses to occur. Until recently the Service has paid more attention to larger streams where adult salmon spawn; it now seems clear that it is even more important to care for tiny feeder streams, often not more than two feet across, where young silver salmon and trout find shelter and food all year.

Alaska's seas are carrying an increasing burden of substances potentially harmful to commercial fisheries. Some, like polychlorinated biphenyls (PCBs), DDT and its derivatives, and certain heavy metals, come from distant sources. These oceanic pollutants may or may not have begun to affect fisheries. There is reason to be concerned because of their ability to affect the production of fish-food organisms over wide areas and because of the effects of contamination on the marketability of fish.

Other pollution sources are closer to home. Crude oil and petroleum products are spilled or dumped into coastal waters from hundreds of service stations, thousands of boats (including fishing boats!), and many pipelines, loading facilities, tankers, and offshore drilling platforms. Steps are being taken to dry up these sources of oil pollution, but as the number of sources goes up and the volume of oil handled increases (as it will, dramatically, with the development of additional oil fields), preventive measures have to become more strict.

All too aware of the threat to their livelihoods posed by marine oil development, commercial fishing interests have put political pressure on the state to regulate potential oil-pollution sources more strictly. In 1971 the state legislature established a "sanctuary" off limits to petroleum leasing in the heart of Bristol Bay. Organized fishermen in Prince William Sound 95 brought suit against the proposed Prudhoe-to-Valdez crude-oil line in 1970 to prevent inevitable oil spills. Commercial fishermen played a leading role in getting the state to buy back petroleum leases in Kachemak Bay in 1976 and to prohibit further oil development there. There has been talk of establishing extensive marine sanctuaries to protect Alaskan fisheries but, as yet, no action.

Serious chronic pollution exists in small areas around fish processing plants in Alaska where unused fish and shellfish parts are dumped into bays with poor water circulation. Alaska's two pulp mills in Sitka and Ketchikan have created small biological deserts by discharging fibrous wastes and waste-sulfite liquors into the nearest salt water. Both mills agreed to a cleanup program which was to allow recovery of these waters beginning in 1975, but when softening pulp markets put these mills in rather marginal situations in 1975 and 1976, the company in Ketchikan refused to comply with the plan and the schedule. The Environmental Protection Agency permitted the company to delay compliance for three more years. Other coves in southeastern Alaska, used for many years as sites for long storage and rafting, have suffered from the physical and chemical effects of massive bark fallout as well as from severe soil disturbance as rafts and loose logs rose and fell with the tides. Simple changes in site selection and log-handling practices should alleviate these problems.

The Alaska Department of Fish and Game has sustained a program of salmon stream and lake improvement for many years, the principal activities being the removal of natural migration barriers, removal of log jam and debris barriers, construction of fish passes to allow salmon to surmount or by-pass obstructions, and regrading of streams in Prince William Sound lifted upward by the earthquake of March 1964. Often these actions have been coupled with artificial rearing and restocking and removal of sculpins or other fish preying heavily on salmon eggs and fry. The state legislature gave impetus to these programs by creating a Hatcheries Section through a $3-million bond issue in 1970 and establishing a Division of Fisheries Rehabilitation, Enhancement, and Development in ADFG in 1971.

Water not only has to be kept clean, there has to be enough of it for salmon reproduction. Alaska sorely needs legislation protecting stream flows from excessive tampering. One way to do this is to establish minimum-flow rates for particular streams — rates which will maintain the stream ecosystem in healthy condition for all life, including valuable fish species. State legislation to do this was introduced in 1962 as part of a model water code, but the entire section of the code dealing with conservation failed to pass. In 1972, 1976, and 1977 minimum-flow legislation was introduced, failing each time. Biologists and fisheries administrators continue to place high priority on this legislation, especially in view of the reawakening interest in hydroelectric projects.

Although there are major threats to fish habitats, especially from petroleum activity, actual damage to date has been highly localized and often temporary. From an economic and political viewpoint, problems relating to the divvying up of harvestable stocks among foreign, Alaskan and other competing American fishermen have been of far greater concern.

The ideal of every fishing nation is to have exclusive rights to harvest stocks in the biggest possible area close to its shores, and to have free access to compete in all other waters with other fishing nations. However, a kind of golden rule prevails in international gamesmanship: Protect against others that which you want them to protect against you. If a nation's fishing fleets are equipped to fish long distances from home the nation may support a principle of narrow zones of exclusive rights (say, a 9-mile or 12-mile territorial limit). Nations whose fishing is done at short range are likely to want broader zones of exclusive fishing (say 200-mile limits). Other factors, 97 many of them unrelated to fishing, complicate this equation.

Up to 1975 the United States claimed a 3-mile territorial sea extending out from mean low water. This zone and the submerged lands beneath it were (and are) under state jurisdiction by virtue of the Submerged Lands Act and Alaska Statehood Act. Beginning at the outer bound of the territorial sea, the United States claimed a 9-mile contiguous fishery zone in which it had exclusive rights unless specific exceptions were made by agreement. Beyond this, the United States declared jurisdiction over creatures that burrowed into, crawled over, or tiptoed across the outer continental shelf, with its seaward limit where water depths exceed 200 meters. High-seas fisheries on free-swimming species above the shelf were until 1976 subject to a host of specific agreements embodying the dual principles of (a) freedom of fishing on high seas and (b) the special interest of nations in the conservation of fish stocks of the high seas off their coasts.

A persistent sore point with Alaskans has been that Alaska's specific fishery interests in securing and protecting bigger shares of various nearshore and offshore fisheries often have been ignored by federal officials from the Department of State. The diplomat's view of preferred trade relations with other nations weighed Alaska's concerns very lightly; to put it more pointedly, Alaskan fisheries were pawns in a bigger game.

Very early, Alaska felt it would benefit from congressional adoption of a 200-mile jurisdiction limit, a position that high federal officials opposed. As negotiations in the Law of the Sea Conference dragged on and on, and as other nations began to declare 200-mile limits, more coastal states added their pressure for extended U.S. jurisdiction. The Fisheries Conservation and Management Act of 1976 finally established an exclusive fisheries management zone out to 200 nautical miles seaward of high tideline. The hope and purpose of this act is to promote the recreational and commercial marine fisheries of the nation, and to provide a way for sound resource decisions to be made jointly by states and the federal government on a regional basis. The act does not eliminate the need for bilateral and multilateral agreements with other nations with respect to particular fisheries, but it does let the United States bargain from a position of greater consistency and strength.

As Richard Cooley discussed so lucidly in *Politics and Conservation: The Decline of the Pacific Salmon,* [5] competition between Alaskan and other U.S. fishermen has played an important role in the political and economic history of Alaska. Alaska regulates the domestic fishery, but under its own and the U.S. Constitution cannot discriminate unreasonably against nonresident fishermen. This problem frustrated attempts to set up a system of entry limitation — which many felt would help prevent overfishing — because no Alaskan politician could stand behind a proposal that left some local fishermen high and dry while granting fishery rights to Outsiders.

The years 1972 and 1973 saw a breakthrough. In 1972, voters approved an amendment to the Alaska constitution allowing the state to ''limit entry into any fishery for purposes of resource conservation, to prevent economic distress among fishermen and those dependent upon them for a livelihood, and to promote the efficient development of aquaculture in the state of Alaska.'' Early the following year the governor submitted a bill to the state senate proposing a solution to the entry-limitation problem in salmon fisheries. The bill, amended and passed in 1973, creates a regulatory and quasi-judicial commission to administer an entry-permit system that can respond flexibly to the problems of the diverse array of salmon fisheries. The number of permits is to be limited for each area; permits will be issued to fishermen meeting standards of past participation and economic dependence. A prime goal of the latter standard is to reduce or eliminate the part-time, avocational fisherman who can afford to fish even when it is not profitable, driving average incomes for all fishermen to submarginal levels. As long as the statutory basis and standards of the Alaska Commercial Fisheries Entry Commission are sound, it is argued, legal attacks will be deflected onto specific regulations and decisions, leaving the commission fundamentally intact.

Limited entry was actually put into practice for 19 different salmon fisheries in 1975. The percentage of permits issued to residents (73 percent) was only marginally greater than the 71 percent of gear licenses going to residents before the limited-entry law passed. Thus, the basic law does not appear to be discriminatory. However, voluntary sales of permits from nonresidents to residents are occurring, and Alaskan fishermen have now secured a bigger share of the fishing opportunity. Any scheme of entry limitation will meet many obstacles in practice. However, most Alaskans want to give limited entry a try, as evidenced by a resounding defeat suffered in 1976 by a referendum to repeal the program.

Headlines of an article in the *Alaskan Advocate* for August 18, 1977, read "COOK INLET SALMON: SPORT FISHER-MEN DEMAND A SHARE." The article recounted recent developments in a decades-old battle between sport and commercial fishermen for Cook Inlet fisheries. The same competition occurs every year in the Southeast, especially for king and silver salmon, and in Prince William Sound. Subsistence, recreational, and commercial fishermen all want salmon in the Copper River run. The salmon of the Yukon River and Kobuk River are sought by subsistence and commercial interests.

Historically, commercial interests have been favored overwhelmingly in this competition. Subsistence and recreational fishermen have been unrepresented or outvoted in the Board of Fisheries, a citizen board (separate from the Alaska Department of Fish and Game), whose regulations are the primary means of allocating runs. Since board members are appointed by the governor and are subject to confirmation by the legislature, the predominance of commercial interests on the board reflects a political perception that other interests are economically and politically weaker.

Will Natives use their improved political power to force a new balance between subsistence interests (almost wholly Indian and Eskimo people) and commercial fishermen? The reason for being uncertain is that many Natives now fish commercially, especially in southeastern Alaska, Bristol Bay, at the mouth of the Yukon and Kuskokwim rivers, and in Kotzebue Sound. More enter the commercial fishery yearly. Incorporation of Native groups under the Alaska Native Claims Settlement Act probably will stimulate more Native fish-processing cooperatives, which will have a strong vested commercial interest in the coastal and river fisheries as opposed to the waning subsistence harvest.

In general, recreationists have not yet built a politically effective case for increasing their share of salmon harvests. Sport fishermen have won concessions in a few places, notably the Kenai Peninsula and other Cook Inlet fisheries where the number of recreationists is large and their economic impact exceptional. It seems likely that commercial fishermen will have to make room for sport fishermen in other areas (Prince William Sound and much of the Inland Passage waters of the Southeast, for example), as time goes on.

Alaska's commercial fisheries, then, are in a curious state of mixed hope and despair. Halibut and the all-important salmon stocks are at very low levels, with disaster and near-disaster years striking with discouraging frequency. Almost unnoticed, more and more salmon-spawning streams, critical inshore nursery areas, and important bays and estuaries are experiencing or are threatened with serious pollution from many sources. On the other hand, fishery management is anything but stagnant. The new federal extended-jurisdiction act holds promise of tighter control of foreign fishing. The state has embarked on the difficult but important experiment of limited entry, with the support of the majority of commercial fishermen. This program could provide the fisherman with a chance to maintain a reasonable share of the total harvest, and with a salable property right should he wish to get out of the fishery. And, finally, the new commitment of the state to encourage private salmon culture operations indicates a willingness to try every feasible avenue for rebuilding runs to their dimly remembered levels of two or three generations ago. State fishery biologists believe it is possible to double the average annual salmon harvest from its present level of about 56 million fish. Their means of doing this are varied, and some are experimental: protecting against overfishing, improving spawning habitats, and stocking with artificially reared fish.

As you try to assess what significance new trends in the fisheries may have for the style of the fishing life, you realize that each of the three major hopes for improving and expanding Alaskan fisheries carries some implicit thrust for deep social change. Take limited entry, for example. If limiting entry decreases the extreme risk once characteristic of salmon and shellfish fisheries, one result should be an incentive for a boat owner to improve fishing gear and boats so as to catch fish more efficiently. If efficiency improves but the total allowable catch is constant, the quota of boats in a fishery must go down over time. If this occurs, the industry will increase efficiency at the expense of employment — exactly as occurred in farming in the United States with mechanization of agriculture. If efficiency doubles and stocks remain the same, only half of the people who now fish will be fishermen. What effects would this have on the life of coastal communities and the relative power of fishermen in state and local politics? With a rural population perennially unemployed, is it really wise to eliminate fishing opportunities where many would gain some income, in order to permit a few to gain a reliable profit? If a boat owner has one fishing permit but three sons who want to follow the sea, how do the ''surplus'' boys gain a mooring?

Potentially, the rise of artificial rearing as a method of increasing salmon stocks could also affect the nature of the fishing lifestyle. A rearing facility requires year-round operation at a fixed location, often far from a community. To make this kind of venture attractive to private industry the operators have to be assured of a certain percentage of the catch of returning fish. Today independent fishermen are many and rearing-facility operators are few, with political decisions seeming to safeguard the traditional fisherman. But will this be true after a generation of success and expansion of the artificial-rearing projects? It is possible that those who operate the facilities will elbow their way into a bigger share of the run; a portion of the fishing opportunity will pass from individual boat owners to the shore-based business venture.

The adoption of the 200-mile zone by the United States poses even greater changes in the nature of our fisheries, if expansion of bottom fishing happens as many hope and expect. Bottom or mid-depth fishing on the high seas for big volume, low-unit-value fish requires vastly larger boats with big capacities and great range. Processing plants have to be big as well. It is conceivable that a major fishery could develop which involves relatively few fleet owners and a bare handful of shore processing plants in Alaska — or none at all. Alaskans in this kind of fishery would be mainly deck hands and fillet-machine operators.

From a global nutrition standpoint it doesn't matter very much whether pollock and sole are caught by Americans or Japanese. From our national perspective it may matter quite a bit because of the balance-of-trade benefit we derive. To Alaska, the issue is how the economics of an expanded fishery relate to social costs and benefits.

Logging

Almost a third of Alaska can support forest growth. For millennia these forests supplied Native people with the raw material for heating, cooking, housing, boats, utensils, and art and religious objects. Wood-burning river boats, mines, canneries, and new communities in the nineteenth and early twentieth centuries accelerated timber use, but supply still far outstripped use except very locally. Truly intensive harvesting, given Alaska's small population, depended on the development of export markets. These have come slowly everywhere except in coastal areas of southcentral and southeastern Alaska where the size of the trees and low-cost water transportation allowed an export industry to grow. Today 97 percent of Alaskan-cut timber is exported. Almost all of it goes to Japan as pulp, cants, chips, or lumber.

Of the 119 million acres in Alaska classed as forest land only 28 million acres meet the accepted definition of "commercial": that is, they can grow at least 20 cubic feet of wood annually or contain at least 8000 board feet of sawtimber per acre. Even that standard is too broad to fit Alaskan conditions, and the true acreage of profitably manageable timber is far less. Interior Alaska has most of the commercial forest acreage, but stands are mostly immature because of frequent fires; harvestable stands are far flung and remote from markets. Major expansion of the forest industry in the Interior probably will not come for several decades.

Alaska's present timber industry is centered along the coast from Ketchikan to Kodiak. Tree growth is best and commercial logging is most intense in the south near tidewater; both diminish northward and higher up the mountainsides. Of 5.75 million acres of commercial forest in the coastal region, about 3.3 million acres are presently accessible in an economic sense. The annual allowable cut from accessible forest lands is about 864 million board feet, of which about three fifths are now being harvested. Logging is most intensive in the Ketchikan-Wrangell area, where essentially all of the allowable cut is being used.

Forest managers began to gain practical experience with

modern logging only about twenty-five years ago. It will be another half century before forest management will encompass a full cycle from the felling of old-growth trees to the economic maturity of second growth. Hence most of the important questions about tree regeneration, timber management, and ecological consequences of timber harvests are still unresolved or are answered only "by guess and by gosh."

The two most abundant and commercially important trees of the coastal forests are Sitka spruce and western hemlock. Hemlock germinates in deep organic litter and can grow in dense shade; it dominates the virgin forests of southeastern Alaska. However, timber interests currently prefer Sitka spruce, which germinates best in mineral soil and requires more light then hemlock. Clearcutting — the cutting of all trees in an area in one season — happily offers both the cheapest way of harvesting trees and the best environment for Sitka spruce, and is the only type of logging done in the Southeast. Everyone hopes spruce will still command the highest prices in the mid–twenty-first century when the time comes to harvest the areas cut in the 1950s.

There are several other important reasons for clearcutting in southeastern Alaska, given the ability of the pulp industry to utilize timber with substantial percentages of defect, which is typical of virgin forest trees. For one thing, the amount of wood added to a Panhandle forest stand each year reaches a peak at approximately 100 years. After this the forest increases in volume more slowly; in many old stands in coastal Alaska the amount added by growth is canceled by rotting and wind breakage. Thus the greatest amount of wood (though not necessarily the best quality for all purposes) can be produced per acre with even-aged stands cut at intervals of around 100 years. Looked at from that viewpoint, clearcutting is the logical way to replace the slow-growing virgin forest with a vigorous young stand.

The two factors most decisive in determining where logging 105 can be done, and the size and shape of clearcuts within the accessible commercial forest area, are erosion potential and vulnerability to windthrow. Coastal Alaska has high rainfall and shallow soils. Steep slopes are extremely vulnerable to sheet erosion, gullying, and land slippage after logging when the rain-shielding tree canopy is gone and the soil is churned up by heavy machinery and logs. The shallow, wet soils are also poor support for tree roots during severe winds. Even in undisturbed coastal forests, winter storms may topple acres of trees on exposed sites. Logging can make the problem worse by removing strongly rooted trees at the edges of stands, exposing formerly sheltered trees to the wind. The likelihood of windthrow also supports the preference of forest managers for clearcut systems, since trees left after selective logging might well be lost later.

Logging practices also are influenced by the requirements of other public forest values such as wildlife and recreation. The major wildlife needs presently considered in logging plans are (1) to protect salmon and trout habitats, (2) to protect bald-eagle nesting sites, and (3) to maintain cover and food for wintering deer. Most recreational activities in southeastern Alaska are water based, a fact which has led to plans for "leave strips" of uncut timber to shield logging areas from recreationists in small boats and from travelers on ferries.

Management Policies

Until settlement of Native claims in 1971, few people could hope to own timberlands, although they could bid for government-owned stumpage. Timber volumes cut from private holdings have been negligble. Ten coastal Native villages selected land with commercially valuable timber under provisions of the Alaska Native Claims Settlement Act, and Interior Natives selected prime valley-bottom spruce stands, so this picture will change somewhat in the future. However, by far the bulk of Alaska's timber is and will be on state and federal lands.

The state's forestry program, perennially understaffed and in the shadow of the oil and gas and lands operations of the Department of Natural Resources, is administered by the Forestry Section in the Division of Land and Water Management. The policy base of the program is founded, on the one hand, by a state constitutional mandate to manage forests on a sustained-yield basis, and on the other by an administrative decision to prohibit exports of timber before primary manufacture. In Interior Alaska, the state program consists almost entirely in selling small amounts of white spruce stumpage to local mill owners. Small sales of birch, white spruce, and cottonwood have been held in southcentral Alaska, and a fairly major sale of insect-damaged timber was held on the west side of Cook Inlet in the mid-1970s. State timberlands in the eastern Gulf of Alaska area and near Haines in the northern Panhandle have supplied the bulk of state-sponsored timber harvests. An active export industry exists in the Haines-Skagway area. In 1970, a Haines-based company shipped to Japan the first wood chips and the first green veneer core stock ever exported out of Alaska. The state made its largest timber sale in 1969 at Icy Cape near Yakataga, an estimated 206 million board feet of spruce and hemlock. Logging under that contract reached full-production levels (16 million board feet) in 1972, bringing the total volume cut on state lands to 78.3 million board feet that year, the highest in the state's history.

The U.S. Forest Service manages nearly 5.3 million of the 5.75 million acres of commercial forest in the coastal zone, and its policies dominate timber affairs in Alaska. The two present national forests in Alaska were established early in the history of federal forest management, with Afognak Forest and Fish Reserve (now Chugach National Forest) created in 1892 and Tongass National Forest in 1907–08. Two pervasive and fundamental policies have shaped timber industry development on those lands since the turn of the century: the primary processing rule and the evolving concept of multiple-use land management.

The primary processing rule is a direct outgrowth of the traditionally strong bonds between Forest Service administrative units and local political and economic institutions. When first established as nationwide Forest Service policy by the National Forest Act of 1897, this rule prohibited exports of unprocessed timber out of the state or states within which a national forest lay. The policy no longer applies to shipments within the United States except in the case of Alaska. The Secretary of Agriculture presently allows a small volume of raw-timber exports to foreign countries from the 48 contiguous states, but not from Alaska (although a minor variance allows cedar logs to be shipped out of Alaska "in the round"). The Service's purpose in retaining the export prohibition in Alaska is to encourage local population growth and a more diverse, less seasonal, forest-based economy than might prevail if logs were shipped unprocessed. In the first half of the present century impatient Alaskan businessmen thought the main effect of the policy was to prevent any timber development at all. However, there were many economic barriers to the growth of the timber industry during that period which probably would have delayed expansion even if raw-log exports had been allowed. [6]

Another criticism of the policy has come from economists who argue that the extra cost of processing is — at least in the case of certain major export products — higher than the value added. Local processing also forces stumpage prices down, reducing revenues from this source to both the federal treasury and the state, the latter getting 25 percent of stumpage fees from national forests. More importantly, the employment benefits presumed to accompany local processing have been questioned. People unemployed before construction of lumber and pulp mills in southeastern Alaska, mostly Native people, are still unemployed because they lack the interest or skills to get the new jobs. Temporarily at least, unemployment may have increased even faster than employment, since more job-seekers often moved to new mill locations than could be employed.

Primary processing once stuck in conservationist's craws because they saw the smoke from pulp mills and sawdust burners hanging low in still valleys, the outpouring sulfite liquors and bark choking Silver Bay and Ward Cove. They also thought that the unfettered growth in mill capacity would lead to the ever-broadening spread of roadbuilding and logging. There is little debate on the point today, perhaps because the uncertain profit outlook in recent years has kept the rate of logging fairly steady.

The Forest Service continues firm in its position on primary processing in Alaska and is supported by the state administration and businessmen in the Southeast. The existing large lumber mills and two pulp mills are financially sound, evidence that even if processing requirements are costly to timber interests, their effect is overcome by low stumpage rates, efficiencies of scale in large-block clearcutting, other forms of subsidies (local tax forgiveness, logging road subsidies, and so on), and at least periodically favorable market conditions.

However, timber companies required to process logs in Alaska may be operating close enough to the margin that new standards of environmental protection or any of several market factors could delay use of the one-third of the allowable cut presently unutilized. In the decade beginning in 1957, the Forest Service prepared and offered a single contract calling for the harvest of much of this uncommitted timber, located in the northern part of southeastern Alaska. The contract was purchased by two companies before 1968; both relinquished the contract before starting construction of the required mills. In 1968, U.S. Plywood-Champion Papers, Inc., successfully bid on the contract. A suit by conservation groups in 1970 delayed what appeared to be imminent construction of mills at

a site thirty miles north of Juneau. The litigation dragged on
for five years. Meanwhile, the pulp market deteriorated. Perhaps the final straw came in early 1976, when an Alaskan
judge found that the National Forest Organic Act prohibited
clearcutting under procedures used by the Forest Service in
Alaska. Faced with several legal uncertainties, the prospect of
new environmental regulations, and a worsening market, U.S.
Plywood-Champion, Inc., asked that the 1968 contract be canceled. It seems unlikely that such a huge sale will ever again
be offered in Alaska.

Another critical but very slippery policy issue is multiple
use and its interpretation. The Forest Service, whose responsibilities today are vastly broader than Gifford Pinchot ever
would have guessed, is not a custodian of a single economic
resource but a steward of diversely endowed public lands. It
manages these lands under the concept of multiple use. How
the Forest Service interprets and implements that concept, and
whether the agency's approach is in harmony with contemporary social needs, public attitudes, and ecological realities, is
at the heart of a running battle in the Southeast as well as in the
other 150 national forests in the United States.

The basic legal statement of modern multiple-use land management is in the Multiple Use–Sustained Yield Act of
1960:

Multiple use is the management of all the various renewable surface
resources of the national forests so that they are utilized in the combination that will best meet the needs of the American people; making
the most judicious use of the land for some or all of these resources
or related services over areas large enough to provide sufficient latitude for periodic adjustments in use to conform to changing needs
and conditions; that some land will be used for less than all of
the resources; and harmonious and coordinated management of the
various resources, each with the other, without impairment of the
productivity of the land, with consideration being given to the relative values of the various resources, and not necessarily the combina-

tion of uses that will give the greatest dollar return of the greatest unit output.

This sentence could have been written by the German, who, according to Mark Twain, "dives into the Atlantic of his sentence and comes up on the other side with his verb in his mouth." What does this statute mean? Well, this language is a lawyer's delight, but several characteristics of multiple use are definable. First, the five surface-renewable resources listed in the act (grazing, recreation, timber, water, wildlife) have no predetermined rank order. Each is to be given equal consideration. A resource should achieve prominence in a particular area because of the peculiar capabilities and limitations of that area, or because of clear preferences within society, or a mix of the two. Second, the act recognizes that no piece of land can be all things to all people. A national forest, like a house, can serve various functions for different people; but common sense dictates that some parts be used exclusively for one purpose or for a dominant function plus compatible secondary uses. Third, the need for flexibility of management in time and space is made clear. Fourth, land-use decisions are not to be based solely on dollar or other quantifiable values, but on the combination of tangible and intangible values appearing to be in the best public interest.

If, as many conservationists have argued for years, the Forest Service enters the complex decisions of multiple-use management with a bias favoring timber, it comes by the bias honestly. The National Forest Act of 1897 and the Weeks Act of 1911 explicitly emphasized wood production as the main responsibility of the Forest Service. Generations of foresters have geared their thinking to that end; today, it should be remembered, the top decision-making echelon of the service was trained in production-oriented schools in the period 1940–1960.

The Forest Service has been, and is, in rapid transition

toward a broader comprehension of public interests in national forests. Now, more sophisticated planning processes have been begun, with vastly more public involvement than ever before. Since early 1977, especially, top Forest Service people have promised a thorough re-evaluation of resource priorities in Alaska. The extent to which this evolution has taken place differs from forest to forest depending on differences in personnel and land-use preferences expressed with the forest by its human "constituency." Lands in Chugach National Forest, for example, are intensively used for recreation but have relatively little timber of commercial value. The program of this forest is weighted toward providing recreational opportunities based on wildlife, winter sports, hiking, and scenic enjoyment. In Tongass National Forest, the Service sees its prime responsibility to be development of a stable forest-products industry. The Tongass budget and staff are directed overwhelmingly to timber-related programs. Until recently, the Regional Forester's plans called for eventual logging of an overwhelming majority of the accessible timber in Tongass National Forest. Less than 20,000 acres of such timber had been withdrawn permanently from logging up to the end of 1972, in contrast to the 3,386,000 acres included in four major timber sales. It is true, of course, that almost three-fourths of the land in Tongass National Forest cannot produce a commercial timber crop, and that some of those lands have significant wildlife, recreation, wilderness, and scientific values. Yet disagreement remains as to whether the forested areas are being allocated fairly.

The 50-year timber contracts existing up to 1975 took most of the flexibility out of the management of the commercial forest zone in southeastern Alaska. Timber-volume commitments had to be met under these contracts regardless of how much area it took to meet them. (The effect of this was clearly visible when, in 1970, in response to heavy pressure from local conservationists to include an area then under a timber contract within a Wilderness Study Area, the Forest Service agreed to defer scheduled cutting for five years but immediately began laying out a logging operation on another island in a contingency area.) Short of exposing itself to lawsuit by unilaterally breaking the contracts, the Forest Service, even if convinced it had goofed, could only strive to reduce timber commitments through negotiation.

How much timber to cut, therefore, is the key question of forest stewardship in the Southeast. There seems little doubt that the supply of timber will be ample in the foreseeable future to support the forest-products industry at its present level, at an annual harvest volume of about 500 million board feet. Even critics of Forest Service logging policy admit that this level of activity would be acceptable. However, the owners of the big mills have their eyes on the 300–400 million board feet of uncommitted accessible timber still remaining. It is that same old-growth forest that wildlife managers, hunters, fishermen, and wilderness enthusiasts covet.

Through early 1978, only 282,282 acres of commercial forest land had been withdrawn from logging by congressional or executive action within the coastal zone from Kodiak to Ketchikan. This is 4.8 percent of the region's total commercial-forest acreage, but a smaller percentage of presently accessible timber. Almost two-thirds of the withdrawn timber is in Glacier Bay National Monument. Two large scenic areas (Tracy Arm, just south of Juneau, and Walker Cove, near Ketchikan) and four small Natural Areas, all in Tongass National Forest, contain the rest of the reserved acreage.

Those who want to secure more virgin timber from disturbance pin their hopes on the National Wilderness Preservation Act of 1964. The history of Wilderness proposals for Chugach and Tongass national forests demonstrates, through a rapid escalation of official and citizen proposals for Wilderness, the political emphasis placed on the Wilderness system as a counterweight to timber sales. The Forest Service proposed no Wilderness-Study Areas (which might later be sent to Congress for Wilderness designation) until 1969, when it tentatively identified six areas totaling 2.27 million acres. The proposals contained lower-than-average volumes of timber per acre of commercial forest land, and a high proportion of the commercial forest land included in the Study Areas was inaccessible. Countering this "rock and ice" wilderness offering, conservationists in southeastern Alaska in 1975 identified 45 areas in need of protection from full-scale logging, including 6 million acres they proposed for Wilderness status. These proposals gained political stature when most were included in H.R. 39, Congressman Udall's bill for new federal conservation lands in Alaska. Of the 5 million acres in this proposal, 1½ million were "commercial" timberland. The Forest Service then proposed 19 new areas in Tongass and Chugach National Forest "suitable for wilderness study," totaling nearly 4 million acres and 1.15 million acres of commercial forest. Taking all proposals together but eliminating overlap, Wilderness proposals by late 1977 had totaled 8 million acres, or 40 percent of all national forest lands in Alaska. No one expects this amount to be designated Wilderness, but it will be a great surprise if Congress does not place in Wilderness nearly as much potential logging acreage as was sold to Plywood-Champion in the ill-fated contract of 1968.

The argument over Wilderness is stealing the show from the ongoing and highly important program of identifying very small but very important areas reserved, temporarily or permanently, from logging. Usually critical for wildlife, these areas include:

1. *Nest sites of bald eagles.* These birds nest in old, broken-topped or wind-formed evergreen trees within a few yards of the sea. Nests are used time after time, though not always in successive years. Since 1967 the Forest Service has marked a no-cut area 330 feet in radius around each nest site found in

timber sales areas. Recent studies suggest that in many sites the no-cut area should be enlarged. In 1972, the Secretary of Agriculture announced the designation of a 10,788-acre eagle-management unit on Admiralty Island. The area contained 25 to 35 nesting eagles in 1971.

2. *Freshwater spawning and rearing areas for salmon and trout.* Streambanks must be protected from disturbance causing erosion, trees and debris must be kept out of the water, and trees must be left along streambanks to prevent excessive summer warming of water.

3. *Wintering areas of black-tailed deer.* Deer in the Southeast are near the northern limit of their range and are highly sensitive to deep snow, winter food shortages, and excessive exposure to cold winds. The old-growth forest provides a necessary winter habitat. It decreases snow accumulation on the ground, shelters deer from storms, and contains enough food in natural openings to carry deer through the winter.

4. *Breeding habitat for migratory birds.* Many species of songbirds nest in old-growth forests of southeastern Alaska and disappear from or are reduced in number in cutover areas.

When it was standard practice to clearcut in large blocks — a system adopted to fit the needs of the young pulp industry in the 1950s — it was almost impossible to balance recreation, wildlife, and industry needs within a single drainage or other small management unit. These logging techniques left drainage-wide areas of esthetically devastated land which later would grow through successive stages of dense, biologically monotonous forest. Forest Service adoption in 1973 of a 160-acre limit to clearcut size greatly improved the chances for a meaningful multiple-use management system. Further reductions may occur in the next few years. Small clearcuts create a patchwork of virgin forest, thrifty second-growth, new regeneration, and currently logged land. The needs of many wild animals and those of an array of recreationists, scientists, and others can be fulfilled in such a forest environment. It is true that more miles of road must be built early in the process of harvesting trees on a watershed under the small-patch system, but the eventual mileage required is essentially the same.

How much uncut forest would have to be left within a timber management area under those conditions? Obviously there is no set percentage because land forms, forest characteristics, and the distribution of critical wildlife habitats varies so much from place to place. Equally important, goals have to be specified. What size of deer population would management strive to maintain? How much reduction in populations of climax-forest songbirds would be accepted? How wide a green belt should be left along streams and in favorite anchorages for recreationists? How many recreationists should be planned for and of what sort?

The Leopold-Barrett report[7] grappled with those questions in relation to the effects of logging proposed under the 1968 contract of U.S. Plywood-Champion Papers, Inc. These two scientists tried to estimate how much timber would have to be left to protect wildlife populations and related values at "reasonable levels" and ensure that no species was eliminated from the local biotic community. Their conclusion was that about 85 percent of all timber could be cut in the Admiralty Island area if logging were done over a 100-year period, but only about 70 percent if the 50-year period written into the contract were followed. These recommendations have to be studied to see if they apply to other parts of coastal Alaska, but they represent a useful first approximation.

Scientists — geologists, hydrologists, biologists, and others — have a unique need for natural areas for research. These ecological reserves function as benchmarks against which humanity's effects on other areas can be gauged. They also serve as outdoor classrooms for advanced students and teachers and are refuges where genetic variety in plants and animals can be maintained. Four Research Natural Areas have been designated by the U.S. Forest Service, and one by the Bureau of Land Management, in coastal Alaska forests. Over twenty additional areas have been listed by scientists as desirable. Most Research Natural Areas are under 5000 acres in size, and most can be located in areas already withdrawn from timber harvests — Wilderness areas, national parks, state parks, and others. Even a fully developed system of Natural Areas in coastal Alaska would have little effect on the timber industry.

Outlook and Choices

Richard Behan[8] once wrote an essay entitled "The Myth of the Omnipotent Forester" in which he warned his fellow foresters about making social decisions on their own. I almost wish I hadn't read it, because one could wish for scores of such omniscient beings in southeastern Alaska, where every Forest Service decision reverberates through the life of the whole region.

There is no question that the Southeast is moving at breathtaking pace away from an old perspective dominated by an increasing forest-products industry, declining fishery, and burgeoning (though localized) population of government employees in Juneau. Today each of these prospects is upside down. In answering the demands of wildlife and wilderness enthusiasts for a greater share of the region's resources, Congress and the Forest Service have little choice but to cut sharply into the logging and pulp industry's expectations of rapid growth. The fishing situation, while not yet moving expansively, is at least turning an optimistic face toward strengthened catches and reduced massive uncertainty. And the capital move, if consummated, will change the whole character of Juneau and surrounding communities.

The Southeast timber industry will be dominated for many years by the demands of the two existing pulp mills (and the associated lumber mills). The two 50-year contracts with those pulp mills will continue to be the channels through which the bulk of Southeast timber harvests will get to market. There seems little chance for a truly "independent" timber market to develop, apart from the mills and their contracts, despite the timber now in private (Native) ownership and despite the continued Forest Service policy of setting aside 15 to 20 percent of the yearly cut for small operators. Likewise, Japan will probably continue to buy most of the region's timber products, as it has since the late 1950s. World demand for products of the kind we produce surely will rise, but Alaska will never be a relatively cheap place to log or manufacture wood products; no sustained surge in demand for our wood can be expected for a long time to come. In short, the timber industry may have reached a long plateau in which neither total volumes nor product mixes are likely to change greatly. Volumes will be kept from increasing rapidly by the withdrawal of significant areas of timber for wilderness and similar uses. Slow increases in volumes handled each year might occur as waste is reduced, growth rates increase on cutover stands, and the barriers of economic inaccessibility are pushed back by increased efficiency. Prospects for a healthy timber industry are good, but spectacular growth is improbable.

In fact, growth in the timber industry seems to have been traded for improved prospects for wildlife protection, recreation, tourism, and — to the extent logging threatened salmon production — the fisheries. We have decided against playing brinkmanship with these other assets by fostering fast expansion in timber. It seems a good trade to me. Southeast Alaska may continue to be the most stable region of the state, its steadiness supported by the prominence of renewable resources in its economy as well as by the diversity provided by tourism, mining, and government jobs. Some might call the region a backwater because it may be relatively unaffected by sudden bursts of economic activity through petroleum development. In a very real sense, however, the Southeast may anticipate the challenges of slow growth that could face the whole state when the oil runs out. The way southeastern Alaska communities respond to this challenge will be a crucial lesson for us all.

The outlook for timber in interior Alaska is far more speculative. Theoretically, a pulp and log industry could develop in the Cook Inlet region and central Alaska that could eclipse coastal logging in terms of sheer volume. Enormous technical barriers now stand in the way. They range all the way from the extreme costs of protecting forests from fires during their century or more of growth, to the difficulties of piecing together a "working circle" of substantial available timber volume in the face of diverse ownerships of the land.

More important, we still have not even begun to tally up the costs and benefits of large-scale industrial forestry in the Interior, nor asked what the alternatives are. We do not know that logging can be repeated on any particular site; there is a risk that we can't economically manage timber on a sustained-yield basis. We do not know how wildlife would be affected by widespread forest management either for white spruce sawlogs or for aspen pulp stock. We haven't examined alternative land uses, such as agriculture. Most basically, we haven't asked whether it suits our Alaskan style better to use a capita-intensive, export-based industrial-forestry approach to the Interior's forests; to swing far in the opposite direction toward a locally oriented, highly dispersed "subsistence" forestry strategy; or to fashion an intermediate strategy emphasizing a range of forest products feeding into domestic markets.

Farming

Agricultural scientists say there are between 18 and 20 million acres of arable land in Alaska. Only about 20,000 acres have been planted in recent years. The difference roughly measures the gap between reality and the expectations of some of Alaska's small group of farmers and agricultural researchers.

Many kinds of farming are being done in Alaska today, ranging from tiny window-ledge vegetable gardens to 2000-acre barley farms, from commercial greenhouses to controlled-environment pork raising. All feed resident demand. Local produce appears every summer in markets from Anchorage to Fairbanks, usually at premium prices and never displacing imported produce even at the height of the Alaskan harvest. Essentially all field and row-crop production comes in July and August, squeezed between the frosts of May and the snows of September.

Those who think in terms of using millions — rather than thousands — of arable acres pin their hopes on export markets. The candidate crops are feed and cereal grains, especially barley and wheat. Experimental plots and small commercial farms have demonstrated that yields of 50 to 60 bushels of barley can be obtained per acre in interior Alaska, possibly averaging slightly better than midcontinent yields. So far, there has been no test of the idea that an export-grain operation can be profitable, however. The reason is that plantings of a few thousand acres saturate Alaskan markets (mostly pork growers and owners of saddle horses), but to ship adequate quantities to pay for overseas transport and make it worth a buyer's while would require that at least 50,000 acres be harvested yearly. Private capital hasn't come within a country mile of that risk.

After a year of intensive public debate, the state decided in 1977 to underwrite a trial of the grain-export idea. An area of about 60,000 acreas of state land with suitable soils was chosen for the project, on the Alaska Highway near Delta Junction, 100 miles southeast of Fairbanks. The concept is to clear 50,000 acres of this land (the country has a growth of small black spruce and aspen) with state funds, survey farm-steads and build roads, and make the agricultural rights available to farmers who would put up a small share of initial capital and pay the full value of the land back over time. Economic estimates suggested that farms would have to be 2000–3000 acres in size to be efficient; the whole enterprise is a far cry from the 160-acre homesteads that have been the mode for Alaskan agriculture since 1916. The state will underwrite loans for farm equipment and may provide capital for a grain drying and storage facility.

The legislature adopted a cautious approach to the project in 1977, authorizing $300,000 for testing efficient clearing methods and $100,000 for environmental baseline studies. As the state will have to advance nearly $20 million for the project, exclusive of road and school costs, it is not a foregone conclusion that the Delta barley project will get firm state support. Even less certain is whether farmers will appear who are willing and able to get the actual grain raising under way.

The reasoning behind the project rests on three presumed benefits. First, the grain can be grown and exported at a profit, adding to the state's economy. Second, the services that build up around the grain-growing activity will make other agriculture more feasible, including red-meat production and row crops. Third, the world needs food and the United States needs exports to balance a trade deficit.

Alaskans as a whole don't quite know what to make of this proposal. The idea has drawn fire from some quarters, skepticism from others, and shrugs from many who don't oppose the idea but simply don't believe it will work, or who argue that if the enterprise has merit, private capital will be available. To some, the very existence of massive state involvement indicates a high level of risk.

Beyond the economic questions lie a host of others. Competition for land is a central one. By pointing out that crops can be raised on many millions of acres and by insisting that all of   121

these lands be kept available for future farming, agricul-
turalists have brought out advocates for other resources on the
same lands: recreation, wilderness, wildlife, forest products,
power production (several million acres of excellent soils lie
upstream of the proposed Rampart Dam on the Yukon River).
This is a time in Alaska when ideas of competition for land set
everyone's teeth on edge, far outstripping today's real or the
future's probable conflicts.

Another source of opposition is the fear of environmental
degradation when ecosystems are converted from wild to
tame. Alaska's farmers are held accountable for (or asked to
defend) the ecological mistakes and environmental arrogance
of American agriculture: soil erosion, overgrazing, water pollution from pesticides and fertilizer run-off, mining of ground-
water, air pollution from dust, whistle-clean cropping that
eliminates wildlife, and so on. "It is possible to do it better
here," Alaskan farmers say; but opponents answer, "Where is
the evidence that you will? If farming turns out to be at the
frayed outer margin of profitability, won't environmental care
be the first expense you cut?"

Still others argue that grain-export agriculture on a large
scale, with big farms, huge capital requirements, and high
energy use for tillage, fertilizing, harvest, and transport, simply does not suit Alaska. Alaska farmers themselves are a bit
ambiguous on this score, being torn by the opposing desires to
expand northern agriculture and yet to avoid public subsidies
and retain family farming. The alternatives seem to be poles
apart. Either we adopt a midcontinent farm system of cor-
porate-owned holdings — agribusiness — or we putter along
at the present rate, letting a few farmers sell lettuce or eggs or
hay if they can, almost totally ignored by the public at large.
No intermediate choice has been defined to bridge the gap.

Actually, it seems likely that an intermediate and mixed
style of agriculture will evolve in Alaska under a combination
of laissez-faire and interventionist public policy. Large chunks
of arable public land will be dedicated to nonfarm uses, and

Native owners of private land with farming potential will also decide against farming in some cases. The world's poor may have to get along without very much Japanese beef raised on Alaskan barley. Even if the available cropland is reduced to 10 million acres, or 5 million acres, however, a significant export agriculture could develop. Meanwhile, arable land on the city fringes needs to be protected from escalating land costs and taxes so that fresh produce in growing amounts and variety can be bought at competitive prices. On a tiny scale, but significantly just the same, Alaska faces the Lower 48's problems of suburban invasion of farmland. Techniques to solve the problem are known (vigorous planning, tax-rate manipulations, purchase of development rights) but need to be applied with a will.

Northern agricultural research has already shuffled genetic cards to produce an amazing variety of vegetable and fruit crops adapted to Alaskan light and temperature conditions. These have been adopted immediately and eagerly by enthusiastic suburban home gardeners. The field is wide open for continued developments of this kind, broadened by technological innovations such as use of solar energy and social efforts like community gardens for city residents. Livestock raising in confined areas and controlled environments also has real potential. Economically serving as important substitutes, home food production has the greater benefit of involving people in one of humanity's oldest and most satisfying activities.

Alaska has almost no counterpart of the Scandinavian family forest-farm, where wood and wildlife products harvested in fall and winter add to income produced from crops grown in summer. There is a potential for this to occur, especially on Native-owned lands in the Tanana and Yukon valleys. Such holdings could produce, on units of a few hundred acres, crops such as firewood, posts, sawtimber, berries, moose, waterfowl, hay potatoes, cabbage, grains, pork, and so on in surprising variety.

Perhaps my message is that there is nothing inherently 123

wrong with farming as an Alaskan social and economic enterprise, and that more thinking needs to be done by individuals and governments to selectively nurture an array of agricultural enterprises. Farming is — or can be — an honest and intimate relationship between man and nature. Visually, farmland could add beauty and variety to the countryside in parts of the Interior and southcentral Alaska. A successful agriculture, it seems to me, will focus on diversity and innovation, not on the massive transplanting of American grainbelt agribusiness to the northern margin of the arable world.

Tourism

As early as 1900, cruise ships began carrying tourists to Alaska. There were tours of Glacier Bay by then, and curios and postcards of Alaska sprinkled the shops of Seattle, Portland, and San Francisco. However, thirty years ago Alaska's wildland recreation potential, poorly known and economically unattainable to most Americans, scarcely had been tapped. The writings of legendary hunters like Charles Sheldon failed to attract many recreation seekers to the North — and may have had the opposite effect on all but the most rugged outdoorsmen among their readers. Only the territory's townspeople consistently hunted, fished, hiked, and picnicked in the hinterland for recreation, and then only close to the meager road system.

In the 1950s newcomers followed the postwar defense-construction boom northward. Driving the defense-stimulated new highways, using surplus military all-terrain vehicles, and capitalizing on the growing knowledge of bush pilots, they widened the search for recreation far beyond the range of prewar residents.

Tourism and nonresident recreation added a new dimension to Alaskan outdoor recreation during the 1960s, when national affluence shrank the economic distance that once had made Alaska so remote. Still another surge in tourism came in the early 1970s, when an increasing number of well-to-do Japanese travelers discovered Alaska. By 1973, more than 200,000 tourists were visiting the state yearly, at least ten times the number who had vacationed in Alaska two decades earlier. Simultaneously, Alaskans continued to take part in outdoor recreational activities more often than is typical of other Americans.

It has always been hard to get any firm information about the tourist industry. Beyond overall estimates of total numbers coming by ferry, cruise ship, air, and highway, the data are generally less reliable than tips passed by your friendly bookmaker.

The tourism sector of the economy involves a huge diversity of activities and facilities, from multistoried hotels to wilderness safaris. Educational and capital requirements also span a wide range. This "industry" is rather labor intensive and offers more opportunities for unskilled people with modest capital than most other industries. The season of greatest activity is June through August, with a month of wind-up and wind-down at each end of this short period. Though tourism probably reflects national economic conditions in a general way, the year-to-year relationship is not always close. According to the State Division of Tourism, 280,000 tourists visited Alaska in 1976 and spent about $90 million in the state. (However, something like one-third of that total expenditure went to non-Alaskan corporations and hence didn't really enter the region's economy.) About 25 percent of the visitors drove up the Alaska Highway, 31 percent came by ferry or cruise ship, and 44 percent came by airline. Airlines have been bringing an increasing share of tourists north, while relatively fewer have driven up the gravel-surfaced Alaska Highway.

Although at least a few tourists visit practically every cove, creek, and community in the state, tourists and tourist services are concentrated in the larger towns along the marine highway and road system. A handful of medium-sized towns off the road system, like Barrow, Kotzebue, Nome, Bethel, King Salmon, and Kodiak, see tourists for a few hours on short-stop flights by scheduled airlines in the summer months. A few privately owned lodges, catering mostly to ardent anglers, are dotted around the most popular fishing lakes of the Southeast, the Kenai Peninsula, Susitna Valley, and Alaska Peninsula. Even the remotest parts of the state may be well known to out-of-state recreationists: the Hula Hula Valley in extreme northeast Alaska and St. Paul Island in the Pribilofs come to mind.

There are two fairly distinct kinds of tourists, and their very different expectations demand distinct management response. One kind of tourist takes part in highly organized group tours, requires a high level of direct services (tour scheduling, air and bus transport, hotel accommodations, interpreters, and so on) and spends accordingly. These tourists are fundamentally spectators. Insulated from wind and weather and the hazards of wild country, the success of their trip depends on seeing things they were programmed to see, avoiding inconveniences like strikes and overbooked flights, and purchasing the right mementos. In an extreme case such a tourist — if he happens to be sick while in port — may never set foot in the state. The energy cost of this kind of tourism may be high, and capital costs of facilities are high. The direct effects of these tourists on the wildland environment are usually low, however, because they rarely set foot on real soil, pick flowers, catch fish, or hunt game.

The other kind of tourist is more of an individualist and active participant. Avoiding guided tours, he and his family or a few friends may drive the road system randomly, fishing here and beachcombing there, flexibly adapting to what the day offers within limits of time, money, and pre-decided goals. Or the participant tourist may book a cabin at a lakeside lodge, kayak a river, hike in the mountains. Such tourists are the only visitors to reach the back country. Their expenditures are likely to be much less than the packaged tourists'. They are intimate with the landscape through several senses, smelling woodsmoke and poplar resin, feeling rain and wind, seeing beauties close and far, and itching from mosquito bites. They compete with resident recreationists for campsites, the solitude of rivers, and fish and game.

The product of the tourist industry is human experiences; the test of product value is quality. Some business people in Alaskan tourism have acted as if quality truly counts, but too many accept the cynical credo that a sucker is born every minute. Meanwhile, public land agencies have paid almost no attention to what the visiting recreationist experiences, devoting their meager recreation budgets to providing access and physical facilities.

With at least seven federal and five state agencies, a score of city and borough governments, twelve Native regional corporations, and hundreds of businessmen involved in tourism and recreation, building coherence and efficiency into Alaskan tourist programs is a frustrating task. An umbrella coordination group exists, the Alaska Parks and Recreation Council, but in its thirteen years its meetings have led to little visible improvement in historically fragmented, sometimes conflicting approaches to recreation management.

A typical example of the problems facing the Alaska Parks and Recreation Council is the Topsy-like growth of recreational uses of Harding, Birch, and Quartz lakes near Fairbanks. Three of a handful of lakes accessible by road in central Alaska, these areas have felt the impact of unilateral developments by private groups (scout camps, private cabin sites), state agencies (fish stocking by the Alaska Department of Fish and Game, access road construction and land sales by the Division of Lands, campground construction by the Division of Parks and Recreation), and federal agencies (land sales by the Bureau of Land Management (BLM), recreation camp development by the Department of Defense). Trout stocked in Quartz Lake attracted fishermen; lacking any other convenient place they used the boat launching site as a place to dispose of trash. The Division of Lands sold dozens of recreation cabin sites around the lake without adequate provision for public-use sites. The Division of Parks and Recreation had no funds to keep up with even minimum needs for sanitation. Harding and Birch Lakes, even more intensively used, are showing signs of pollution and conflict among water-oriented recreationists.

Most recreation program directors readily admit that beyond some undefined threshold the quality of recreational environments and experiences declines with each additional demand, but the momentum of development-oriented programs seems little affected by that admission. Part of the problem is that money for old and still-popular ideas is easier to get than funds for new and untried ones; part is that there is essentially no information yet available to make the concept of carrying capacity "operational."

Carrying capacity, in terms of recreation resources, has two main components: the ability of the biophysical environment (the "land") to absorb human use without changing excessively, and the threshold range of demand at which the "average" user feels crowded. The land's capacity varies with the type of use made of it (vehicular or foot traffic, overnight or day use, and so on), the nature of the soil, climate, and biota, and many other factors. The psychological response of users is affected also by a great array of factors, including expectations brought to the area, the design of facilities, and terrain features. None of these has been studied adequately in Alaska, and most of them have not been investigated at all in the northern settings.

For his part, the landholder and recreation administrator can only ignore the issue, assume that carrying capacity has not been reached (or, if reached, will merely result in an exchange of users from those with exacting requirements to others with broader tolerances), or attempt to limit usage. Most landholders still assume that the problem is years away, but a growing number of administrators are testing and implementing various use-limitation techniques. The most important example is the 1971 decision by the superintendent of Mount McKinley National Park to substitute buses for the bulk of the surging car traffic using the park's single, dead-end, access road. The program has been highly successful. Park visitors (who can choose between a concessionaire-operated tour bus and a free shuttle-bus service provided by the NPS) have, by a surprisingly wide margin, expressed satisfaction with the system. In 1974, another step toward control of visitor use in the park came with the establishment of quotas for backpackers in certain popular valleys. The top of Mount McKinley, now trampled by dozens of mountaineers and even hang-glider buffs, could benefit from a quota system.

There are other indications of a general concern for carrying-capacity issues among Alaskan recreation resource managers. Rarely does a park master plan or environmental-impact statement circulate that does not contain an estimate of eventual limits to recreation use. Unfortunately, there is no firm basis whatsoever for these estimates. By lending an air of spurious concreteness to the report they may do more harm than good.

What draws tourists to Alaska is the expectation of seeing wild and beautiful country and wild animals. Wildness, then, is a central characteristic of the setting for Alaskan outdoor recreational experiences. How can wildness be protected and managed, and how does the concept of Wilderness in the National Wilderness Preservation Act fit Alaskan conditions?

Huge areas of the North are wild today by anyone's definition, not because of conscious protection but because no one has gotten around to disturbing them. One of the critical problems today is to protect the wildness of at least some of those lands, federal or state, until administrative review and congressional or legislative decision determines whether they should be designated permanently as Wilderness.

Federal lands identified as official Wilderness Study Areas are protected adequately under law; other potential candidates are not. The de facto wilderness issue became acute in the early 1970s on many national forests around the United States, several important suits being brought into court to define the Forest Service's legal responsibilities. In 1973, while arguing the problem with the Sierra Club in the district court in San Francisco, the Forest Service agreed to an out-of-court settlement stipulating that the Service would prepare an Environmental Impact Statement for each proposed logging sale in de facto wilderness. The Forest Service thus has to justify, in a public document requiring hearings, a decision to log in most of the remaining wild country it manages. Coming at the height of an Administration-led effort to increase logging in national forests, this settlement significantly slowed the rate of loss of national forest wilderness. In 1976 the Department of Agriculture began a new review of Forest Service roadless areas all over the nation, perhaps signaling a more enthusiastic support of the wilderness concept within the service.

Policies of the Forest Service mainly affect Southeast's wilderness. Policies of the Department of the Interior, on the other hand, provide or withhold wilderness protection for the bulk of the state. The public land withdrawals of 1972 under section 17 (d)(2) of the Alaska Native Claims Settlement Act effectively stopped land disposals and major projects on 83 million federal acres outside of the Panhandle. Simultaneous withdrawals of most remaining federal lands under section 17 (d)(1) slowed developments and land transfers on the rest. By the end of 1978 the national-interest lands debate will have brought forth a new act affecting the vast majority of Alaskan wild country. Many will either be designated as Wilderness or as Wilderness Study Areas. The fate of lands held by the Bureau of Land Management is less clear. Supposedly subject to wilderness review under provision of the 1976 BLM Organic Act, BLM lands may or may not be exempted from that review by the 1978 Congress.

Other facets of the de facto wilderness-protection issue received less national attention but are crucial in many parts of Alaska. A prime example was the attempt in 1974 by the Alaska Department of Highways to obtain easements for numerous proposed roads the department wants to build across (d)(2) lands. The department actually began construction of one such highway, the Copper River Highway from Cordova to the Interior. The Sierra Club and Alaska Conservation Society promptly filed suit to stall construction until Congress could decide what management systems should be applied to the uninhabited (d)(2) lands the route bisected. The suit was settled out of court in 1975, basically agreeing to the conservationists' position.

Closely tied to the problem of de facto wilderness is the question whether wilderness, unlike virginity, can be regained. Conservationists have argued this somewhat inconsistently. They have urged wilderness withdrawals on the grounds that impending human disturbances would destroy their wild character forever. However, faced with Forest Service resistance to wilderness proposals in areas of the eastern United States once logged or farmed, wilderness proponents have taken the position that time has healed the wounds to the extent that many eastern woodlands now qualify under the Wilderness Act. The argument on both sides may be politically opportunistic, but the problem remains: Can wilderness be re-created? If so, how soon? The problem is partly ecological: Renewal of original living communities will happen at widely varying intervals after disturbance depending on the nature of the stress and the character of the site. The question is also a social and political one. Time until recovery obviously depends on the standards set for judging recovery, in much the same way that definitions of pollution are fundamentally a reflection of public tolerances.

After a Wilderness area is established, the knotty problems of management come to the fore. The most pervasive and perplexing is to protect wildness from its friends. The problem is acute in many backcountry areas in the 48 contiguous states. It seems to resolve into two basic aspects: first, finding out how ecosystems in a particular place respond to disturbance from hikers, horses, and so on; and second, devising ways of restricting use to levels that will not jeopardize these ecosystems. The ecological problems are getting scientific attention, at last, but on a far smaller scale than is needed. The question of rationing wilderness visits has not been resolved except by trial and error in a few areas.

In Alaska there will be other management issues of importance. Wilderness areas along the southern and southeastern coast of Alaska contain important salmon and trout populations. To what extent will it be possible to maintain these runs at optimum levels, if doing so requires clearing streams of natural log jams or landslide barriers, maintaining weirs, building hatcheries, and sometimes (as after the 1964 earthquake, which tilted coastal areas of Prince William Sound) even re-creating lost spawning habitat? Another issue is the control or noncontrol of natural wildfires in Alaska, a question intimately tied to wildlife management and recreation opportunity. Still another is the extent to which hunters and others will be able to use snowmobiles, motorboats, and airplanes in Alaskan Wilderness areas. There is little comparison to be made with the approach used in other states, where Wilderness is usually a small island surrounded by lands with ample access. A more liberal approach needs to be used in Alaska. On the other hand, conservationists don't want Alaskan wilderness to be second class in terms of quietness, solitude, and naturalness. And finally, many Alaskans think of wilderness as wild country where a few people live, widely dispersed and requiring no intrusive public services, since they live in large part off the land. Whether Congress is willing to change its classical approach enough to allow homes in Wilderness is doubtful.

Looking at these issues in the context of the history of public-land management, it seems fair to conclude that one of the main reasons why conservationists fought so hard for the 1964 act, and why they continue to press for large Wilderness withdrawals, is to be found in the long dominance of commercial interests in federal land management. In a nutshell, conservation groups see Wilderness as the only existing defense against continued degradation of public land values. In Alaska this defensive tactic will, I hope, result in the preservation of fine stretches of wild and beautiful country. At the same time there is a real danger that Wilderness status may cast land management in some areas into a rigid mold unsuited either to the landscape and its resources, or to the public.

Businessmen, urban Alaskans generally, and many resource managers in public agencies accept without challenge the idea that tourism is a good thing for Alaska. Yet there are many Alaskans who are less than enthusiastic about present levels of tourism, who question that more would be better. Like rural people in popular tourist areas around the world, rural Alaskans dislike being considered exhibits or part of the scenery. Some of the popular "bush tours" by local airlines have a strong element of callousness and paternalism. Rural people also have deep concerns about the effects of nonresident hunting and fishing and guided safaris on the land and its wildlife. An article entitled "Tourism's Ugly Head" in the *Newsletter* of the Association of Village Council Presidents (Yukon-Kuskokwim Delta region) put it in no uncertain terms:

"We have been trying to explain to the decisionmakers that they should not move to destroy our culture," said David Friday, chairman of Nunam Kitlutsisti, an AVCP organization, "and now people inside Bethel want to try and make money off our culture . . . We do not want a lot of people bothering us and the land."

Rejecting the idea of guided tourism packages, AVCP reasoned that birdwatchers could endanger animal life by disturbing nests and leaving eggs or young open to predation. Other 133 visible damage, like leaving tracks on the tundra by using off-road vehicles was cited. Clearly, though, the people simply wanted to be left alone.[9]

The elements of a strategy of tourism and recreation management that suits Alaskan social and environmental needs thus begin to take form. Tourism can contribute substantially and permanently to the state's economy, and there is no reason that it should not, if we think through some of the inherent problems:

1. Organized tours that reach primarily the urban centers and the most popular hinterland attractions where adequate facilities are available can satisfy a major element of the traveling public with greatest return to the economy and least cost to the land and its resources. No community should be made a tourist stop, however, without its full knowledge and approval.

2. Quite a few opportunities exist for the private sector to offer services to small parties of active recreation seekers. For example, backpack trips, river trips, guided photography tours, and wild-country cabin rentals all can attract customers and provide, in return, a fine experience. Much of this will take place on public land, where the manager must be sensitive to the ease with which crowding, litter, and animal harvests by recreationists can damage the land's basic assets.

3. Wilderness Areas, especially, need a whole new set of management concepts in Alaska. Excessive restrictions on motor usage in all Wilderness Areas would drastically limit use and might eventually lead to the repeal of Wilderness designations. On the other hand, a too-liberal policy about access could quickly degrade our wild country. The idea of cabins in Wilderness Areas, where people can live for a few months or years, should be considered carefully.

4. The conflicts between nonresident tourists and resident recreationists must be discussed openly. Many of these revolve

around the taking of fish and game. There are many ways to resolve these problems without illegally discriminating against either group.

5. To date, the private and public sectors involved with tourism and recreation management have thought in terms of quantities — recreation demand, numbers participating in given activities, miles of road and trail access, campground units, and so on. The key to successful tourism management really lies with a central focus on quality of re-creating experiences.

6. Now that 44 million acres of former public land have been returned to Native Alaskans, their rights as private property owners must be respected by outdoor recreationists. This change, plus the parceling out of public domain to various federal agencies and the state, brings new urgency to the need for communication and cooperation. Whether we like it or not, our old freedoms with public land recreation are diminished. Only with careful (but restrained) regulation can we keep from losing more.

Subsistence Living

Subsistence — living off the land — is what people did for a million years before money was invented. Probably no one in North America now lives without money in its various forms, so in that sense pure subsistence is extinct. But in Alaska there are many rural people whose tradition of pure subsistence is a bright and recent memory, whose social fabric still shows its strong influence, and who still depend both psychologically and economically on "living off the land" for part of their sustenance. They are in a transitional or partial subsistence way of life. The subsistence issue touches still more people than that, however, because countless urban

Alaskans, economically able to buy food, feel good when they are able to bring wild meat or berries, mushrooms or firewood, into their homes with their own hands. Far down below the masks of an industrial culture they answer to the instincts of an earlier time. I am one of that group myself.

In this decade, subsistence living has become the focus of a broad, varied, and often sharp public debate in Alaska. No voice denies that the subsistence lifestyle should be protected for those who must or would like to live it, but how subsistence is to be distinguished from nonsubsistence (for example, commercial or recreational uses of wildlife and fish), and to what extent it should be protected and given priority, are bitterly contested issues.

One of the early aspects of the debate, oddly enough, involved only Natives. Made landowners by the Alaska Native Claims Settlement Act of 1971, Native people had to decide how to select their third of the 120 million acres available. On one side were village people who felt that land used for fishing, hunting, and other gathering activities should have priority. On the other were a smaller number of very influential, politically active Natives whose interests lay in land with money-making potential: oil and gas lands, timber lands, mineralized areas. If the two resource sets were on separate areas the problem was how much of a limited entitlement to use on each type of land. If petroleum and fish were in the same lands, the problem of developing one without hurting the other rose to the surface. The issue affected the internal organization of several large regional corporations and caused several changes of leadership in those areas. The problem is far from settled.

Contradictions in federal laws became another catalyst for the subsistence debate. The Settlement Act explicitly stated that in exchange for land and cash the Natives gave up all aboriginal title to fish and game, presumably putting Natives and non-Natives on equal footing. The 1972 Marine Mammal

Protection Act and the Endangered Species Act of 1973, however, gave Alaskan Indians, Eskimos, and Aleuts rights to take
various species for subsistence and handicrafts. The conservationist's 1977 bill to establish new parks and refuges in Alaska
(H.R. 39) provided for subsistence but not sport hunting in
new parks and defined subsistence users in such a way as to
prevent anyone from qualifying who had not been substantially dependent on subsistence in 1971, or who was a descen-
dant of someone who had. The bill also allowed subsistence
users to set regulations for wildlife harvests on certain federal
lands, subject to the approval of the Secretary of the Interior.
These contradictions and proposals smoked out strong statements by both recreational groups and subsistence users, at
times with racial overtones. They also served as another touchstone for arguments of state versus federal jurisdiction.

Aside from these legally based arguments, it is inevitable
that competition for limited wildlife resources would lead to
friction. The decline of several caribou and moose stocks in
the early 1970s and the growth of commercial salmon fishing
in the Yukon Delta and Kotzebue Sound areas made matters
worse. Given a demand that seemed to exceed supply, managers face the age-old problem of setting up priorities of uses
and users and defining classes of users so those preferences
can be implemented.

The whole situation must have been bewildering to con-
gressmen and -women who found themselves in the midst of
the debate in 1977. Residents of big cities or suburban and
rural areas where even the term *subsistence* is practically
unknown faced a yawning canyon between two cultures — urban American and Native traditional — with the
mixed culture of smalltown Alaska a mesa in the middle.
Congress, it has been said, deals best with problems that can
be expressed in economic terms. If true, Congress couldn't be
at its best in this issue where human longings, nonmonetary incomes, culture shock, and dynamic social change dominated.

The subsistence issue has at least one positive aspect. People generally accepted the desirability of protecting subsistence lifestyle opportunities and had to admit the need to protect the land so that it would continue to produce wildlife. This in itself elevated political concern for protective land-management systems. In addition it was recognized that no single landowner in the patchwork quilt of Alaskan land stewardship could adequately protect year-round habitats of mobile species like caribou. Cooperation among landowners, long a desperate need, got a major boost.

In my opinion, subsistence living, or any honest mixture of subsistence and cash income, is a fine way of life. If the responsibility of majorities in a democracy is to protect minorities, this minority way of life merits that care. Furthermore, to those who hope to maintain the wildlands and wildlife of Alaska forever a constituency of rural people who demand wildlife habitat protection is an extremely valuable political ally.

Some fundamental requirements for protecting subsistence living should be understood.

Probably the most basic fact is that subsistence-living opportunities are very limited. The sun sets the subsistence table, and in the North the feast is Spartan. If we accept the population of Alaska in the mid-1700s (about 70,000) as a rough measure of the number of people the country can provide for on a subsistence basis, Alaska's 430,000 people today could obtain on the average only about one-sixth of their livelihood directly from the land. Thus, subsistence opportunities cannot be offered to an unlimited number of people. In addition, recreation and commercial harvests, though given lower priority in some cases, must be allocated a share of that potential subsistence resource.

Second, if the subsistence constituency is to continue permanently, Native racial background cannot be a criterion for entry. In the course of time Natives will step over the threshold of the subsistence way of life as we define it legally for the necessary management purposes, entering the nonsubsistence economy. Someone will have to take their places. It seems only right, too, that entry into the subsistence life should be possible by choice as well as inheritance. This does not negate the need to protect, first of all, the opportunity to continue in a subsistence lifestyle for those who now live it.

Third, the institutions used to decide who has the chance to harvest fish and game should be able to distinguish carefully between situations where the supply is truly too small to meet everyone's needs, from those where conflict is only imagined. There is no need to give subsistence users sole access to snow-shoe-hare harvests (for example) if hares are abundant enough to meet all demands. Where preferences have to be given, valid subsistence needs have to come first. All users, however, must be included fairly in the decision process.

Fourth, some sort of limits may have to be set for the kinds of equipment that can be used to take animals for subsistence. Laser beams may be a far-out example, but wide-tired Super Cubs are not. At some point a line has been passed where a tradition has been left behind, and the preference should be given to those who will use accepted harvest technologies. The others, once called subsistence hunters, will have to compete as recreationists or commercial harvesters.

It is impossible for me to say whether the satisfaction I get from putting caribou or berries into my freezer is as great as that of an Eskimo in Point Hope who kills a seal. I cannot stand in his shoes. Knowing that my need is real, I must recognize that so is his. I can only hope there continues to be room for us both. If not, Alaska will be less.

CHAPTER VI

An Embarrassment of Riches

If Croesus' wealth is in Alaska, it is buried far under our tender living skin, black as coal, black as crude oil, spangled purple as copper ore, drab as uranium. How big that ultimate cache may be, no one pretends to know. Prudhoe is undeniable, but so is the continuing disappointment in the once-touted oil province west of the Colville River, the dry holes along the Kandik and Nenana, the pittance in upper Cook Inlet. Coal by the sealskin pokeful heated cookfires in the Alaskan Arctic for centuries, but will North Slope coal by the millions of tons ever fuel the dampening fires of world industry? The hard-rock lottery and the petroleum punchboard: hidden stakes in a gambler's game.

No question about it: What Alaska is and will be hangs in balance on the answers to those questions. How big the treasure, how rich the profit? Who will get what there is? How will they spend it? Who will be trampled in the rush, who shunted aside to wait and watch? What will be built, and what destroyed? What old images lost, what new ones smelted? Will discoveries sputter through a century like a string of half-wetted firecrackers, or will the whole keg go up like a Roman candle?

Those are crucial but formless questions that need substance and a sharper edge. Some things are known about our subsurface estate — an elegant phrase for crude oil and raw minerals — some likely developments are apparent, and some of the broad channels for the flow of wealth are being mapped. Some critical junctions of state and federal policy can be examined for the choices they offer for the future of the North.

On the Shelf

Geologists paint estimates of Alaskan petroleum and mineral reserves with a coarse brush, knowing that trying for too fine a line is akin to asking a draftsman to draw a mirage. Recent estimates have pegged undiscovered, recoverable oil reserves at anywhere from 12 to 94 billion barrels. In other words, the amount of oil yet to be discovered in Alaska may equal only the amount already found, or may be eight times as much. The state's official estimate is about 75 billion barrels, which means that undiscovered oil in Alaska would equal one-fourth of total U.S. undiscovered reserves onshore, and two-thirds of the nation's undiscovered offshore oil. Alaska's estimated 380 trillion cubic feet of natural gas would be one-tenth and one-fifth of the nation's onshore and offshore reserves, respectively.

Who controls this potential resource? Solely because of the Prudhoe Bay fields the state controls essentially all of Alaska's known oil and gas reserves. However, geologists agree that offshore potential — federally controlled — is far greater than onshore. Probably only 4 to 6 percent of undiscovered reserves are under land owned by Alaska Natives, and about 10 percent is under state land.[1] The rest is in federal hands. Clearly, Congress and the President control the tap of Alaskan petroleum production. Except where Prudhoe's first-in-line position put the state in a relatively decisive position for setting the pattern of arctic oil and gas exploitation, both Natives and the state often will find themselves piggybacking federal projects.

Estimating coal reserves is a chancy game, too. Today's firmer estimates are based almost entirely on coalbeds on land and rather close to the surface. Huge beds are suspected offshore in the Chukchi Sea area far north of Nome and Kotzebue, but mining is so problematic there that few people bother to come up with tonnage guesses. Also, huge deposits of coal far under the surface of the western North Slope, now beyond technical reach and economically far out of sight, could someday add reserves as big as the total for all other states combined. Ignoring this deep deposit, geologists estimate that there are about 24 billion tons of bituminous coal and 558 billion tons of subbituminous coal within 3000 feet of the land surface in Alaska.[2] Ninety percent is north of the Brooks Range. Sulfur content ranges from very low to marginally high by today's air-quality standards. Most of the state's coal has relatively low heat content and only a few deposits of coking coal are known.

If you need to be a hard-core gambler to risk estimates of petroleum and coal, however, only a Merlin on an amphetamine high would try to guess Alaska's total metallic mineral wealth. Compared with coalbeds and oil fields, mineral deposits are tiny targets. They are also much more diverse in geologic origin and physical properties. Using the "Blind Man's Buff" technique of assigning a value to minerals in Alaska on the basis of mineral values in well-worked mining regions of grossly similar geology, various rather staggering estimates have been made. They are not very useful.

However, some things can be said about the general character of these potential resources that are important to public policy. First, dozens of useful minerals — some of them not commonly found in other states — occur in Alaska in amounts ranging from "significant" to "huge." Second, extremely few of these deposits or occurrences are commercially exploitable now or in the immediate future. Third, the diversity of mineral resource occurrence, grade, minability, and demand is so great that significant mining activity is likely to continue for a very long time. Even in a time frame of 100 to 200 years, the state could consider mining as a whole to be a permanent activity while approaching any particular mining project as a venture of distinctly finite life. Fourth, a strong element of uncertainty will remain about the viability of proposed or even ongoing mining projects because of market and technological changes. This implies that even short-range forecasts of mineral production will be surprisingly hard to make.

Across the Counter

Petroleum and mineral production today is small compared to levels thought possible toward the end of this century.

Oil production in early 1978 reached almost 1 million barrels per day. Three-fourths of that production came from Prudhoe Bay, whose wells ran at unexpectedly low start-up volumes because of accidents at two pump stations and the effect of early decisions imposing high pipeline tariffs. The only natural gas being sold in 1978 was a portion of the upper Cook Inlet production not reinjected to maintain pressure in that and the adjacent Kenai oil fields.

In the next five years, few if any new fields can be discovered and readied for production. Daily production from Prudhoe Bay, however, should at least double. Natural gas from Prudhoe Bay conceivably could be heading southeastward through the AlCan Pipeline at the end of this five-year period. In five to ten years, Prudhoe gas production is nearly certain, and oil fields now showing promise during exploratory drilling, neighboring the Prudhoe field to the east and north, probably will be in production, raising Trans-Alaska Pipeline volumes to around 2 million barrels per day. Upper Cook Inlet production will be less than it is now because the field has passed its peak.

Beyond those expectations, production estimates vary wildly, depending on assumptions made about new discoveries in places barely being explored today, or slated for leasing in the next five years. Economists at the University of Alaska in 1975 felt that reasonable estimates of oil production could run from 4 to 10 million barrels per day by 1990.[2]

Only one coal mine was in operation in 1978, a small open-pit mine northeast of Mount McKinley along the Alaska Railroad which shipped its modest 700,000–tons-per-year output to power plants supplying Fairbanks. Extensive subbituminous coal deposits in the lower Susitna River Valley at the upper end of Cook Inlet show good possibilities for production by the first half of the 1980s. Production could be very modest if it is used in the Anchorage area for power generation or could be much higher if the coal is converted to a liquid or refined solid fuel and exported. From one to several 100,000–barrel-per-day plants producing solvent refined coal could be built to use the upper Cook Inlet reserves.

When (if ever) North Slope coal will be mined is wondrously speculative. Little activity seems likely before the end of the century. Eventually, coal in northern Alaska may be mined and shipped as raw or refined coal or used at the mine as a base for a petrochemical complex.

Mineral production in Alaska has been low to the point of near invisibility in the past two decades, but gold and gravel production values rose in the mid 1970s. There was a surge of interest in gold when the United States released gold prices from long bondage at $35 per ounce; in a year or two they had risen to $110–$150 per ounce, at which price some claims could be reactivated. Gravel use increased sharply with pipeline and general construction booms between 1973 and 1976. Total nonpetroleum mineral production, mostly from gravel, stone, and coal, had a gross value of about $120 million in 1976.

The Cash Register

Everything we call a natural resource, by definition, brings a measure of wealth to humanity. The wealth may be in elevated spirits, as with wilderness resources; in nutrition, as with racks of drying salmon; or in bank accounts. With no intent to belittle other kinds of resource wealth, I will turn attention to the economic rent Alaska is getting and may expect to get from nonrenewable resources. Its sheer magnitude, its sensitivity to public policy, and the unparalleled social importance of how it is spent set mineral revenue in a class by itself.

Hard-rock and placer mining is commonly perceived in Alaska as an industry scrambling for marginal profitability. Perhaps Kennecott Copper made a windfall from the huge nuggets of native copper at the north end of Rex Beach's famous Iron Trail. Perhaps one or two large corporations and a few hardy individuals made a killing in the sluice boxes. But these, most people believe, are the few exceptions that prove — and are necessary to support — the rule of frequent failure. More than that: Mining is seen as so beneficial in itself, in terms of the metals produced and the jobs created, that the public should prop it up with timbers of state or federal subsidy. As a result, Alaska does provide a limited variety of small subsidies and imposes no tax beyond "normal" corporate and individual income taxes. Tentative suggestions of a severance tax have been loudly shouted down.

There is, however, a latent opposite view. Minerals are one-time resources (absent significant recycling); when they are taken from the ground, the public at large (and especially future publics) should receive some compensation for their "loss." Fish, timber, and petroleum pay such rents; why not minerals? If a mineral deposit cannot now support such a tax, the thought goes, why not leave it in the ground until it can?

Some kind of royalty payment, I believe, will be required of miners before very many more years have passed. The real argument even today is not so much *whether* such a tax should be paid but *when* it should be imposed and at what point in the ledger sheet of an individual firm. One side, arguing against a royalty or severance tax until the mineral industry is more firmly established in the North, wants the tax imposed on net rather than gross earnings. The other view, holding that mines should not be developed until they can support a royalty payment, argues for a tax on gross mineral value. Whatever decision is reached, at some time in the future the state very likely will be receiving substantial income from hard-rock mining, not as spectacular as oil revenues but probably much longer in duration.

Coal presents a very similar situation. Today's personal income and public revenues from coal are trivial. Tomorrow's may be huge. As the horizon for coal development in upper Cook Inlet moves closer, the need for a hard look at environmental and taxation requirements will become more obvious to the State of Alaska.

Many Americans think the state is already rich, when in fact it is fiscally less sound than before oil was discovered at Prudhoe Bay. In 1960, 98 percent of the state's current operating budget (unrestricted General Fund) of $28 million was coming from recurring sources, mainly income taxes. By fiscal year 1978 the total General Fund budget had risen to just under $800 million and the state had no cushion left. In fact, we were spending much more per capita on government services than was coming in from taxes. Sixty-one percent of the unrestricted General Fund budget was coming from nonrecurring sources. In the 18-year period since 1960, Alaska's population had not quite doubled (226,000 to 420,000), but state government employment had risen from 3900 in 1960 to about 15,500 in 1977. Obviously the state had been trying to provide more and more services to its citizens — paying off on a promise of statehood — nurturing this expansion with sporadic windfalls from one-time sources.

The most memorable windfall was the $900 million in

bonus bids received in September 1969 for Prudhoe leases. But even this massive sum was soon dissipated when legislatures geared budgets to expectations of the huge oil-production revenues everyone hoped would begin in 1973 or 1974. The prolonged planning and construction period for the Trans-Alaska Pipeline put a severe crimp in those hopes, but the tap of government growth, once turned on, couldn't be turned off. By 1975, the General Fund balance was dropping toward rock bottom, inflation bulled costs through the ceiling, and the pipeline startup was scarcely in sight. The state imposed an unprecedented "reserves tax" in 1976 on holders of North Slope oil and gas leases which, due to a rebate provision, was really an enforced loan from the major oil companies. The $450 million in reserves-tax revenues tided the state over through 1976 and 1977, barely spanning the gap before Prudhoe production began.

For several decades the state will get an enormous amount of revenue from petroleum. Yearly income almost certainly will be several billions by the mid-1980s. The big unknowns, of course, are how much additional oil will be discovered, its net worth after deducting production and transportation costs, and the rate of state taxation. (In that regard, oil discovered on outer continental shelf lands, on National Petroleum Reserve Alaska, or on Native lands will not be taxable by the state. Oil-related corporate or private income will be taxable in all cases, however.) Considering Prudhoe Bay's proven reserves alone, and assuming an average total production tax of 25 percent and a wellhead oil value of $9 per barrel, the state will receive at least $25 billion over the 15–20-year life of that field. In comparison, state receipts from all petroleum leases and production taxes from 1959 through 1975 amounted to only $1.3 billion.

Another potentially huge source of petroleum revenue is natural gas, usually produced with the oil but often continuing for years after oil production falls away. So far, Alaska's natural gas has been worth relatively little. Cook Inlet production has been burned off, reinjected to keep up oil production, or sold in Anchorage. Prudhoe natural gas seems destined to be piped to Canada and eventually to the West and Midwest, but the economics of the line and the eventual net worth of the gas at wellhead are very much in doubt.

A Honey Tree in Bear Country

Alaska's known petroleum and coal reserves are a prize big enough to have caused the corporate bears of the world to lift their moist snouts to the breeze and set off on a trot for the North. Our potential resources of coal, oil, gas, and minerals are a cache of honey big enough to cause a snarling melee around the honey tree and all the way up the scarred trunk. Only a shocking disappointment about the size and number of combs will disperse the tangle, and only the whiff of other honey, it seems, can thin its ranks.

It has taken Alaskans nearly a decade to understand that, for at least our lifetimes and perhaps most those of our children, petroleum will more powerfully and completely mold our lives than any other materialistic force. Concern about oil and gas development has come full circle in just a few years. At the instant of discovery near Prudhoe Bay the first thought was of coming economic wealth. Through the years of pipeline delay environmental issues like caribou protection and oilspills dominated the public press. Then, with 25,000 new pipeline workers on the scene in Alaska's smalltown society, the word "impact" rang with sledge-like blows from newsprint and television screen. Today we are thinking about petroleum revenues again, but this time with as much apprehension as avarice. As T.S. Eliot said,

We shall not cease from exploration
And the end of our exploring

Will be to arrive where we started
And know the place for the first time.[3]

There is no longer any doubt that oil and gas resources require the fullest and most thoughtful treatment possible in Alaskan public policy. However there are those who doubt that the state really can exert much control over petroleum development. Considering that the federal government calls the tune for development of most of the potential resource, that Native corporations may control a significant share, and that the state itself is ambivalent about development goals and therefore not certain to exercise or know its full measure of power, this skeptical view is not lightly dismissed. It may be, as some believe, that the state can reach the accelerator but not the brakes: that it can increase oil and gas activity much more easily than slow it down.

My own belief is that the state has a great deal of control within its reach: levers of decision-making connected to both the quantitative and the qualitative facets of petroleum development. The crucial ingredients are the will to use those levers and the knowledge to use them effectively. On the quantitative side, the state can decide when to lease its own lands, stretching out or compressing the exploitation period for its own reserves. The state already has affected the rate of exploration of federal offshore lands (though the delay in the initial Nixon schedule for outer continental shelf leases under Project Independence was certainly not wholly or even mainly a result of Alaskan lobbying). And oil development on Native lands can be influenced by the amount of activity on adjacent state lands and by a variety of state policies toward environmental protection, roadbuilding, and taxation which create the overall "climate" in which private decisions to explore for oil and gas are made.

An intriguing and diverse set of policy levers are capable of influencing some extremely critical *qualitative* aspects of pe- 149

troleum resource development, ranging from direct intervention to protect communities, natural environments, and nonpetroleum industries jeopardized by petroleum development,
to decisions affecting the use of oil and gas revenues.

A closer look at these opportunities shows both the inherent
difficulties and the prospective benefits of state guidance of petroleum development.

Hands on the Pump

The direct way to control the rate of petroleum development
is by speeding up or slowing down production. (By "slowing
down" I mean dampening the flow of new production, since it
seems unlikely that production from existing wells will be substantially reduced by a policy decision of government, although some reduction might occur in response to economic
forces.) Currently the state's petroleum-management system
and in most situations the federal government's as well are
based on the simultaneous granting of drilling leases and the
right to produce whatever may be found. The first and most
important point of control is in the decision to lease, itself.
There is some chance that federal offshore lands may be sub-
jected to a two-step decision process which would involve
both a determination to lease exploration rights and a later,
more-or-less-independent decision to begin production.
Congress actually established that system in 1976 for petroleum development west of Prudhoe Bay in the vast National
Petroleum Reserve (Alaska). However, because the primary
reason for this system is to cope with the high uncertainty surrounding the environmental effects of offshore development, it
is unlikely that the state will adopt the two-step process for its
onshore and nearshore holdings.

The overriding reason to lease and develop state petroleum
lands is to make money. This focuses attention on the state's
fiscal picture as the prime factor determining when leases will
be sold. Refining a complicated issue down to basics, the two

primary questions are: 1) How will current state expenditures be related to current income? and 2) How much will future benefits be discounted in favor of present income? If costs of expanded government services continuously push up against the barrier of current revenues, the ingrained and compelling urge for growth will stimulate new resource sales for both immediate income (bonus bids) and the hope of long-term increases in oil and gas production revenues. If, on the other hand, the state keeps expenditures down and diverts surplus current income into a "safehouse," out of reach of yearly operating budgets, growth will be reduced (but not eliminated) and pressures for more leasing bled off.

Even from a strictly financial standpoint, it is not clear whether development now is worth more or less than development in the future. Economists usually discount future income so heavily as to assure that almost every calculation favors present resource exploitation. Occasionally (as with oil between 1973 and 1975) the value of a resource rises so sharply that earlier production would have sacrificed income. Oil and gas resources may be subject to that kind of unexpected leap in real dollar value either because imports are cut off or because uses shift (as from electricity generation to medicines, food, and petrochemicals). Another financial factor affecting the timing of lease sales is the judgment whether bonus bids would be at or below peak levels at the proposed sale date. This is an uncertain art at best, relying on how a person weighs information on the "money market," the financial condition of potential bidders, the extent of prior exploration in the area, timing of competing lease sales, and so on. Furthermore, the bonus bids are a very small part of eventual income from a successfully developed field and are important only if the state needs money in a hurry. The state very nearly opened submerged lands in the Beaufort Sea to leasing in 1976 solely to meet an immediate need for cash and despite its reluctance to set in motion another round of environmental and "impact" problems just when the Trans-Alaska Pipeline project was cresting. 151

The reserves tax was imposed instead, and the Beaufort sales are now scheduled jointly with nearby offerings of the federal government in late 1979.

There are, of course, many other considerations in leasing decisions. Oil-field conservation, for example, may dictate lease sales to fill in unleased areas within a producing field or to prevent drainage by wells of another and neighboring landowner. Sales may be scheduled to make the most use of a major trunk pipeline, replacing oil from a declining field with enough from new discoveries to keep the pipeline at capacity. Perhaps most important, sales may be held at intervals suited to the capacity of the whole society, including its economy and work force, to absorb and meet the needs of the inevitable demands of petroleum development. Norway's leasing of North Sea holdings is carefully timed so as not to unleash excessive inflation or to force the use of immigrant labor. Several Arab and North African nations similarly keep their oil production at levels below the maximum for internal social reasons as well as (at least occasionally) to keep world prices at optimum levels from their viewpoint.

All current projections indicate that revenues from Alaska's Prudhoe Bay production will exceed state needs for at least a decade, beginning in 1980. Adjacent fields close enough to use the Trans-Alaska Pipeline almost certainly will prove able to buoy North Slope production when the original Prudhoe fields sag. If this is true, the state has little financial reason to offer any more "frontier" lease sales in the foreseeable future. Quite the contrary: There are many reasons why a prolonged schedule of state leasing should be adopted as a partial brake to rapid growth catalyzed by expected offshore discoveries and, perhaps, by discoveries in Native-owned lands onshore.

Surplus Income and the Permanent Fund

Government budgets usually rise to meet revenues available — and sometimes to exceed them. State and local government expenditures are already 16 percent of Alaska's gross product and are rising in constant dollars at 10 percent per year, even before production taxes and royalty oil sales from Prudhoe Bay are in hand. Because government expenditures can stimulate immigration, add to or (by being withheld) dampen the flow of dollars in different regions and social sectors, and change the level and kind of public services available, the question of what Alaska does with its wealth is a first-order public issue. The sheer size of the potential "surplus" of revenues, too, is to be reckoned. Alaska's state operating budget is now about a billion dollars. If the level of service were maintained but inflation added costs of 10 percent per year, by the mid 1980s the budget might have doubled. By comparison, oil revenues could easily be $15–$20 billion per year.

Ever since the 1969 lease sale Alaskans have talked about squirreling away some petroleum revenues for the stormy days of the more distant future when oil gauges read "EMPTY." In 1974, voters endorsed an amendment to the state constitution that allowed a permanent fund to be established, receiving at least 25 percent of certain oil revenues annually. Pipeline delays seemed to indicate that there was no hurry to set up the fund, however, so it was not until recently that the legislature began looking at fund policy and management problems. By early 1978 some clear expressions of public preference had shown up for what to do with permanent funds, but the priorities to be given to these different preferences and the important questions of fund management were still unresolved. People are in a mood to build the fund faster than the minimum required — whether out of a straightforward desire to increase the joint savings account or out of mistrust of politicians' ability to command the wisdom of Solomon in revenue expenditure is hard to tell. There is strong support for investing in renewable resources development; less but still majority interest in getting the most income possible from investments of the principal; and considerable enthusiasm for using the fund as a 153 low-interest loan institution for private or community projects.

No one has analyzed the implications of such uses of the permanent fund. It is apparent that the several uses are different and even contradictory. Flooding the Alaskan economy with low-interest loans for home mortgages, entrepreneurial ventures, and community enterprises could boost inflation, strain private banks, and result in very low returns to the fund. Excessive investments in dams, pulp mills, sawmills, hatcheries, canneries, fishing boats, grain elevators, and similar renewable resource projects could cause overcapitalization, overexploitation, and general industry collapse. Investments in power projects such as the massive Susitna River project, which could produce surplus power available at low enough cost to attract energy-intensive manufacturing, would cause immigration, city growth, and environmental degradation. These are by no means blanket condemnations of the various investments mentioned, but they do suggest that we have a lot to learn about being rich.

Four general objectives for the permanent fund are consistent with the kind of Alaska I believe desirable. First, the fund should make sure future generations of Alaskans share the benefits of our exploitation of exhaustible resources, because they surely will have to pay some of the costs. Second, the fund should be managed to result in the least possible added population, because the rate of growth will be at least as high as we can cope with anyway. Third, the permanent fund or some other channel though which mineral revenues flow should assure that renewable resources are protected from degradation during our era of rapid petroleum, coal, and mineral development. And last, the fund (or other channel) should be used to protect and improve the general quality of Alaskan life through high standards of land and water stewardship, cultural activities, community improvement, and public safety and security.

154   It may be that the wisest approach now to our coming

wealth is to put as large a share as possible into the permanent fund. If 50 percent or more of the designated oil revenues were placed in the fund (amounting to 28 percent or more of all current oil revenues) and all or part of the fund interest were returned as well, the chance of a "whoopee!" approach to state spending would be reduced. The lion's share of fund investments could be made in high-return securities Outside, reducing the growth-inducing effects of local investment. This cautious initial approach could be changed when the state has done some soul-searching and gained experience in investment management.

The permanent fund is a grand experiment in long-range decision making toward the public interest. The fund could be a major intergenerational transfer of wealth or a complicated sink for ever-eroding income. It could be a powerful instrument for reaching broad social goals or a means of perpetuating business as usual. With the experimental design still in doubt and the investment coffers still like Mother Hubbard's cupboard, it is too soon to guess the outcome.

The Commoner's Royalty: The 12½ Percent Solution

When the state sells oil and gas leases to private firms it retains ownership of one-eighth of all oil and gas produced as well as the right to tax the corporation's seven-eighths-share. The "royalty" oil and gas can be accepted in kind (the state owns and physically controls the use of 12½ percent of production) or sold at the wellhead to the leaseholder, who then disposes of it along with the rest of production. Obviously the royalty oil and gas represents significant wealth to the state, and its disposal has aroused intense, often acrimonious debate.

If we continue to sell royalty oil and gas to producers at the top of the well, the issue would be diverted to the questions of revenue disposal just discussed. If we accept physical possession but then transport the oil or gas to non-Alaskan markets, the issue would again be one of money wealth. The reason for the heated debate, however, is that the legislature has all but forced the state to sell its royalty share to companies who contract to refine the crude oil and separate components of the gas into the building blocks of petrochemical manufacturing within the state. Some people have proposed that the state form its own company to do the same thing. The idea is that the value added in manufacture will increase Alaska's share of the total worth of the resource. Those who argue this case see a chance — very nearly the first — to create a major manufacturing sector in Alaska's economy.

Three small refineries now use Cook Inlet oil and a fraction of early Prudhoe production fuels to produce heating and motor fuels for use in Anchorage and Fairbanks. A small fertilizer plant exporting urea to the Northwest and a gas-fired thermal power plant in Anchorage complete the roster of current in-state use of Alaskan petroleum. These uses do not necessarily demonstrate that tremendously scaled-up plants using essentially all of the daily stream of royalty oil and gas from Prudhoe would be economically feasible. North Slope producers certainly have not built plants in Alaska to refine their seven-eighths-share. According to most consultants, the extremely high cost of plant construction and labor, the tiny local market, and the distance refined products have to be carried to Outside markets make unsubsidized local refineries generally a bad risk. The key word, however, is "unsubsidized." Firms may be willing to set up small plants in Alaska, using a fraction of a contracted amount of oil, which lose money, if in exchange they can sell the remaining crude oil outside the state. Alternatively, the state might subsidize the local plant by selling the crude oil at less than top price or through many other devices. Subsidies are unpopular with Alaskans, but politicians seem much less emphatic on the subject. Clandestine subsidies could easily escape public notice in the thick forest of contract verbiage.

The more fundamental question is whether it makes sense for Alaska to embark on a path of petrochemical industrialization. Business and labor interests in Anchorage and Fairbanks think it does. Some people in other communities are somewhat uncommitted but, in any case, wouldn't want a plant in their community. Conservationists, fishermen, and village Alaska are opposed to the whole idea, mostly because they anticipate the myriad pressures of new Alaskans elbowing for a share of the state's limited renewable resources.

Some question exists, too, about the long-range wisdom of walking the path of industrialization based on exhaustible resources. The effect is not to diversify the economy (an oft-quoted object of northern economic development) but to vastly increase its dependence on a set of resources sure to run out in a generation or slightly more. We would be building sandcastles in the top half of an hourglass. From the nation's standpoint it may not make a great deal of sense to build new refining capacity in a harsh, costly, and remote place; to import a skilled labor force; and meanwhile to watch existing refinery complexes in the South slowly shrink away. The short-term gain to parts of Alaska's economy might be indisputable, but the net gain to the nation, zero or negative.

Other Choices

Leasing policies, revenue saving, and royalty disposal are important points of leverage in a strategy for petroleum-resource management, but they are far from the only ones. Another significant aspect is to try to talk Uncle Sam into an approach to federal petroleum reserves that dovetails best with state management and creates the fewest possible negative side effects. An Alaskan economist has argued convincingly that the pace of federal offshore development itself will be scarcely responsive to Alaskan pleadings to either speed up or slow down.[4] However, the federal government can be expected (indeed, already has begun) to pay attention to risks to local resources like the fisheries and to help reduce unwanted effects on Alaskan community life. Requirements for ecological research before leasing, withdrawal of environmentally sensitive tracts from sales, organizing of traffic to avoid fisheries problems, oil-spill prevention, fast and effective means for compensating for pollution damages, funding of onshore planning by communities, careful siting of major facilities: All of these and more are among the ways now being designed and tested to soften the impacts of federal petroleum development.

State, federal, and private cooperation could sharply reduce the total investment for development facilities (pipelines, roads, stripping plants, tank farms, and so on) and simultaneously decrease the amount of wild country lost, wildlife disturbed, and construction side effects experienced, taking Alaska's "oil era" as a whole. For example, making sure that one trunk pipeline serves as many fields as possible over the longest time will make multiple pipelines unnecessary. Putting several gas or oil pipelines into one narrow corridor served by one access road and sharing gravel pads will diminish private and public costs (an opportunity missed in the case of Prudhoe Bay, despite early pleas from conservation groups to build the oil line along the trans-Canada route now chosen for Prudhoe natural gas). Delayed-development techniques involving either government-contracted exploration or compensation from government to private firms for postponing development following discovery could allow a steadier rate and better geographic distribution of petroleum development. Following the Norwegian model, we could accelerate or slow exploration effort itself to assure the selected pace of production, though in frontier and wildcat areas the uncertainties of discovery could make this a clumsy tool. Perhaps the main point is that strategic development planning can pay off even more handsomely than the project-by-project tactics adopted to date, which inevitably pays more attention to cosmetics than to body health. The dif-

ficulty is to overcome ancient turf defense, political shortsight-
edness, outdated models of "free enterprise" long since abandoned in the oil industry, and real or imagined economic
barriers.

Controlling Coal and Mineral Development

Although the horizons for the exploitation of coal and mineral resources are still some time off, development is sure to
occur and will be fiscally, socially, and environmentally significant when it does. Can Alaska survive as a unique place to
live, as a magnificent wildland state, during a long era of mining? If we can survive petroleum, we should have the attitudes
and institutions to cope handily with coal and minerals — but
this is not to belittle the challenge.

Quite likely the most critical aspect of mineral development
planning, from the standpoint of maintaining the qualities of
village Alaska and the wilderness landscape, is transportation.
Today's miners, like yesterday's, think that roads are the only
transport facility that really suits their interests. The very maze
of roads they envision, however, would destroy the unique
values of rural Alaska. A different solution has to be found,
and probably can come only over time through imaginative
planning.

At the outset we have to stop building roads on speculation,
hoping to assist exploration and discover something worth carrying over the publicly financed roadway. Mineral exploration
is being done by air out of necessity today and could continue
to be done that way indefinitely as a matter of social policy at
very little cost to consumers. Once we get over the delusion
that roads are necessary for and will automatically result in settlement of broad-based regional economic development, roads
rarely will be the transport mode of choice for either the mining firm or the public.

If not roads, then what? Many alternatives are possible now 159 and there will be more. Coastal mines logically will be served by ship; icebreaking ore or slurry carriers can extend this choice into ice-dominated seas from Nome to Barrow. Railroads are much preferrable to highways because they respond to transportation needs without entanglement with the issues of land management and community change that always accompany new extensions of the road network. Slurry pipelines are equally or even more benign from that viewpoint, and have real advantages for those minerals and coal products that can be turned to slurry form. High-value minerals — even certain types of copper — can be carried by aircraft. A recent study indicated that aircraft could be the cheapest way to carry copper from proposed mines in remote parts of northwest Alaska unless the government presented the mine developer with a free surface transport facility.[5] In some parts of Alaska, like the middle Yukon River valley and its northern tributaries, rails or roads running westward to a Bering Sea port and *not* connected to the Fairbanks-Anchorage axis could avoid most of the problems of excessive access to wilderness, competition for fish and game, and frantic village change.

Another reform of considerable environmental significance is to switch from granting full ownership of mineral lands in the public domain to the discoverer, to granting only the rights to mine. Leasing systems of one kind or another have been proposed for many years and fought successfully by miners. However, major mining companies privately admit that such systems of land tenure are certain to come and will not have much effect on the mining industry. It is the traditional frontier "small miner," with visions of having a cabin on land of his own which he can mine in peace, who most bitterly opposes the change. From the public's point of view, the transfer of full title conveys rights beyond those necessary to mine, creates inholdings that are continual aggravations to surrounding land-management agencies, and weakens control over mining activities as needed for water, air, land, and wildlife protection.

Many aspects of mining directly cause environmental problems ranging from nearly insignificant to extremely serious. There are so many kinds of mines, mining operations, environmental issues, control technologies, and cost-benefit tradeoffs that I will not try to discuss them here. A word about strip-mining reclamation may be valuable, however. A sound national mine reclamation act was finally pushed through Congress in 1977 after years of effort, but certain escape clauses in it may prevent its being applied in Alaska. (At this time a legal analysis is in process to answer this question.) It would be extremely unfortunate if this were the case, because few ecosystems need human help in restoration after mining as much as the North. Strip mining in the tundra-covered North Slope will trigger permafrost thawing on a huge scale, making re-vegetation almost impossible using any techniques now known. Even in the Beluga coalfield area in the "banana belt" of upper Cook Inlet, vegetation regrowth is much less certain and sometimes much slower than in Ohio or West Virginia. Acids draining out of freshly exposed coalbeds could threaten some spectacular commercial and sport fisheries. We need firm ground rules for large-scale mining in Alaska, responsive to our peculiar conditions; and we need them before major investments are committed to mineral development.

A final issue of mineral development I want to discuss is what public land should be open for mineral exploration and mining and under what general conditions. Ever since the General Mining Law of 1872 established the ground rules for miners, prospectors and miners have enjoyed great freedom to look for, claim, and develop minerals on public lands. For several decades this freedom has been eroded by withdrawals of land from unreserved to special-use status such as national parks and wilderness. This process, which has taken place throughout America's public lands, is just now reaching its climax in Alaska with congressional debate over the national-interest lands issue. Understandably, miners are appalled at the amount of land conservation interests want placed off limits to exploration and mining. Conservationists, in turn, have taken what they think is the only sure path to prevent losses of wilderness, wildlife, and general environmental assets that have accompanied the traditional system of mineral development. Miners argue the irrationality of making rigid land-use decisions today given in poor knowledge of underground resources and protest the locking away of potentially valuable or even nationally critical resources. Conservation spokesmen counter by saying that the net worth of many Alaskan minerals is far lower than the value of the surface environmental assets above them, that there are many other places the minerals can come from, and that in any case a future Congress can unlock the door to a park any time it is clearly necessary. To which, in reply, miners say that by the time Congress realizes it is necessary to mine it will be too late, considering the decade or more required after discovery to bring a big mine into production.

A complicated compromise is being strung together right now, and only its general outlines can be seen. First, some land in Alaska will be declared off limits to mineral prospecting and entry, indefinitely, and with no special unlocking mechanism provided. Most if not all new national parks and all Wilderness probably will be treated this way. The total acreage (not a very significant statistic, but a very visible one) so withdrawn will be less than conservationists want and more than miners want, possibly 30–50 million acres of federal land. Existing national parks and refuges now closed to mining (some 20 million acres) also would be in this category. New non-Wilderness refuges, national recreation areas, national monuments, and perhaps national preserves, probably will be closed to mining-claim entry but open to controlled exploration and potentially opened, in case of formal declaration of national need, to mining. In effect, the storehouse door will be closed but an inventory process will go on and a key to the lock will hang on a nearby hook. Perhaps another 40 million acres is likely to be treated in this way. Most remaining federal lands — some 140 million acres — will be opened to prospecting and mining, as will most of the 150 million acres of state and Native land.

Like so many other Alaskan issues, the question of mining versus conservation is a highly emotional, polarized one, fraught with ideological conflicts and warped by exaggerated fears and misunderstandings on all sides. The adversary style of legislative processes makes matters worse, even when reasonable compromises are being sought. Wide and fertile ground for agreement exists, but that ground will not be plowed until the question of who will control the land is resolved, and the serious business of resource management is taken up.

CHAPTER VII

City and Country

In fine weather the flight from Seattle to Washington, D.C., is a delight to a confirmed landscape watcher. The variegated patterns of farmsteads and towns unreel from the east until your aching neck or a pre-emptory call to choose between chicken and beef intervenes. First the soft green coastal plain where every place is a good place for settlement. Then the deep snow belt, where people only visit. Here is the mountain country of Idaho and Montana, the influence of valleys big and small overwhelmingly dominating the lay of towns and their linking roads. And now the high arid prairies with communities forced toward water, and with water forced toward towns now outgrown themselves. The irrigated circles and squares of cultivation, huge and blurred, unnoticeably stencil a casual geometry on ranch and rural crossroad.

More water in the Midwest, its abundance releasing village and city from the bondage of drought. Instead, the rigid will of the surveyor imposes his predictably imperfect squares on road and small settlement. Internally the cities mirror the mania of parallel lines, but the cities themselves spring up at odd intervals along the big rivers that cut their bias across the coarse cadastral cloth. Still farther east, the built environment defies interpretation by a stranger from a seat in a fast-moving jet. Too many patterns are superimposed on each other; patterns deriving from musket-era defense, soil fertility, falling water, foreign and transcontinental commerce, and the car. Pervading all, the surging megalopolis fills the spaces and destroys the design.

What is the geometry of the North?

The settlement patterns of ancient subsistence cultures almost perfectly explain the design of village Alaska. It is an organic geometry, a close expression of the pattern of natural biological production. Even short-term settlement was possible only where wild food could be gathered dependably and where shelter could be found or built against storm and cold. Northwestern communities along the Bering, Chukchi, and Beaufort seas are where lookouts could see open leads, especially in spring, when the coming of seal and whale was a desperately urgent thing. These ancient people were wise in the ways of ice, aware of patterns our color-coded satellite images are only now revealing to us. In the Interior, settlements were on riverbanks, where the winding waters gave access to migrating fish and shifting game populations. The abundance of salmon affected community locations in southeastern Alaska perhaps more than any other single factor, but access to the sea and to interior trade and war routes, as well as shelter from winter storms, played their parts, too.

A good number of these ancient sites have been taken over by non-Native populations in the last fifty to seventy-five years. Commercial fishing and logging depend on the same basic resources as the subsistence culture, so the broad overlap is not surprising even though the requirements of deep-draft, long-distance shipping have shifted the locations of some villages. The basic relation of rural communities to the natural features of their local landscape has not changed.

In contrast, there is little or no fit between natural features and the bustling towns of commerical Alaska. The arcane requirements of a national defense strategy based on medium-range bombers and early missilery cannot be deduced from the local terrain around Anchorage, nor do surface features explain the oil-service towns of Kenai and Soldotna. Nothing visible in the landscape around Juneau — a town squeezed by mountains into a blind channel — would lead anyone to predict either its birth as a mining town or its survival as a seat of governance. Perhaps it is apocryphal that riverboat Captain Barnett got stuck on a sandbar in the Chena River one summer day, unloaded his cargo of mining-camp supplies, and called the place Fairbanks, but equally whimsical events have had equally concrete results all over the North. Certainly no one would have planned to put Fairbanks where it is, given an inkling of its abundant environmental disadvantages.

Village Alaska evolved out of countless years of interplay between people and nature — a local, specific, intimately known, overwhelmingly significant nature. Rural places have a relationship with hill and creek and shoreline, a relationship which permeates community character. These places have, as Rene Dubos called it, a genius: a fitness between the built environment, the natural environment, and the inhabitants such that each would be naked without the others. Urban Alaska has been superimposed on a landscape in answer to distant forces only remotely related to the local environment. Alaska's new towns of commerce are certainly not without character, but their character has to do almost solely with the activities, viewpoints, and gossipy interactions of the newcomers who people them. They have no genius of place. Fairbanks would be Fairbanks even if it were fifty miles west at Nenana or seventy miles southeast at Delta.

If urban Alaska has yet to find its genius, village Alaska is in real danger of losing or burying what it has.

Native populations statewide are increasing and will continue to increase for several decades because there are so many Natives just entering marriageable age. The ebb and flow of people among villages, regional centers, and Anchorage and Fairbanks will continue to favor growth in the larger towns. Most rural villages probably will retain their 1976 population size, but Fairbanks and Anchorage and the steppingstone centers like Bethel and Kotzebue will grow in Native population. Some of the smallest settlements may decline to the point of abandonment, a process that has been going on for some time. For example, there were several hundred villages in the Aleutian Islands in the eighteenth century, but less than two dozen in 1970. In northern and western Alaska there were 181 villages in 1950, but by 1970, despite a 70 percent increase in overall population, the region had only 168 villages.[1]

These trends could change, of course, either with unexpected upheavals such as economic hard times in major cities, or with more subtle forces like land ownership by village stockholders nudging individuals toward the choice of remaining in — or going back to — villages. The current state program of building high schools even in small communities, a program given impetus by a 1975 court decision finding that to fail to build local schools was discriminatory, might dampen the townward migration, too. Nevertheless, the tide still is setting toward the cities in the North, while in the nation as a whole that tide has reached and passed its zenith.

Villages of Tundra and Taiga

It would be very wrong to ignore village Alaska, however, even if these population shifts continue. A great many rural people still elect to remain in the small communities despite penalties such as broken families, lower incomes, and poorer community services. For that reason alone, the villages need attention in public policy. There is another reason, too, of long-term interest to urban Alaskans and to many young people in other states who dream of going north. Village Alaska offers a change of life pace, a different set of social values and criteria for success, for anyone strongly impelled toward rural living. If Alaska is different, as I have argued it is, village Alaska is a big part of the reason.

Most rural Alaskans live in places with no formal government. They pay no local taxes. They have very low incomes and pay very little in state or federal income taxes. But villages ask for public services: schools, police protection, fish and game enforcement, wildfire protection, airports, local roads, power generation, water supply, health care, and other services. There has been a strong net flow of dollars from the nation at large and from the bigger towns and cities of commerce-based Alaska to rural places. Some decry this "subsidy," but I don't see it that way. Industrial Alaska and its associated service activities, and even elements of the national economy, are sustained by the discovery and exploitation of natural resources of the Alaskan countryside. The city is fueled by rural resources, but the only way village Alaska can benefit (other than by moving, which has high personal costs and risks) is through the redistribution of this wealth by means of services, welfare, or revenue sharing. Furthermore, it is city concerns and city values that have upset and denied the subsistence lifeway, and therefore a city responsibility to help create new ways.

The character, vitality, and even survival of village Alaska is very closely linked to how city and country residents interact to deliver or withhold housing and utilities, education, and transportation and communication. Some of these determine the convenience or livability of the physical environment of the communities. Some affect the type of choices made by villagers when faced with the decision to stay or leave, and influence the individual's ability to pursue that choice successfully. Others determine how accessible one village is to another, and to the people of Anchorage and Fairbanks. Even more may be at stake when the *process,* rather than the *product,* is brought into focus. How decisions are made, who makes them, how services are financed, what institutions develop to set priorities or operate facilities once in place — these are all major elements in a continuing process of social evolution in rural communities.

The Hardware of Inconvenience

Huge sums of money over the years have flowed from industrialized America to the Alaskan bush in the form of welfare, other transfer payments, educational and protective services, transportation facilities, and utilities. An unbelievable bureaucratic friction has scraped a high percentage of the worth of every dollar launched on its erratic trajectory from Washington, D.C., and Juneau toward rural Alaska. No coherent goals have guided this flow, unless the unspoken but widespread assumption that what is good for cities must be good for villages can be considered a goal. No comprehensive approach has ever been seriously proposed, no integrated priorities set, no measures of performance required or even desired. Each of scores of agencies has tried to deliver its particular hardware or software up to the fluctuating limits of annual budgets. Villagers are left with the failures, the half-completed jobs, the impossible maintenance costs of "successful" demonstrations.

Housing and utility programs are without question the most disjointed, thoughtless, and friction-laden of these endeavors. The concept, language, and hardware of "infrastructure" and "development" have been delivered to rural Alaska through the vehicles of public agencies, often unordered by villagers, frequently with missing essential parts, always without a full prior understanding of price. Then, as a staff member of a Native association in Bethel once wrote,[2] "the other village" is created, dragging the traditional village along its wake of spiraling costs and demands for more jobs and more technology to support its basic structure. "The other village" takes many forms: schools, power plants, fish-processing stations, community halls, health centers, airports, docks. All are artificially emplaced and uncertainly supported within the traditional village by external funds and manpower. The traditional village scarcely influences this new village, but the impact upon old ways is enormous.

169

The Yukon Delta community of Emmonak, for example, was chosen as the site for a federal project to build a water-supply facility. The bureaucrats' idea was to demonstrate how modern technology could make village life convenient. This structure is a marvel. It contains showers, a washeteria, flush toilets, saunas, and a centrifuge/incineration plant for treating sewage. It cost $2 million. The federal agency disavowed any maintenance responsibility, so the 450 people of Emmonak faced an operation cost of $130,000. Construction, increased shipping, fuel needs, and other associated aspects of the plant caused unprecedented growth of the village; but soon the new people had nothing to do and nowhere to go. Ultimately the village council refused to accept the operation responsibility for the water utility; the federal government now owns a decaying totem to technology. In Alakanuk the state built a similar plant with similar operation costs. At Scammon Bay, a water plant, four years in construction, froze up after six weeks of operation. It was costing a home owner $70 to $120 per month for the water — and this in a region where the average cash income for a family is less than $4000 a year. In 1977 about half of the 230 or so villages in Alaska had no sewage treatment facilities. The others had high-technology systems that often did not work. Which group is better off?

The technical culture of urban Alaska and the Outside, then, has been delivering extraordinarily costly Trojan horses into village Alaska, out of which at night came hordes of bill collectors. Blame can be assigned to almost anyone: distant bureaucrats blindly applying development concepts and technologies totally unfit for the rural North, engineers from warm and populous places who prescribe impossibly complex and miscast designs, Native legislators who seem to be just as eager to deliver "projects" to their constituents as anyone else, village leaders who incautiously say yes when they should say no. But assigning blame is a sterile exercise. The learning and application of hard lessons is the important thing.

From an engineering and economic perspective the main

lesson is that the simpler the utility, and the closer in scale to conservatively estimated needs, the better off everyone will be. Happily, some engineers are thinking small and simple. One of the benefits of this utility strategy is that villages can once again loosen up and stretch out over a larger area to take advantage of favorable terrain and natural amenities, rather than being pulled inward toward the central power plant or water utility by the stricturing girdle of delivery costs. Another advantage is that villagers can take on a fuller responsibility for both payment and operation when scale and level of complexity and dependability are within their grasp.

The larger lesson relates to cultural change. If transition from subsistence to money economies and cultures is inevitable for rural Alaska — and history to date strongly suggests that it is — surely it would be better for the leap to be made from the self-sufficiency of the hunter to the self-sufficiency of a wage earner coming reasonably close to paying his or her way in society. The Trojan horse process, in contrast, shuttles villagers into the bewildering and degrading world of welfare. The key questions about the coming of modern technology to rural settlements, then, are not only what kind but where, how (in the sense of the process for purchase, delivery, management, and maintenance responsibility), and at what rate? Who will ask those questions? Who will answer them? Will the corporations imposed on rural life by the Alaska Native Claims Settlement Act be able to cope with the basic cultural aspects as well as the technically easier problems of engineering, financing, and management? Will the eyes of state and federal agencies be opened? There is, today, little basis for hope.

A Long Way From Home

Rural education services are and have been beset by serious problems. Until statehood, one or another federal agency controlled rural schooling. After statehood the state began to take over rural schools a few at a time. By 1977, the state operated 134 rural schools while the federal Bureau of Indian Affairs continued to operate 44. A major shift in responsibility began in 1975, with state legislation establishing 21 Rural Education Attendance Areas in which local people assumed administrative responsibility (but not financing) of village schools even in the absence of organized local government.

Many Alaskan villages formed around schools built by missions and agencies. These schools used English as the sole language, partly because of the policy favoring rapid "integration" of Natives into the new cash economy, and partly because the young teachers sent into BIA schools rarely stayed long enough to learn Eskimo, Aleut, or Athapascan languages. The subject matter taught was basic Dick and Jane, rarely modified in any way to fit the student's life outside the schoolhouse. Young Natives who went to school beyond eighth grade had to leave the villages. Many transferred to public schools in Fairbanks, Anchorage, or the larger towns in southeastern Alaska. Others went to BIA's high school near Sitka. Still others left Alaska entirely to attend BIA Indian high schools. The entire process of rural education was authoritarian, the Natives taking no significant part in decisions. Thousands of children were permanently scarred by the system, their natural adaptiveness and skills broken and buried by self-defeating behaviors taught by the school environment.[3]

Five overall trends in rural schooling began or were greatly strengthened with the coming of statehood. First, local village schools became public schools in the sense that any community resident could attend, which meant that non-Natives began to go to these schools at least in small numbers. Second, secondary and post-secondary schools and community colleges began to spread into rural settlements, lessening the need for young Natives to make long journeys and leave their families for months at a time to continue school. Third, skill centers and other vocational training opportunities became available in the larger communities of rural regions. Fourth, serious efforts began in the 1960s (and still continue) to develop bilingual schooling in the villages, relying mainly on Native teacher aides to provide the teaching in the local language and local cultural traditions. And last, local responsibility for curricula and school administration has been growing rapidly since the passage of the 1975 REAA Act.

The potential results of these trends are deeply significant for rural development. Families may stay together longer; at least they will not be forced to split asunder when a child has to leave home to go to school. More non-Natives may move into some villages as the barrier of local schooling is removed. Acceptance of school administration responsibilities may be a substantial step toward development of organized borough governments in the rather large districts defined as Rural Education Attendance Areas. (On the other hand, early experience with REAAs suggests that because local people do not have to raise money to help support the educational system, the new areas may actually delay the development of local government by making it unnecessary.) The outcomes of the bilingual and vocational training programs are less easy to deduce, though their objectives are quite clear. The sense and significance of Native traditions should be understood better at an intellectual level by young Natives taught in bilingual and cross-cultural programs, but whether this knowledge will be incorporated in a meaningful way into the outlook and life choices of young adults later depends on reinforcement from home and peers. Likewise, the development of work skills is certainly important for the young Native in rapid transit away from the subsistence economy, but opportunities to use those skills in village Alaska still are extremely scarce. Locating a vocational program in a rural area may delay by only a few months or a few years a young person's move into the city. In some ways the program makes such a move nearly inevitable for a person who, at a critical time in life, learns drafting or ac-   173 counting instead of the skills needed in a semi-subsistence village society.

Pathways

Villages are where they are partly because of the transportation methods historically used by their residents. Conversely, the location of villages and the distances between them largely dictate the kind of transportation services available to them. Major changes in transportation technologies and costs immediately affect family and village economies, social and economic exchanges within and between rural regions and with urban Alaska, and the extent to which non-Natives visit and use the resources of the hinterland.

Dog teams and paddled boats dominated transport in rural areas until just a few years ago. They fostered settlement patterns consisting of relatively large numbers of small communities. Long-distance exchanges of goods and services were minimal, but short-distance social and economic interchange was easy and cheap.

Then came successive waves of motorized craft, big and small. Late in the nineteenth century and early in this century, goods from Outside began to trickle into villages annually from cargo carried by steamer to a few coastal towns like Juneau, Sitka, Cordova, Kodiak, St. Michaels, and Nome. Riverboats distributed goods to communities along the Yukon River. Slowly this shipping fingered out into smaller places. As schools, missions, canneries, and government offices spread into rural Alaska, the demand for regular freight service increased; Native people began to use the service as well.

Inland settlements had to await the development of commercial air transportation to receive these services. In 1936 and 1937 Harold Gillam of Fairbanks struggled to establish Alaska's first freight and passenger service. Bush pilots had already logged 5.6 million passenger miles in unscheduled (and unorthodox) charter trips by then. In the 1940s and 1950s, an extensive web of regular air transportation had tied most rural Alaskans with Fairbanks, Anchorage, and the Pacific Northwest. Cash from welfare or earned income had to be available for a person to purchase the goods and services now offered. In the 1940s and 1950s, outboard motors and the new boats designed to use them were adopted widely by villagers along inland rivers as well as the coast. A dramatic change in summer hunting, fishing, and visiting patterns followed. In the 1960s, the snowmobile was adopted as the favored winter vehicle, displacing dog teams as rapidly as the outboard motor had displaced canoes and hand-paddled boats earlier.

A communication revolution has occurred in two stages since the 1920s throughout rural Alaska, parallel to and interconnected with the new transportation technology. Bush air service depended on the existence of radio communication, and by the time airports and air service had come to nearly every village of modest size in Alaska, radios had become a common and favorite means of communication. Family news, reports of fish and game occurrence, word of visits by government officials, emergency calls, orders for groceries, and calls for Public Health Service doctors and dentists crackled between village and city. Then, in 1974–1976, satellite-beamed television brought state-of-the-art popular communication to rural places. In a fantastic cultural leap, industrial America and Native youngsters by 1977 had agreed (for the moment) that the Bionic Woman was the ultimate siren. Dick and Jane were dead.

Urban Alaska and its business partners in Seattle and other U.S. cities benefited from (and in most cases actually supported) the ship and air transportation facilities on which rural areas now rely. Oddly enough, however, urban Alaskans have never believed in shipping and air transport as deeply as in roads. Non-Native Alaskans have had an abiding belief in 175 highways as the sine qua non of economic progress, no matter how dusty, rutted, frost-heaved, or costly roads may be in reality. Alaskan roads have not nourished economic activity to anything like the extent assumed by sourdoughs and the business-labor community. Nevertheless, they have had real influence on the use of commodity resources, on population distribution, on the character of villages they pass by, and on recreational opportunities for town dwellers.

For over a century, Canadians and Americans have argued whether roads and railroads should precede or follow economic development in frontier areas. The era of transcontinental railroad construction (from 1866 to 1890 in the United States, somewhat later in southern Canada) was based on the belief that early investments in surface transportation would stimulate mineral, timber, agricultural, and other natural-resource exploitation and eventually would pay handsomely on the investment. The nations were willing to take the risk, grant railbuilders huge areas of free land, and massively support agriculture and other economic activities in the Plains and Far West, not on a careful analysis of costs and benefits but simply because the settlement of the West was the dominant business of the times.

Provincial and federal governments in Canada adopted the early investment policy as readily as the United States and carried it forward to the present in much less ambiguous form. National and provincial ownership of railroads is a logical extension of the belief that public support of costly transportation infrastructure is a fundamental element in economic development. So is the growing network of roads in northern British Columbia, Yukon, and the Northwest Territories.

The strength of the build-first–pay-later policy had waned greatly by the time it was to be applied in Alaska. In part, this was due to increasing reliance on economic cost-benefit calculations in public works projects, which clearly would place massive, costly, and speculative northern highway or rail projects at a disadvantage. Probably pragmatic politics were more important. The territory was as close to a political cipher as one could imagine during the every-other-year dip into the pork barrel. Congress saw little evidence of self-generating Alaskan growth, in the 1930s and 1940s, which would even remotely justify authorizations for major transportation projects. Seattle shipping interests certainly did not lobby for road or rail connections to Alaska. By the time Alaska achieved statehood, the tide of Manifest Destiny was gone, the rail and highway network was essentially complete in the other states, and Congress had turned its thoughts elsewhere.

Before World War II, Congress authorized 2700 miles of rural roads of all classes in the territory. Highway mileage almost doubled from 1939 to 1948, when defense needs catalyzed major road construction. (The most famous and important of all Alaskan roads, the AlCan or Alaska Highway, was completed in 1942 as a part of national defense strategy.) Since 1959 the state has built only one major new highway, the Anchorage–Fairbanks route via Mount McKinley National Park, paralleling the Alaska Railroad. Even with a favorable federal-aid program providing 18 federal dollars for every local dollar, road reconstruction, maintenance, and city-street needs have soaked up Alaskan highway funds. According to estimates publicized in 1977 while the legislature debated an increased gasoline tax, highway users generated only two thirds as much in taxes as road maintenance was then costing the state.

In addition to the main network of roads qualifying for federal funds, the state also has a program of locally funded pioneer and mineral access roads. This program (and a closely related "local service road" program) sought to build low-standard roads to mines, potential agricultural areas, and other hinterland sites with special economic potential. Local service roads are funded entirely by the state, while private funding of at least 50 percent is required for pioneer access and mineral 177

ALASKA

access roads. Most roads built under these statutes have been
short and close to existing settlements. The 400-mile winter
haul road to the North Slope, built in 1968–70 and classed as a
local service road, was an exception. (That "road," a bulldozed track that needed to be nearly rebuilt each year, was
abandoned in 1973 for a different route selected for the Trans-
Alaska Pipeline.) The pinch of finances has kept appropriations for the program down to very low levels, but oil-fueled
state budgets could change the picture rapidly.

The $900 million windfall paid to the state in 1969 for
Prudhoe Bay leases brought an amazing variety of wishbook
proposals to the surface. One, in the form of a map resembling
remnants of spaghetti on a platter, was an official Department
of Highways' vision of Alaska's future. It displayed the department's long-standing goal of connecting every town of 1000
people or more in an interlacing road system, regardless of existing or feasible service by air or water. Once printed on slick
paper, the spaghetti maps began to achieve an aura of public
policy despite the absence of public discussion, cost-benefit
analyses, comparison with alternatives, or evidence of consistency with land uses and regional social goals.

However, these grandiose proposals turned out to be paper
tigers. Highway funds continued to be blotted up by urban system improvements and rural road maintenance, and growth in
other state services soaked up the windfall. Furthermore, by a
quirk of history the spaghetti maps were set before the public
at exactly the least propitious time. In the early 1970s, rural
Alaskans were making it abundantly clear that they did not
want to be connected by road to Anchorage or Fairbanks.
Meanwhile Alaskan conservation groups were sharply
challenging several major road extensions, and the entire Federal Aid to Highways program was bedeviled by environmental and mass-transit groups at the national level. Given
strong backing from Alaskan political leaders, the Department
of Highways could have bulldozed through this opposition.

The 1974 gubernatorial campaign, however, saw the whole process of highway planning exposed to public debate, with the winning candidate pledging to reorganize the department into a transportation agency.

The mystique of highways in Alaska has been based on several assumptions borrowed from mid-century American experience, plus several that have not been heard in other parts of the nation for almost one hundred years.

The borrowed assumptions are that Americans will continue to cherish their cars for decades in the future; that roads decrease the cost of goods and services in remote communities; and that city residents need highways for access to recreation sites. The first may or may not prove true, but the basic question is, what does this have to do with rural Alaska? Other Americans have been hooked for half a century on automobility and can scarcely conceive any real alternative. Rural Alaskans, in contrast, have developed other ways of living and other methods of transport. Neighbors within towns can be visited on foot, and friends in other communities can be reached by boat or snowmobile at far less cost than an automobile could be bought and kept running in the Bush. Urban Alaskans have brought their auto habits with them, and for them the existing road system is available, some 6500 miles in extent. Even Alaska's city people use a wider variety of vehicles than highway officials like to admit. In Anchorage and Fairbanks, for example, an extraordinary proportion of residents own airplanes. In Juneau and other Southeast communities, fleets of pleasure craft rocking gently in small boat harbors attest to the heavy use of the incomparable Inside Passage.

The assertion that roads decrease the cost of rural living is often accepted because rural people *want* to believe it. Road proponents have never presented evidence that can be examined closely. Project costs are inevitably underestimated and traffic volumes often overstated. More fundamentally, any savings to rural consumers could exist only because non-Alaskan taxpayers pay the lion's share of road construction costs and because all Alaskan taxpayers will be billed for the husky deficit between maintenance costs and highway tax revenues. What would have to be charged if users had to pay in full for rural road maintenance? From 1974 to 1977, Alyeska Pipeline Service Company charged truckers $1.07 per mile for use of the North Slope Haul Road before it became a public road; the fee was to defray maintenance costs. Even with the present public subsidy, freight costs to small communities along the road system are high. In 1977, residents of the tiny community of Central, 128 miles from Fairbanks, paid truckers $5.20 to $5.60 per hundredweight for items in less-than-a-ton lots. At this rate, a can of peaches costing 79¢ in Fairbanks would carry an extra 34¢ charge for shipping by truck over the proposed 750-mile-long road to Nome.

Several generations of Americans have used highways to get out into the country for recreation. Is this a good argument for building more roads in Alaska? On the basis of the present and continuing trade deficit due to oil imports, and considering the declining position of pleasure driving in our national priority list for petroleum usage, one could expect roadbuilders to lean less on it as a project justification. This is especially true in the North, where long extensions of the road system flirt with economic unacceptability, and where cost-benefit calculations are highly sensitive to traffic projections.

Access for city people to the country is exactly what most rural Alaskans dislike about new highways. Village Alaska sees itself on the receiving end of a host of ills brought by thousands of travelers. The countryman recognizes an enormous gap between city values and his own. He feels threatened by both the direct, tangible urban invasion and by the rapid change inevitably attending the coming of the road. He doesn't want the stress forced on himself, his family, his community. The takeover of sparse village business opportunities by outsiders, the increased incoming flow of alcohol, the increased dust and noise, the danger to youngsters accustomed to using streets as playgrounds, the new threats of vandalism, the reduction of game and fish: All urge rural people to oppose roads.

The early American frontier gave rise to an entrenched notion that roads and railroads "open up the country" for resource exploitation and settlement. Americans who came north in the gold rushes and military booms of the first sixty years of this century carried this idea with them, and it has been an essential part of the conventional wisdom surrounding Alaskan economic development. Probably there is no generally "right" answer to the chicken-and-egg argument about transportation investments, which rapidly transcends economic analysis and enters the realm of political philosophy and perceptions of social growth.

The majority of Alaskan road projects have had a very ambiguous relationship to later settlement and economic growth. The Elliot, Steese, and Taylor highways were built to serve thriving gold-mining areas but failed to catalyze any further activity that could sustain a significant local economy when placer operations went broke. Highways have provided access to the western Chugach, Kenai, Talkeetna, Wrangell, and Alaska Range mountains for many years without triggering any mining other than small and ephemeral operations.

The differences between Alaska and the American West are clear. In the West, almost any long highway or railroad, planned with any reasonable regard for route, would cross extensive areas of arable soil or harvestable timber. This is simply not possible in interior and northern Alaska. And though minerals may be as abundant in Alaska as in the Rocky Mountain region, we are much farther from markets and from relatively inexpensive labor. Access may be necessary for mining in Alaska, but it is not enough in itself to overcome other barriers.

Transportation networks obviously are related to settlement and growth patterns. Borrowing again from the Old West, Alaskan sourdoughs have often urged roadbuilding as a certain means of settling the country: of fulfilling the Jeffersonian dream of a nation of hard-working, self-sufficient, landowning yeomen. It is worth a closer look at federal and state land and resource policies, specifically as they relate to settlement.

Settlement Perceptions and Policies

Alaska was rather thoroughly settled, of course, long before whites came. The Euro-American invasion changed this aboriginal pattern and superimposed a vastly different settlement pattern upon it. When economists and modern historians speak of "settlement" they refer to three processes: the infiltration of Native communities, the dispersal of non-Natives over the countryside, and the growth of urban places. These processes were scarcely affected at all by conscious public policy in Alaska up to the time of statehood. The federal government, in fact, had no single and coherent approach to settlement. It was simultaneously permissive and tightfisted in its dealings with people asking for land. Generally it let economic incentives control the timing, pace, and location of settlement.

The land scandals in the Old West gave pause to the federal government when it considered the Alaska situation in the nineteenth century. Then, one by one, land-disposal laws began to open up the territory: the General Mining Law in 1884; the Trade and Manufacturing Site Laws in 1891; the Homestead Act in 1898; a coal-leasing act and Native Allotments Act in 1906, the latter allowing individual Natives to get title to small acreages used and occupied; the Native Townsite Act in 1926; the Small Tracts disposal law in 1945. The General Land Office (which later became the Bureau of Land Management) accepted applications for everything from cemetery plot to cement plant with neither grin nor grumble. At the time of statehood, 272 million of Alaska's 365 million acres were open to a wide range of legal private entry and land often was pre-empted simply by "squatting." The 54 million acres in wildlife refuges, defense withdrawals, parks, a petroleum reserve, and Indian reservations were polar opposites to vacant public domain, being closed to nearly all settlement and mining activity. Of the rest, 48 million acres of national forests and power-site classifications were under some form of multiuse management and 1.3 million acres were in private lands (half of it in unperfected entries).

Before statehood there was no land-use planning process to help or hinder the accretive process of settlement. Homesteads could be filed anywhere, regardless of whether agriculture was feasible. Mining claims were patented with only a barely perceptible nod at the provision of law requiring proof of a commercial deposit before title transfer. Business sites, Native allotments, recreation cabin sites, and other small tracts were parceled out in a rummage-sale atmosphere. No federal, territorial, or local agency had land-use planning responsibilities. Towns grew in leapfrog patterns, making it increasingly hard to provide urban services to satellite settlements. Dumps accumulated, ground water became polluted, jumbled commercial and residential uses intermixed haphazardly: It is amazing how so few people could do so much environmental damage without even trying.

The homesteads just beyond suburban fringes seemed the worst problem of the lot. Too far from town to be served economically but too close to be ignored, settlers five to thirty miles from towns imposed unusual financial burdens on school districts, fire-control agencies, welfare organizations, road-maintenance crews, and police departments.

In the 1960s, national interest began to focus on the anachronistic policies of public-domain management and land disposal. Despite the mining, timber, and grazing lobbies' vig-   183 orous opposition, Congress passed the Classification and Multiple Use Act in 1964, giving the Bureau of Land Management temporary authority (originally from 1965 through 1969, later extended through 1970) to classify land for various uses and to plan for its management.

In Alaska, with 60 percent of all U.S. public-domain lands, federal-disposal programs changed drastically after 1968. Transfers of federal public lands to private interests all but ceased in January 1969, when Public Land Order 4582 completed the freeze of public land to protect Native land rights until Congress could settle claims. Within a short time it was clear that the old frontier policies of federal land disposals had changed forever. No federal lands were available for sale in Alaska in 1972, or subsequently, up to the present. No applications for small tracts have been accepted since 1968. The processing of old (and a handful of new) homestead entries continued through the early 1970s, but the federal homestead program obviously had plowed its last deep furrow. In 1970, the Public Land Review Commission recommended repeal of the Homestead Act and other changes to control freewheeling entry on the public domain. Although rather timid in following through on their own bold stand that "The policy of large-scale disposal of public lands reflected by the majority of statutes in force today should be revised . . . ," the commission's recommendations clearly showed the direction of new American attitudes toward public lands.

The Classification and Multiple Use Act authorized the Bureau of Land Management to identify lands that would remain permanently in federal hands and to classify and manage these areas. Millions of acres at the base of the Alaska Peninsula, Wrangell Mountains, and Tanana-Yukon uplands were classified by BLM as it slowly built up momentum in its stewardship role. After a hiatus from 1970 to 1976, while the Alaska Native Claims Settlement Act had federal land affairs in Alaska in an uproar, the Bureau regained comprehensive management authority with the passage of the Federal Land Policy and Management Act of October 21, 1976. This act eliminated homesteading and most other land-disposal programs in other states but continued homesteading until 1986 in Alaska. However, no land can be disposed of until the present blanket land withdrawals are lifted (expected by the end of 1978) and until a broad planning and land-classification process identifies land for disposal.

The opening mandate of the natural-resources article of the Alaska State Constitution — ''to encourage the settlement of its lands and the development of its natural resources by making them available for maximun use consistent with the public interest'' — has the real pioneer flavor. However, the state's attitude toward its real estate was from the outset very different from that of the federal government. First, the state knew it would have far less land available to it in the critical first decade; it had to select and use land carefully. Second, it needed all the land and resource revenues it could get. Third, the state was not interested in large blocks of land for conservation purposes. (Most Alaskans thought the federal government was doing all that needed doing, and more, in that field.) Fourth, direct and indirect expenses of land ownership were high, and incautious land selections could put the state in the red.

To cope with these problems, the state quickly decided that it would sell lands only at fair market value or above, unless other considerations were paramount; that it would retain subsurface mineral rights on all lands it sold or leased for other purposes (this was actually stipulated by Congress in the Alaska Statehood Act); and that land classification would be required before disposal, except for mineral leasing.

The state has classified land essentially on demand. Therefore, cumulative acreages classified for agriculture, private recreation, residential use, and open-to-entry are rough estimates of the extent to which the state as landowner has been in the settlement business. By this measure, the state's in- 185 volvement has been very modest. Through 1975, the state had classified 81,000 acres for agriculture, although in 1977 that figure doubled with the launching of a state farming project southeast of Fairbanks. Private recreation-lot sales totaled 42,000 acres and residential lots totaled under 9000 acres. Residential-lot sales have not changed patterns of settlement, being almost lost in the welter of subdivision sales on the fringes of rapidly growing towns. Private recreation-lot sales, on the other hand, have had a somewhat more noticeable (though still very limited) effect on settlement. The offerings typically have been around lakes from ten to fifty miles from a major town, linked by road to the major community. The sales have been conceived as benefiting a transient summer population, but in fact the "summer colony" sometimes has evolved into a permanent community struggling to provide the services normally desired by townspeople.

The open-to-entry land category was added to the classification system in 1968, when a powerful legislator insisted on a land program giving individuals the opportunity to select their own lot location. The open-to-entry program involved: (1) classification of a large block of state land as open-to-entry; (2) first-come–first-served filings on lots up to five acres in size, the individual selecting the location and shape of his own lot and erecting stakes at corners to mark it; (3) choice by the individual whether to lease or buy. The state had no control over the pattern of filings or uses made of the land after entry.

By the end of 1973, open-to-entry lands encompassed 2,-544,090 acres. Over 4000 applications had been filed for about 20,000 acres of land. As could be predicted, the first applications were for the choice sites in each open-to-entry block: water frontage, view sites, lots with timber for cabin building, sites near good hunting, and sites close to access points.

Judging from prices obtained at private recreation-land auctions and from the number of open-to-entry applicants, both programs were popular. Urban Alaskans yearn for a place by a lake to spend weekends and vacations. A wide variety of Alaskans (and some nonresidents as well) took advantage of the open-to-entry program because, with the slowdown in land disposals by the federal government, this state program was one of the few ways to get land cheaply. Real estate speculators took full advantage of the activities, too. "An increasing number of individuals," a note in a 1972 Division of Lands *Newsletter* stated, "who have open-to-entry sites are listing them for sale with local realtors or are running advertisements in the local newspapers. Some are asking $4000 to $5000 for a site with no improvements of any kind, and on which only a filing fee of $10 and a few years of annual rental of $40 per year has been paid." On August 15, 1973, the division announced suspension of the open-to-entry program for at least a year to look into these and other abuses.

An initiative placed before voters in the fall of 1978 provides the most extreme expression of pioneer land hunger in modern Alaska. This initiative would require a crash program of land disposal by the state until 30 million acres of state land had been doled out to private individuals in parcels ranging up to 160 acres in size. All applicants would have to be residents, and long-term residents could get more land than newcomers. The state could not exclude land that might be unsuitable for homes or in any other way hamper the giveaway by planning or regulation. The initiative provides no controls over abuses such as "commutation" — the use by large corporations of dummy applicants to gain control over vast areas of land. Many responsible public figures oppose this initiative, but few have the courage to say so.

Settlement in the Southeast has followed a different pattern. The channels and sounds of the Panhandle provide free highways to practically every habitable site in the region; settlement has neither bottled up while waiting for a road to be built nor been excessively restricted to a few travelways. Another source of this difference is that most of the land in southeastern

Alaska has been a national forest or national monument since the turn of the century, very hard to convert to private ownership. The overall pattern of community location in the Southeast, therefore, was set by 1900.

Congress allowed the state to select only 400,000 acres from Tongass and Chugach national forests combined. The federal administrative view has been that the state has to show that lands are needed for community expansion and recreation before selections are accepted. Only a tenth of the entitlement had been selected up to 1977. Under the Alaska Native Claims Settlement Act, Native villages in the Panhandle were allowed to select up to 23,040 acres of land apiece, a smaller entitlement than other villages but a fairly ample one from the standpoint of community space requirements.

Southeastern business and community leaders sometimes express frustration at the relative scarcity of land for community expansion, arguing that land prices are in consequence unnecessarily high and economic activity hampered. Federal land ownership often is the scapegoat. Often as not, however, the real culprits are the physical limits to readily developable terrain coupled with the adoption of sprawl-producing systems of growth in both private and public sectors. The American approach to city expansion is not well suited to the effective use of small spaces.

God, Geddes, and Frank Lloyd Wright

Can a society exert a conscious control over settlements to create patterns suited to its own style, purposes, and ecological setting? Throughout human history, many societies have tried. In our own nation, the settlement of the West happened in partial response to such conscious decisions ranging from general Jeffersonian policies to specific delineations of railroad routes. For nearly a century, however, and as the land began to "fill up" and national life became more industry oriented, we have been slipping into a new pattern of thinking. Broad designs of settlement, we now say, cannot be planned. They will result as a by-product of an infinite number of small decisions made by innumerable people, mainly in that mythical center of social life, the marketplace. To attempt to intervene in this process, so the thought goes, is fruitless and socialistic folly.

Intervention, however, can take many forms. Intuitively I agree that a full-blown plan, imposed by public officials onto society, probably would not "work" nor be a good thing even if it did. But if that extreme is to be avoided, so is the opposite fatalism. There should be an intermediate level of intervention in which guiding principles for settlement, growing out of a broad consensus, become the touchstones for independent but mutually supportive decisions at all levels of public life in some critical aspects of private activity. The coercive elements of such a process could be relatively unobtrusive and highly selective, while the delivery of public benefits is amplified.

Alaskan society is still transitional, formative, flexible — call it what you will — and reasonably open to the molding influence of public policy. The challenge is to do the molding with a vision primarily centered on the style and quality of Alaskan life, responsive to the realities and opportunities inherent in both the ecology of dollars and the ecology of life and landscape.

Three equally important, interdependent goals comprise the fundamental underpinnings of a grand strategy for Alaskan settlement: to encourage and maintain community diversity, to retain the wild character of landscapes, and to create the best possible human environment in cities.

Alaskan communities today are incredibly diverse — probably more so today than ever before. There are unorganized constellations of widely scattered families in the Bush, hardly qualifying as communities but in fact exhibiting, in times of stress, strong communal responses. There are tiny 189 villages with clear coherence and social organization along traditional Native cultural lines, thinly overlaid with the trappings of American community structure. There are regional centers, more highly organized and economically and politically connected with urban Alaska, steeped in change and cultural conflict. There are urban centers, of non-Native origin, located off the "statewide" road net and for that reason more Alaskan than typically American. And there are Anchorage and its *doppelgänger*, Fairbanks, closely mimicking but not quite becoming Anytown, USA. Alaskans know that these places are very different and they feel rich for the choices offered. There are, however, homogenizing forces threatening this diversity which only a conscious exertion of public choice can thwart.

No one can read letters to editors of Alaskan newspapers, listen to the congressional debates about new parks for Alaska, or examine Alaskan opinion surveys without coming to the conclusion that wildness is a highly valued Alaskan asset. By "wildness" I mean a general characteristic of landscapes, complex in its derivation but easily recognized once experienced, which can pervade and dominate sparsely inhabited as well as unsettled places. I do *not* mean only Wilderness, a very specific statutory land designation designed to describe the commercially forgotten nooks and crannies of long-settled states. Scattered cabins and villages do not mar wild country in the Alaskan context as long as the habitations and inhabitants are spiritually as well as economically connected with the landscape. Commercial and even industrial activities can sometimes be carried out without grossly assaulting wildness, though at some threshold point (admittedly a subjective one) the palpable disruptions of air clarity, water purity, soil stability, silence, and vegetation mosaics destroy that character.

The third of this triad of goals is one my intuition tells me is extremely important, but one which I am ill equipped to detail. Cities are where most Alaskans live, and it makes sense to bend our energies into creating optimal urban environments for that reason alone. Beyond that, it seems clear that to save wild country we have to make the towns as attractive and satisfying as possible, lest the city drive its residents into desperate flights of escape into the fragile, easily abused northern countryside. (On the other hand, part of a frontier society's perception of a satisfying city indisputably is one that you can leave behind fairly quickly when you want to. Northern city people should have convenient and — if they choose — frequent access to the country.)

If those are acceptable objectives for societal effort, what are the critical points of leverage at which events and processes of settlement can be guided most effectively? At least five stand out: 1) choice of transportation programs, 2) government approaches to public-land disposal, 3) patterns of revenue flows into rural and village Alaska, 4) urban planning, and 5) "new towns" or "development cities" policies.

Of these, quite possibly the most powerful, and the one most difficult to derail from channels of habit, is transportation policy. The needs that decision makers perceive and the responses they make to them are derived from long-standing American patterns, exerting an almost irresistible force molding the North into southern lifeways. We have, for example, a national penchant for public subsidy of roads. In any local area, where the tax levied to supply the subsidy always seems insignificant in relation to the specific benefits received, roads will always be the transportation mode of choice as long as the traditional subsidy prevails. Streams of subsidy can be redirected, however, as exemplified by the acceptance of Alaska's ferry system as a Marine Highway (ah! the magic of the name!) and the federal subsidy of ships for the system. Over time, both federal and state governments could change subsidy policies, the one through the growth of mass-transport and rail constituencies and the other through purposeful allocations of resource revenues into nonhighway alternatives.

In 1977, the old Alaska Department of Highways merged with the state's Department of Public Works (the agency then responsible for ferries and airports) to form the Department of Transportation and Public Facilities. Ostensibly this was done to create a planning system that would weigh different transport alternatives more thoroughly and equally. The hopes of rural people and conservationists were clearly in that direction. People who are less naïve about government reorganization were skeptical — a skepticism hard to set aside today. During the reorganization almost all key positions in planning and policy levels were filled with former Department of Highways personnel. Planning itself was decentralized and lodged in the old highway regional headquarters, where former highway engineers gained new titles. A department work program given to federal DOT officials in September 1977 included, within some progressively worded paragraphs about "multimodal comprehensive planning addressing physical, economic, social, and political elements," some revealing comments. "The primary system of transportation in the state is, and will continue to be, a system of streets and highways," it said. And in the proposal for the next six-year Capital Improvement Program, the stated objective was a Macadamian slip: "To describe the Capital Improvement (Construction) projects to be undertaken on the statewide roadway network to which funding must be allocated at Federal and State levels . . ." [4]

In a state where far more communities are served by air or marine transportation than by road; where aircraft ownership per capita is fifteen times the national average; where river transport is a once successful but now neglected activity; where cold and distance push individual car ownership costs to unbelievable levels; and where frozen, snow-covered surfaces provide myriad opportunities for low-cost rural travel, these statements imply a stubborn disregard of real-world transport alternatives.

Elements of change are to be found on close examination, however. An honestly comprehensive study of transportation alternatives for the Prince William Sound (Cordova–Valdez–Whittier) area was done in 1977 in response to an environmentalist court suit several years before. An embryonic effort was made to expose transportation policies to review outside the DOT and by officials with many perspectives through a State Interdepartmental Transportation Planning Group. And there seems to be a strengthening effort to expose transport plans to more thorough public review. But while these facts suggest the possibility of policy change, they do not yet provide solid evidence for it.

People who have grown up in a country already shaped to the highway and the car may feel this to be an excessive concern about roadbuilding. But roads inevitably bring dramatic change to village Alaska, a change the residents simply do not want to be forced to make. Roads also trigger new uses of land. Village people feel the threat of competition for the land's limited renewable resources, and city-dwelling environmentalists fear the unregulated use and abuse of those same resources. The geographic inflexibility of roads built before it is known where there may be resources worth hauling out of a countryside and the high building and maintenance costs of long ribbons of gravel or asphalt are other less fundamental problems. Alaskan transportation planning should not abandon completely the notion of new hinterland highways, because some may be desirable. Instead, transportation planning must start with an acutely sensitive understanding of the social and environmental uniqueness of what we are and can become, progress through a careful appraisal of needs and alternatives, and end with the allocation of funding to any system chosen to meet specific regional objectives, unhampered by anachronistic bureaucratic barriers.

Land transfers from government to private individual played a starring role in the drama of settlement of the Old West. In Alaska they have had little more than a bit part, mainly serving to provide simple living space for people already on stage.

Today, however, there are signs that public-land–disposal

policies may assert a stronger presence. This is especially true of state lands, because the federal government, having committed the bulk of its Alaskan holdings to Natives, the state, and conservation withdrawals, is unlikely to do more than follow the state's policy lead. Unquestionably there is a highly vocal and continuous demand for private land in Alaska. Although profits from land speculation are one motive, part of the demand stems from feelings closely akin to the get-away-from-it-all, be-your-own-man dream so visibly a part of America's history.

There is no good reason why the state should be totally deaf to these demands. Politically there is no chance that it will be. The crucial question is *how* the state will respond in terms of the location of land disposals, the method of disposal (fee-simple, lease, or development-rights sale), and the follow-up infrastructure of roads, schools, utilities, and community services.

If the state simply releases land on demand, most of the area physically suited to any sort of property development, along the present and future road system, eventually will be transferred. At the other extreme of public policy, the state could release land only at the edges of growing communities, stabilizing existing settlement patterns and leaving most state land "vacant" and in public hands.

It would be a terrible mistake to foster a broadly dispersed new rural population living on fee-simple property and scattered in varying densities throughout a matrix of public lands. For one thing, there are essentially no unspoken-for resources left to support additional subsistence economies or family-run businesses. Moreover, those who would get the land are not really attuned to that kind of hardscrabble life either mentally or culturally, much as some may initially think they want it. A broadcast disposal policy would be economically disastrous to taxpayers, considering the extraordinarily high cost of local roads and the whole gamut of services the purchasers would demand. "No Trespassing" signs would keep townspeople out of the most popular and accessible recreation areas, fish and wildlife populations would erode, and pristine watersheds would be polluted with untreated sewage and wastes. In short, dispersed settlement would conflict with recreation assets of urban Alaska and with economic assets of village Alaska, while wasting the precious public resource of wildness.

With a little time and imagination, the state could establish a land program that would avoid those conflicts and losses. Such a program would use a variety of well-known planning techniques and land-tenure instruments to respond to the land hunger positively but with restraint. Permanent settlement would be permitted only where the required family and property services can be provided efficiently at the time of land disposal or very soon afterward. This policy would limit fee-simple residence-land disposals to areas around and within communities where services can be extended to new subdivisions in a short time and at a cost the community can bear. In rare cases where a new and permanent community is desired, the state would first complete a thorough community plan and then make land available under appropriate tenure systems consistent with that plan. The planning process for locating and designing Alaska's capital city is not a bad model, politics aside.

Normally the state should lease rather than sell land. Leases can meet the individual's true need while keeping permanent property rights in public hands and permitting reasonable control over land use during the lessees' terms of tenure. Clusters of recreation lots can be leased around lakes and coasts, carrying covenants prohibiting year-round residency or limiting one lessee's tenure, so that recreation areas would not become full-fledged communities requiring major investments in services. Isolated wilderness cabin sites can be leased in carefully chosen areas to provide opportunities for extended wild-country experiences. Lease costs should be kept low to permit a broad spectrum of people to get land-use rights, and subleas- 195 ing should be prohibited or regulated to prevent speculation. The total number, density, and general design of leasehold developments can be controlled by classification and planning work done before leasing.

Alaska Natives soon will have full title to huge areas of land around existing villages. Conceivably, compelled by economic hardship, they might sell land for new residences. My guess is that such sales will be on the extremely small scale, with essentially no perceptible effect on settlement patterns except to accommodate modest growth around a few roadside villages.

From time to time the discovery of a major mineral deposit or oil field has led to proposals that the state work with the developer to build a new and permanent town. The 1975 molybdenum discovery near Ketchikan, the earlier fluorite-tin discoveries at Lost River west of Nome, and the Prudhoe Bay petroleum strike are examples. The owners of the Lost River properties succeeded in generating enough political approval to pass a law intended to both plan and subsidize such communities. Hardly anyone is enthusiastic about this idea today. Rural people don't want the intrusion or potential dilution of existing patterns of political power. Conservationists prefer a temporary work-camp approach that will heighten the chance that nature will return once the mine plays out. Existing towns do not want business activity drawn away, and government officials are leery of costs of services. Result: The Development Cities Act rests in peace.

Another set of policy levers for gaining settlement objectives relates to revenue-sharing programs. General-revenue sharing is popular with most communities because it reduces local taxes and can be used for almost any public service. Other revenue-sharing comes as grants or matching funds for specific local projects. Inevitably, a great deal of oil money coming into the state treasury will be diverted back into local communities through revenue sharing. Some problems with this process can be predicted. For example, shared revenues can stimulate gross community wealth without affecting per-capita wealth. Grants for specific kinds of utilities usually are accompanied by detailed restrictions on the kinds of systems (often emphasizing hardware) that a community can choose; in rural Alaska these often lead to oversized, costly, nearly non-maintainable utilities. The same kinds of effects could hit urban centers too, but urban leaders are better able to manipulate the revenue flows to avoid these problems, and the flows are much smaller in relation to overall city finances than they are in villages. In either case, the revenue-sharing process has potential for mischief as well as for becoming a prime instrument for guiding growth and improving the quality of community life.

The fifth and last area of policy leverage I will mention also deals with urban life: the creation of optimal town environments in Alaska's largest cities. The places most urgently in need of determined self-improvement programs are Anchorage and Faribanks; unfortunately the power of those who will gain most from unrestrained growth and the proportion of transients with no historic commitment or future interest in the community as home are also greatest in those towns.

In our society townspeople are responsible for planning the development of their own community. The state's role, however, is far from negligible. The state exercises police powers such as standard setting for air and water quality in accordance with federal guidelines, which influence municipal development choices. The state also has a powerful lever in funding transportation facilities, which gets right down to the fundamentals of community design and community character. Revenue sharing and grant programs can be directed toward maximizing municipal self-analysis and planning rather than to the delivery of loosely connected, often contradictory, packages of software or hardware.

As a neighboring landowner the state can help municipal- 197 ities carry out mutually wanted developments. Finally, state carrot-and-stick energy-conservation programs can influence the urban area's built environment at levels all the way from home design to neighborhood layout.

Alaskan city people want easy access to the countryside. There is good reason to encourage such a feeling: An urban population barred from intercourse with the landscape is likely not to pay much attention to its stewardship. This is of practical importance, considering the dominance of urban votes in Alaskan politics. It will be a difficult balancing act to encourage access to the countryside without unleashing pressures destructive to rural life and environments, and conversely to restrain access as necessary without turning the city to indifference or hostility. Selective encouragement of air travel to distant wildlands, maintenance of wild country very near city centers (as is now the case in Juneau and Anchorage, for example), and energetic, imaginative environmental-education programs in towns are several of many possible tactics.

CHAPTER VIII

Wildlife Stewardship

Vignettes:

. . . A shopper feeds pieces of bread to a raven in a Fairbanks parking lot.

. . . Three youngsters fishing for halibut from a dock in Juneau catch eighteen cod in twenty minutes. Each gleaming body is wrenched free of the hooks, slammed on the boards, and kicked into the sea to drift out with the garbage.

. . . A 30-06 bullet weighing 180 grains pulps the brain of a sleeping walrus. Knife and axe flash. The head is dragged to the boat by its ivory tusks, the huge body left to tip into the sea when the ice pan softens in the sun.

. . . For one sharp timeless moment the dawn moose fuses ancient memories in the watching couple. The moose vanishes into golden willows. The moment of revelation shatters, and the man and woman walk stiffly back to their camp.

. . . In season, salmon once ran redly up the dancing stream. Now the water dives through galvanized culverts and concrete girdles, febrile with the slops of hasty subdivisions. The salmon are gone.

The northerner treats wild animals ambiguously. Love, greed, disregard, oneness, otherness, curiosity, creativity: All are at and under the surface of both public and private relationships with wildlife. Sometimes the conquistador stalks. 199

Sometimes a wondrous event transforms, like that ephemeral flash of green at the instant of a perfect sunrise.

To many Americans the name Alaska is synonymous with wildlife. Alaska is the one state where — people believe — nature's cup overflows: salmon runs beating the streams to a froth, wolves howling at the gates of town, endless herds of marching caribou, and all the other symbols of an untrammeled frontier. No matter whether these visions are illusory, there is no mistaking the urgency of designing an Alaskan wildlife-stewardship program that combines a strong protectionist element with the more utilitarian aspects of harvest regulation and habitat conservation. What characteristics of northern wildlife provide the practical boundaries of such a program? What can be done not merely to save Alaskan wildlife but to build toward a fuller unity of man and nature?

The Nature of the Beast

Scarcity, not abundance, is the natural condition for wildlife in the North, an inescapable consequence of low annual plant production on land and in fresh water. Popular films and picture books have convinced many people all over the world that Alaska teems with wildlife resembling the landscapes behind plaster dinosaurs in museums. The illusion may be pleasantly harmless for the beleaguered city dweller who needs dreams of far green pastures, but it is a disaster for those who have to tend Alaska's natural resources.

There are other important features of boreal and arctic wildlife that have to serve as touchstones for stewardship.

For one thing, and in apparent contradiction to the fact of comparative scarcity, wildlife can be spectacularly abundant at some times and places. A few Alaskan environments are rich by any standards. These are almost entirely coastal or offshore marine areas: the southern Bering Sea with its huge groundfish, salmon, sea-bird, and marine-mammal populations; the eelgrass lagoons of the Alaska Peninsula; Kachemak Bay in lower Cook Inlet with its amazing shellfish and fish production. The sea is even the source of many of the famed onshore congregations of wildlife in Alaska, including the bald eagle flocks along the Chilkat River near Haines, the bears along salmon streams of Kodiak Island, Admiralty Island, and the Alaska Peninsula, and the huge sea-bird "bazaars" along coastal cliffs.

Other concentrations are strictly temporary or are part of the slow ebb and flow of cyclic species for which the North is famous. Caribou from thousands of square miles gather in post-calving migrations. Sandhill cranes soar and glide along the north side of the Alaska Range in clangorous spring flocks. Lemmings scurry through countless runways in the short tundra mosses and sedges in the peak years, only to disappear in a few months. Snowshoe hares increase one hundredfold in four or five years, then vanish from all but scattered islands of sanctuary. White-winged crossbills, red squirrels, goshawks — these and other wildlife fluctuate dramatically in a few years' time. Some of the management implications of local or temporary abundance seem clear, but others are not. Places where animals traditionally congregate obviously need the utmost protection from destructive change. The animal congregations themselves attract hunters or watchers, both requiring careful control.

How to respond in hunting or trapping regulations to cycles or other year-to-year population changes is more of a puzzle. Many wildlife managers believe that harvests ought to rise even faster than wildlife numbers when a game species is on the upswing, then become very restrictive at the population nadir. In this way, the idea goes, fluctuations will be "dampened." Just exactly why they should be, is uncertain. If northern ecosystems consist of or have produced sharply varying stocks of many species, there may be good reason not to tamper. Perhaps plants grazed or browsed by wild herbivores need time to recover strength (nearly all are perennials, depending on nutrients stored in roots, tubers, bulbs, and buds to start growth the next year). Perhaps predatory forms depend on once-in-a-decade surges in prey abundance to nourish an exceptionally big crop of cubs or kits or pups which carry the gene pool until the next fat time.

The rise and fall of wildlife in any one part of Alaska may be the result of another key biotic feature, migration. By far the majority of birds that amaze tourists by their summer abundance leave Alaska in fall to wing to a distant wintering ground. Some mammals migrate out of the state or its inshore waters, too, like bats, some caribou, polar bear, bowhead and gray and other whales, and fur seals. King salmon caught off Yakutat in the eastern Gulf of Alaska are from stocks reared in Washington and British Columbia, an exceptional example of the not uncommon long-distance migration of fish. Migration makes Alaskan wildlife stewardship a national and international matter, the Bering Sea marine mammals shared with Russia and the "Porcupine" caribou herd of Yukon-Alaska being only the best known of many examples. Sacramento Valley rice farmers and Yukon Delta Eskimos are partners in the use and care of the hundreds of thousands of ducks, geese, shore birds, and perching birds that winter in the one place and summer in the other. Whistling swans from the North Slope winter in Chesapeake Bay.

Another generalization about Alaskan wildlife management reflects both human frailties and natural conditions: that it is rarely feasible to manipulate or improve wildlife habitats on a significant scale. For one thing, we simply don't know how. The intimate and detailed knowledge of wild animals and the systems they contribute to is not available. (Some will say that salmon enhancement programs are an exception, but, even there, millions of dollars' worth of trial and error have let fishery biologists re-create or improve the environment of salmon only during the early part of the fresh-water phase of this complicated life cycle.) For another, even if we knew how, the cost of changing ecological conditions over big areas for wild-life benefits alone is astronomically larger than the payoff. Dam builders talk glibly of mitigating losses to wildlife, but the talk is empty.

Alaskan wildlife habitats differ widely in their inherent stability. Arctic and alpine tundras, which cover over half of the state, are comparatively stable in the sense that the general character of a tundra range does not vary much from one decade to the next. Trees and tall shrubs are nibbling at the margins of tundra in the Kodiak Island–northern Alaska Peninsula region and in small areas of the Gulf of Alaska coast where glaciers have just retreated, but the bulk of tundra is unaffected. Tundra fires, much less frequent than forest fires in interior Alaska, occasionally destroy ancient plant communities and set in motion a half century or more of natural reconstruction. The universal conflict of land and ocean adds a note of dynamism to arctic ecosystems as lagoons form and fill, beaches advance and retreat, deltas build, and cliffs erode. But neither fire nor sea nor glacial whimsy greatly changes the tundra during the span of several human generations.

The only human activity which in recent times has put a strain on tundra systems over any extensive area is reindeer herding. Reindeer were brought to Alaska from Siberia in the 1890s to provide Eskimos with a substitute for depleted marine mammal and caribou populations. The herds increased phenomenally to 630,000 head by 1932, far more — as herders soon learned — than the tundra ranges could support for long. Lichens and other forage plants of western coastal tundras were badly abused. Starvation struck the herds. By 1952, less than 30,000 reindeer had survived. Recovery was slow; in 1967 there were just over 37,000 reindeer in Alaska. Caribou disappeared from most reindeer ranges. Doubtless all other tundra animals were affected too, but their responses to the 203 reindeer catastrophe went unrecorded. Reindeer grazing, like caribou grazing, is a natural force to which tundra life is adapted. Trouble comes when human actions subsidize reindeer long after the tundra cries "enough!"

The old-growth coastal forests from Cook Inlet to Ketchikan are also very stable places for wildlife to live, being essentially free of fire and only fractionally affected by avalanches and windstorms that topple ancient spruce and hemlock. Only logging has significantly affected these forest habitats.

The Interior forests are a different matter. The interplay of fire and frost keeps the boreal forest in a state of continuous change readily measured in one man's memory. On the average, over a million acres of Interior forest and scrub have burned every year for the past seventy-five years. Most of the forested Interior has burned at least once in this century. The result is an extraordinary mosaic of habitats, limited in number of dominant species but almost limitless in variety of plant combinations and ages. We cannot yet define how each species of wildlife is affected by fire and subsequent habitat changes. In a general way, though, we know that some animals like caribou, red squirrels, spruce grouse, and white-winged crossbills need old-growth forests at some seasons, while moose, hares, and white-crowned sparrows (to name only a few) need regenerating sapling and shrub growth to reach maximum abundance.

Marine mammals numbering hundreds of thousands and sea birds numbering tens of millions live in the Alaskan ocean ambit. Pollution has not yet greatly influenced these northern ocean areas, except where they are locally affected by town, cannery, oil, and pulp-mill wastes. Caution, however, is critical. No one knows to what extent global marine pollution by DDT, DDE, PCB, and other members of our modern alphabet brew has crept into the North Pacific and Bering Sea. The ocean habitat definitely has been changed by fishery exploitation, however, even if the effects of overfishing on birds and mammals are still a matter of speculation. The threat of future oil pollution from outer continental shelf and state coastal petroleum developments looms monstrous in the minds of most marine biologists today. If only a little oil and gas is found and that little is developed carefully the threat may prove a tempest in a teapot. If the predicted petroleum bonanza is struck and exploited in haste, northern ocean ecosystems could be crippled for decades.

Problems of Stewardship

What are the most crucial issues of wildlife stewardship in Alaska? The Kobuk Eskimo watching a float plane discharge a load of Anchorage hunters on Walker Lake would have one answer. The scholar pondering philosophies of Western civilization would have another. A dedicated member of a national wolf- or whale-protection society would disagree with both. A forester laying out a new timber sale near Sitka, a scientist cataloguing wildlife assets along a new oil pipeline route, and an angler just clipped behind the ear with his fellow salmon fisherman's lure would all see the problem in other ways.

There are, in fact, many levels and facets of reality. It is a fundamental truth that once man invented industry, industry re-shaped man into a form that does not know how to behave in nature, that has not re-cast his ethical systems to suit the new and desperate facts of life. It is also true that in Alaska the coming together of subsistence and industrial cultures in political forums merely masks the chasm between them in terms of full understanding. These realities, nevertheless, are too basic to be dealt with explicitly by either citizen or public servant; they are the stuff of subconscious nightmares and academic intellectualizing. At the surface of practical reality are three issues most people would name as their focus of concern: economic and population growth, intensification and widening of 205 the scramble among wildlife interest groups, and the federalizing of land-use, environmental-protection, and wildlife decisions.

Growth: More of Us, Less of Them

Everywhere on earth, wild things have had to move out and die away in the face of expanding human numbers. Oh, yes, a few species, several of them universally disliked, prosper in the heart of towns. A few more find good livings in suburbia, on farms, and in cultivated forests. But the majority survive in forgotten corners or with thinned ranks in second-grade environments. Increasingly, some become extinct.

Until recently, Alaska was one of the world's corners, not totally forgotten but very little disturbed. Now there is no "away" for wild things to go to; if oil men don't get there, wilderness safaris will. Not that I foresee immediate doom for wildlife or near-term desolation of tundra and forest, but there is no denying the dramatic intensification of land uses set in motion by wealth and human population growth. Much more of our wildlife will live in modified environments, in more frequent contact with people, than ever before. The survival of wild landscapes will be the result of conscious human decision, not accident. Which species will adapt to this new situation, and which will not? We can make some good guesses for some species. Ravens are apparently as happy in garbage dumps as at moose carcasses, but gyrfalcons are very vulnerable to nest disturbance; red squirrels can be numerous in suburbs, but grizzlies cannot. For the great majority of wildlife, however, the answer depends on the style and pattern of growth.

To most Americans it may seem odd to the point of incredibility that anyone is concerned about growth in Alaska. If Montana is mostly wilderness with three-quarters of a million people in 147,000 square miles, how can a place with less than half a million people in almost four times the area be crowded?

Crowding is relative — a matter of mind and psyche more than absolute quantity.

Alaska is crowded relative to what it used to be within easy modern memory. *In Barrow:* Whaling captains were few and greatly respected until 1974. Now, though not quite a dime a dozen, captaincies are not hard to buy with pipeline wages, and are consequently worth less. The ice is starting to get crowded. *In Clam Gulch, Kenai Peninsula:* At the time of statehood, a family could be alone on the razor-clam beaches on a good tide. Today the minus tides of spring bring hundreds to the mudflats, and the clams hide deep. *On the Noatak:* The river didn't carry a canoe from one year to the next until publicity generated by park proposals in the 1970s drew party after party to that far northwestern tundra valley. Examples are almost endless.

Crowding is also a function of supply and demand. Alaska's supply of wildlife is surprisingly limited. The demand for wildlife, on the other hand, is high. Per capita consumption of game meat is far higher than anywhere else in the nation. Because rural Alaskans eat so much game (far more than store meat) and because urban Alaskans hunt more often and (in terms of big animals) more successfully than other Americans, I venture that 420,000 Alaskans use as many pounds of game as 20,000,000 Americans living in other states.[1]

Crowding is a behavioral phenomenon, too. Alaskans outdoors tend to resemble a fire ant in a sleeping bag: Bulk doesn't count for as much as activity. The average Alaskan's outdoor manners are abysmal, judging from debris at campsites and the thoughtless roar of unmuffled snowmobiles that has racketed across my solitude so many times. The imagined freedoms of the imagined frontier turn many Alaskan hunters and fishermen into greedy usurpers of a startling number of physical and psychological resources.

Finally, crowding relates to expectations. No one expects 207 the rewards of Daniel Boone at Coney Island in summer, but the northerner has come to expect them any weekend. We anticipate the looming vastness of uninhabited miles to spread out from any hilltop lookout. We plan to paddle all day without seeing the aluminum spoor of earlier voyageurs on the rocks. We expect frequently to come to a place and a time when there is no sound, an unheard-of experience in the temperate world. Growth robs us of these things.

It is not easy to say whether growth has already diminished the abundance of Alaskan wildlife; there are too many confounding factors. Migratory birds, for example, are probably more seriously affected by harvests and habitat changes in other states, Mexico, and central America than in Alaska. And when big game numbers seem to have declined as moose, caribou, and mountain goats have done in many parts of the state since 1970, nothing so simple as "growth" is the cause. Counting techniques are so unreliable that population changes of 50 percent in a year are arguable, changes of 30 percent are barely significant, and changes of less than 20 percent are rarely detectable. At best, the modernizing and urbanizing of Alaska has not *increased* wildlife in general, even if a few species have benefited from garbage and fires. And despite greatly improved access to wildlife country for subsistence and sport hunters, despite a continuing increase in the number of people hunting, and despite the spending of more time afield by the average urban hunter, harvests of major game species have stayed the same or declined in the past ten years. This does not sound like the early stages of exploration of a frontier; it sounds like saturation.

The Expanding Conflict

Crowding, real or imagined, is generating conflicts in the use of Alaskan wildlife. So is the current and drawn-out settling of land ownerships in the state, a process that started in earnest at statehood, accelerated with passage of the Alaska Native Claims Settlement Act in 1971, and peaked in the national-interest lands issue in the final stages of resolution in 1978. People are battling to protect their wildlife interests for all time by supporting the landowner they think is most likely to take their side in the future. It is hard to separate actual from feared conflicts, and in political terms there is little to choose between them.

Anyone who has watched the Alaskan wildlife conservation scene for the last two decades will have seen three striking changes in wildlife interest-group activities. For one, national wildlife organizations are more intensely involved than ever before. Second, photographers, birdwatchers, hikers, tourists, schoolchildren, scientists, and other so-called "nonconsumptive" interests have become much more vocal. And third, subsistence resource users, especially Natives, have suddenly begun to use political weapons to protect their interests. A little more discussion of these changes will reveal why they have come about and what concerns and conflicts are at the forefront of wildlife stewardship today.

National citizen organizations interested in wildlife conservation have been involved sporadically in Alaskan affairs for many years. To give just a few examples, various sets of these groups tried to force the territory to eliminate bounties on bald eagles in the late 1930s and early 1940s, favored appropriations for wolf-poisoning campaigns in the early 1950s, spoke in behalf of a preserve for brown bear on Admiralty Island, and opposed a huge hydropower dam at Rampart, on the Yukon River, in the early 1960s. Since the late 1960s, however, national groups have become more concerned about a broader range of wildlife issues in Alaska. Today the Sierra Club, Wilderness Society, National Audubon Society, and Friends of the Earth are the largest among an array of conservation groups with Alaska at the top of their agendas. Their 209 prime concern is to protect wildlife environments from destructive developments. In many cases, this means to persuade federal agencies or Congress to establish refuges, parks, or Wilderness areas, thus providing wild-country recreation as well. Another strong interest, but one voiced more stridently by groups like Defenders of Wildlife and Friends of the Animals, is to prevent the killing of wolves, furbearing mammals, and marine mammals.

It is natural that national organizations, especially those with only a loose (or no) locally organized membership but with strong centralized leadership, should prefer to deal with one Congress rather than fifty state legislatures, and with half a dozen federal agencies rather than several hundred in the states. National conservation organizations, therefore, have looked for countrywide solutions to issues of concern to them. The result is a transfer of power from states to the federal government; wildlife decision making has become "Washingtonized," to borrow some atrocious argot from the city on the Potomac. There are gains and losses in this process. Politically, organized national groups and their local affiliates gain access to future decisions at the expense of local interests without national lobbies. Because most funds for federal wildlife management come from taxpayers, federal managers can answer to a broader range of constituents without threat of a "revolution" by one interest group. However, legislation to shift responsibility to federal agencies often is not accompanied by the money to do so; this, plus the tailing off of state-level management which obviously attends loss of jurisdiction, and lack of expertise by newly assigned federal employees, can result in less effective resource conservation. In some situations federal jurisdiction is necessary because international or interstate levels of control are demanded.

The best example of the mixed effects of nationalized wildlife jurisdiction is the complex of changes following signing of the Marine Mammal Protection Act in 1972. The act grew out of popular support from people outraged at widely publicized (and not always accurately portrayed) instances of marine mammal mistreatment or harvest. The plight of whales, the clubbing of seals off Canada's Atlantic Coast, the state-authorized sport harvest of polar bears off Alaska's northwest coast, and the slaughter of dolphins in tuna nets in the Pacific are the most widely known examples. Oddly enough, the act as written had little or no effect on whales or Canadian sealing and did not stop polar bear harvests, but instead shifted them from sport to subsistence hunters. The act took management authority from coastal states and gave it to the secretaries of Commerce and Interior, the latter getting jurisdiction over walrus, polar bear, and sea otter, the former over seals, sea lions, whales, and dolphins. The law prohibited general harvests of marine mammals except by Alaska Natives and tightened controls over imports of marine-mammal products. It provided a process whereby states could regain partial management authority under constant surveillance by the federal government.

A great deal of good may come from a number of provisions of the Marine Mammal Protection Act. The treaty-making power of the President and Congress could be beneficial in working out international problems relating to polar bears, many whales and porpoises, ribbon seals, walrus, and bearded seals, to cite North Pacific examples. Congressional interest has channeled small amounts of money to marine-mammal research, and this funding might increase with time. After a fumbling, controversy-strewn start, federal, judicial, and industry efforts have cut the incidental killing of porpoises by American tuna boats from 300,000 in 1972 to about 30,000 in 1977. (Foreign-flag boats catch a small but increasing share of yellow-fin tuna, however, and these vessels kill many more porpoises per ton of tuna than do U.S. boats.) There is a general gain in statutory authority to protect marine mammals from excessive direct harvests, but this is still an illusory benefit rather than a practical one because few people have been hired to enforce the law and regulations.

In other ways, the act has not been such a good thing. When Alaska lost authority to manage marine mammals it largely lost incentive to continue its research. After five years, and despite the serendipitous injection of federal research money for marine mammals through the Outer Continental Shelf Environmental Assessment Program, this research momentum is still not regained. The same is true of enforcement efforts. State biologists and enforcement officers, intimately familiar with the biological and social aspects of marine-mammal use, had built up an invaluable prestige among Native and non-Native hunters of seals and walrus. This was lost. The few federal replacements — many of them not even resident in Alaska — have little appreciation of the human context of marine-mammal management.

Many people who supported the act and voted for it thought they were eliminating what they saw as unnecessary, cruel, or biologically dangerous harvests. What really happened was that fairly well controlled harvests by sport and subsistence hunters were displaced by poorly controlled hunts by Aleuts, Eskimos, and Indians under a loosely phrased "subsistence" provision. Harvests and waste of walrus have increased as hunters have killed to get ivory. The harvest of polar bear went up to 150 in 1976 when ice conditions brought the bears closer to shore than normal.

Without doubt the most troublesome Alaskan marine mammal problem is the conservation of bowhead whales. These huge baleen whales, growing to sixty feet in length, are very scarce as a result of commercial whaling for the half century beginning in 1848 in the Bering Sea and North Pacific. After commercial whaling had killed itself off, Eskimos continued to take an average of eight or nine bowheads per year until about 1967. The whale meat was tremendously important for a half dozen remote coastal villages from St. Lawrence Island to

Kaktovik on the northern Yukon border. To be a whaling captain or respected crew member was to have the highest possible social status in the traditional village. Then in 1968, and especially in the mid-1970s, whale harvests rose dramatically. Perhaps there were more whales, but certainly there were more whalers, their ranks swelled by young Eskimos whose pipeline wages could buy a boat and gear. As more whales were beached more meat was wasted, and more whales were shot but never recovered.

Meanwhile, the International Whaling Commission had been warning the United States since 1972 that known stocks of bowheads were so low (estimates ranged from 600 to 1500) that the subsistence harvests had to be controlled or stopped. The Department of Commerce did nothing effective either to regulate the hunting or to get credible population estimates. The crisis came in June 1977 when the IWC imposed a moratorium on all killing of bowheads, effective in the fall. Technically the United States could object and permit the hunt to continue, but to do so threatened collapse of the painstakingly developed commission power and credibility of the Scientific Advisory Committee. Backlash effects on sperm whaling and other whaling by reluctant whaling nations in IWC were a clear possibility. The United States did not object, but immediately asked the commission to allow a small and controlled harvest in 1978. The commission agreed to establish a quota of 12 whales beached or a total of 18 struck, a number half again as high as the average take in the first half of the century. Back in Barrow, militant Eskimo spokesmen who vowed that the hunt would go on without regard to a quota seemingly invited one of the bitterest confrontations over wildlife regulations in modern times, comparable to the "Washington Fish War" still making headlines.

The Marine Mammal Protection Act did not cause the bowhead controversy, but it did nothing to prevent or ameliorate it. The research and enforcement supposedly provided by the act did not materialize. More significantly, the exemption of Natives from the general prohibition on harvests gave a racial overtone to the problem, which state wildlife regulation had tried to prevent. And finally, the act and the interrelated Endangered Species Act of 1973 failed to show how a scarce animal and a waning but valuable culture could, together, find their way through a maze of vague and conflicting legal definitions and national and international politics toward a reasonable state of mutual conservation. The bowhead issue is only a beginning; headhunting for walrus by Native Alaskans is likely to follow close in its wake. Sea otters, the smile givers of the sea, also can be killed legally for subsistence purposes, including commercial sale of pelts. A real potential for bitter and explosive confrontation lies in the tangled kelp beds of Public Law 92-522.

There are many other examples of how jurisdiction over wildlife is moving toward Washington, D.C., but in Alaska one stands out among the rest. This is the proposal, in conservationist and administration bills on the national interest lands, to put the Secretary of the Interior at the center of subsistence harvest decisions in Alaska. On the surface the proposal seems to deal with a very limited aspect of wildlife regulation: It refers only to subsistence harvest, applies only to federal lands important for subsistence, and has a provision for the state to do the regulating if it toes the federal mark. However, these limitations do not confine the issue as much as an outsider would think. For one thing, subsistence harvests occur practically everywhere that harvestable fish or game exists, and include every species of interest to recreational hunters and fishermen as well as to numerous others. Second, most of rural Alaska is and will be federally owned, so that the geographic coverage of the action, while not complete, is very extensive. And third, the language which permits the secretary to return limited authority to the state makes the terms rather unattractive to Alaska. The state could very well decide not to bother.

If this provision becomes law and the state refuses to apply for a return of authority, rural Alaska will have a federal regulatory process for subsistence hunting and fishing on federal lands, a state-run process for all kinds of wildlife harvests on Native and State lands, and a hybrid federal-state process for nonsubsistence harvests on federal lands.

The alleged purpose of this proposal is to protect subsistence harvests, giving those uses clear priority over commercial and recreational uses. There is a certain logic in using national-interest lands legislation as a vehicle because it is a part of the many provisions of the Alaska Native Claims Settlement Act, and most subsistence users are Natives. National conservation groups have supported the transfer of subsistence regulation authority to the federal government partly to befriend Native spokesmen who favor this approach (and who might help conservationists get new refuges and parks established via this legislation) and partly as an expression of their general preference for federal pre-eminence in wildlife and other environmental matters. Little thought has been given to the way such a system would work: whether it would correct an interest-group imbalance or exchange one imbalance for another, and whether wildlife itself would benefit or suffer in the long run.

No one can define subsistence — much to the dismay of law-writers and to the benefit of practicing lawyers — but, in Alaska, everyone knows in his own mind what it is. The economic core of subsistence is simple enough: the direct use of wild foods and other products without the exchange of money; but the all-important cultural penumbra defies analysis. The simple way out is to argue that subsistence is exclusively an activity of Natives. By definition, then, any harvest of fish or game for home consumption by Natives using traditional methods is subsistence. Unhappily, traditional methods either are long abandoned and not wanted back or have to be re-   215 defined to include the new traditions of rifle, explosive harpoon gun, motorboat, snowmobile, and (arguably) airplane. The notion of subsistence under this usage would embrace the Native, with an annual salary of $40,000, who hunts geese in spring after chartering an airplane to carry him to and from the marsh. In fact, there may be a strong and psychologically important residue of cultural memory in such an activity which gives the experience a different and fuller meaning than it would have for a California sportsman. If that kind of definition is used to give one group highest priority among people competing for a shrinking resource, however, no one should expect calm acceptance by the people given second consideration.

The basis for the difficulty is that powerful pressure is being exerted to define subsistence in law at the precise time that the phenomenon itself is in bewildering flux. There is no such thing as a pure subsistence lifestyle in North America anymore. That is no reason to belittle or to fail to protect lifestyles, partly subsistence in nature, that are so common and so deeply cherished by rural northerners. While urban people commonly hold the view that the subsistence culture is inevitably and rapidly declining, many rural people disagree that it is or should.

The spectrum of partial subsistence is broad. At one end are older Yupik Eskimos of the outer Yukon-Kuskokwim deltas, living with a few hundred dollars in cash per year in a region of exorbitant costs, surviving by netting fish, trapping fur animals for meat and pelt, and living in high summer on berries and birds. At the other end is the educated non-Native who sets aside a good job to spend a year or more with his family at an old trapper's cabin, deeply fulfilled by the joy of learning ancient survival techniques and fending for themselves. In between are people who in summer fish commercially and in winter subsist; bearded youngsters fleeing the Great American Dream to adopt, at least for a while, an older dream; once and future Native pipeline laborers now at home with family elders 300 miles from the nearest Chrysler Imperial; a Scotch-Eskimo governor's wife who sets salmon nets in Bristol Bay in July; and gruff innocent old miners in log cabins along remote creeks.

These lifestyles cannot be protected without sacrifice. Much land and water are required to produce the goods of subsistence; those who would use the land and waters in ways that would reduce productivity obviously would be curbed. The share of fish and game allocated to subsistence cannot also go to commercial fishermen, guides, commercial trappers, sport hunters, or anglers. And to the extent that wildlife harvests diminish the value of wildland to scientists or hikers and photographers, they, too, are losers. On the other hand, the winners are not only the subsistence participants but all who gain allies in trying to keep land in its natural state: tourists, recreationists, conservationists, commercial fishermen, and others. (It is interesting to speculate about the reduction in intensive land use and energy in *other* states made possible by Alaskan subsistence. Every ton of wild game and fish eaten by rural Alaskans is a ton less of livestock that needs to be raised, less sage and pinyon chained to make room for range cattle, less fertilizer and pesticides used, less corn required, less energy consumed in shipping.)

Both the State of Alaska and the federal government have agreed that subsistence participants should have highest priority among those who want to harvest fish and game. The federal approach at this stage is very uncertain, but the overall tendency seems to be to define subsistence and give priority to it in law and to fix, in law at least, the basic outline of month-to-month resource decision making. The most discussed definition of subsistence would encompass, for all practical purposes, only Natives who were subsisting as of 1971 (when the Alaska Native Claims Settlement Act passed) and their direct descendants. The state, on the other hand, has relied on regulations and administrative policy to give preference to people dependent on fish and game. The state has successfully avoided discriminating on ethnic grounds, although the effect of numerous specific game regulations is to favor the rural person who, more often than not, is Native. It seems that the federal approach identifies a small and inevitably declining class of subsistence users; whereas the state's approach favors a slightly larger group in which shrinkage through emigration or rise in cash income of former participants can be balanced by entry of newcomers who want to adopt the lifestyle. The first strategy will lead to early disappearance of subsistence but has the advantage of limiting pressures on subsistence resources. The other approach encourages permanency of the subsistence interest but could lead to excessive entry and overexploitation or discouragingly small catch limits.

As is so often true, the right hand giveth and the left taketh away. Although both government levels give preference of harvest to subsistence users, they are less firm about protecting the resource base itself. Federal enthusiasm for offshore petroleum leasing (only slightly eclipsing the state's enthusiasm for leasing within the three-mile limit) does not seem affected significantly by the knowledge that massive petroleum development almost certainly will diminish marine fish and mammal stocks. The state's burgeoning program of hinterland acreage giveaways through homesites, homesteads, and open-to-entry lands can lead only to increased pressures on fish and wildlife stocks and habitats. Native regional corporations are perhaps just as eager as governments for economic development, a fact that has caused a good deal of unrest and disagreement within the total Native community. And these are not the only examples.

Subsistence interests cannot win every time, but they do need to be let into the game. The most basic complaint of rural Natives, perhaps, has been that they are unable to take part in wildlife decision processes on a par with other interests. Because it was a state process they had lived with and criticized,

Natives tended to support federal control of harvests on federal lands. The state made a serious effort to win them back by offering major reforms in regulatory systems, including financial support for travel to meetings. The political dilemma is that giving more power to rural people erodes the power of urban hunters. At this writing the outcome of this tug-of-war isn't clear.

A paraplegic in a Rose Bowl game is no worse off than a conservation agency pursuing its mission without the support of its constituencies. The disenchantment of subsistence groups with the Alaska Department (and regulatory boards) of Fish and Game is a serious problem. So is the growing hostility of so-called nonconsumer interests toward the state wildlife-management agency. (In a true ecological sense every human is a consumer of wildlife and wildlife habitats; as popularly used, the term "nonconsumer" identifies someone who likes wild creatures but does not shoot, hook, or net them.) These interests are pounding on the doors of all state conservation agencies of the nation. In my view the agencies' only choice is to unlatch their doors or watch the hinges give way.

Nonconsumer interests tend to picture federal officials in white hats (or at least gull gray). Historically, many federal wildlife programs have had a protective cast, as, for example, the national wildlife-refuge system, the migratory-bird treaty programs, enforcement of import prohibitions on whale products, furs, or rare animals, and endangered species preservation. Philosophically contradictory federal functions such as predator and rodent destruction have been loudly criticized by many wildlife interests, but at least the center of gravity of U.S. Fish and Wildlife Service programs has been favorable to nonconsumers. In contrast, the states have been involved primarily with the use of common resident species large enough to hunt or to catch with rod and line. Their funds have come from sportsmen, and, not surprisingly, their attention has rested on that constituency.

Sometimes it is hard to tell what nonconsumers want   219

Alaska's wildlife managers to do. Various groups have asked the Department of Fish and Game to manage small urban-fringe parcels of land for general wildlife preservation and recreation; for areas closed to hunting so that wild animals will be more easily seen by travelers; for raptor studies; to eliminate bounties; to stop aerial hunting of wolves and polar bears. The department has done all of these things, though not always as enthusiastically or often as their critics would like. Recently nonconsumer interest advocates have begun demanding a total shift in management orientation from *species* to *ecosystems*. Exactly how any agency can manage ecosystems is unclear to advocates, scientists, and disbelievers alike. How a department, with no mandate or authority to manage large blocks of land and with next-to-no influence over land-use decisions made by other landowners, can manage ecosystems, is an even greater puzzle.

Probably the specific things that the Department of Fish and Game is doing that nonconsumers do not like (or is not doing that they want to be done) are less important than the perceived difference in attitude toward wildlife. The game programs (and the term is significant) of the department are dominated by the thinking of people who read Aldo Leopold's treatise on game management as the art of producing wild crops for harvest but who didn't go on to read *Sand County Almanac* with its eloquent argument for a full conservation ethic. Result: Over the years, department spokesmen have acted as though any unharvested surplus of moose or deer or caribou was an affront to their professionalism. They have argued to gain approval for cow moose hunts, often with reasonable biological justification but in the face of public outrage. They have exchanged bitter memos with federal landowners on those rare occasions when the landowning agency wanted to reduce vehicular access to backcountry to maintain wilderness qualities, when the department spokesmen saw only the reduction in ease of hunter access. The department's staff lobbyist in

Washington, D.C., during the national-interest land battles continually opposed Wilderness designations and new parks in areas where sport hunting would be affected. None of this is wrong in the context of orthodox, sustained-yield–oriented wildlife management, but all of it rubs anti-hunting and non-consumer interests precisely the wrong way.

Wolves provide a marvelous study of rapid change in public and agency attitudes toward wildlife. The change from loathing to love which for the nation as a whole took 300 years is being squeezed into 30 years of Alaskan history.

Wolves are built to kill large, hoofed mammals. The hoofed mammals are built to avoid being killed. Survival of both predator and prey depends on just the right degree of superiority of hunter over the hunted, and on just the right difference in birth rates between wolves and their prey. However, wolves and their quarry rarely are "in balance." Browse plants, ungulates, alternate prey, wolves, and other factors — especially snow conditions — interact bewilderingly. Yet despite constant imbalances the interacting species have thrived together for millennia. Humans enter the picture as competitors of wolves, as admirers of the predator and its prey, as wolf killers, and as modifiers of biotic communities. The management dilemma is to define for each unique situation the most desirable interaction between wolves, people, and the large herbivores, and to achieve those ends by practical and ethical means.

Alaskan sourdoughs and sportsmen in territorial days viewed wolves as intolerable competitors for moose, caribou, and other game. They expected the territory and the federal government to take steps to eliminate the predator. In response, Congress and the territory provided an essentially unlimited opportunity for hunters and trappers to take wolves, established a bounty system, and conducted wolf-control programs. The campaign of extermination that eliminated wolves from livestock ranges of the West was begun in Alaska to protect wild game.

Between 1915 (the year of the first bounty payments for wolves in Alaska) and 1958 (the last year before statehood), the territorial legislature appropriated $1,530,743 for wolf and coyote bounties. There are no reliable data on the number of wolves killed in Alaska in this period — certainly tens of thousands — but whatever the figure, the bounty system alone clearly could not provide the degree of wolf control public opinion demanded. Public agencies then undertook active wolf-killing programs. The territory's first full-time wolf-control agent was hired in the late 1930s, when predators became scapegoats for the sharp decline of reindeer, which had overgrazed the western Alaska tundra ranges. Responding to requests from the Alaska Game Commission, influential sportsmen out of Alaska, and even several national conservation organizations, Congress in 1948 appropriated $100,000 to the Fish and Wildlife Service for an Alaska-wide predator-control program. For the next decade, federal agents roamed the territory setting out cyanide guns and poisoned baits and shooting wolves from aircraft. These control efforts apparently did not reduce wolf populations severely except in a few areas such as the reindeer leases of western Alaska and the subalpine Nelchina Basin northeast of Anchorage. They did arouse public sentiment against the use of poisons, which affected public policy after statehood. In addition, the techniques of aerial hunting developed by federal hunters during the 1950s spread to civilian bush pilots; this, too, was to play a role in the debate over wolf management in the following decade.

As the new state took wildlife management responsibilities from the federal government in 1959 and 1960, new public attitudes toward wolves were interjected among the traditional ones. The state legislature continued the bounty program (which was popular among rural legislators as a local welfare program) and in the next eleven years paid $50 each for over 10,500 wolves presented for bounties. But the legislature also recognized wolves as game species, implying that wolves had

222

positive values and providing a basis for flexible, multipurpose, "sustained-yield" management. The legislature decided against establishing a predator-control agency in the executive branch. Instead, the Department of Fish and Game was given broad discretion to conduct control activities.

Together with the regulation-setting citizens' Board of Fish and Game, the department developed a management program based on the premise that wolves are economically and ecologically valuable members of the Alaska fauna, and that their control should be undertaken only in response to clear need. Although powerless to remove the bounty (which they officially opposed), the board established a summertime closure on wolves, instituted a permit system as a means of controlling aerial hunting, and set limits to the number of wolves hunters could kill.

In 1968 the Alaska legislature gave the Board of Fish and Game authority to designate areas where wolf bounties would be paid. The board closed the entire state except for the mainland of southeastern Alaska and the southern islands of that region. The action reduced wolf harvests, although high fur prices somewhat dampened its effect. The legislature enacted a law in 1968 requiring state agencies or persons to get written permission from the board before using poisons to take any wild animal. The only use of poisons on predators since 1968 has been by the federal agent on reindeer leases in Western Alaska.

Shooting wolves from the air is a highly volatile issue in the continuing debate over wolf management. Senior Alaskan wildlife biologists, searching for some way to reduce wolf numbers when predation on hoofed mammals seriously impeded recreational or subsistence game harvests, greatly prefer aerial hunting to bounties or poison. To some Alaskans and several national animal-protection organizations, however, aerial shooting is simply unethical. Public Law 92-159, passed by Congress early in 1972, purported to make aerial shooting illegal. Officials of the Alaska Department of Fish and Game argued that a loophole had been left in the law big enough to fly an airplane through. Still, in July 1972 Alaska's newly appointed Commissioner of Fish and Game announced that as a matter of policy the department would issue no more aerial hunting permits to citizens. The department's problem was to find alternatives to bounties, poisons, and aerial hunting when high wolf populations need reduction.

Before any such alternative showed up, caribou and moose numbers plummeted in several Interior and Arctic districts. In the Nelchina Basin and the Tanana River Valley south of Fairbanks, a combination of sport hunting, wolf predation, and severe snow conditions seemed to be basic causes. In northwest Alaska, subsistence hunting and wolves were the most likely immediate causes of the drastic drop in numbers (from about 250,000 in 1970 to about 50,000 in 1976) of the Western Arctic caribou herd. The Department and Board of Game cut back on caribou hunting despite powerful incentives to permit subsistence harvests to continue. State biologists believed that wolf numbers needed to be reduced as well. A thousand or more wolves loped across the cold plains of the Western Arctic, and in the Interior from one to several hundred wolves roamed the much smaller moose and caribou ranges. Sportsmen demanded severe wolf reductions, but several national animal-protection organizations filed suit in court to prevent any killing of wolves. Caught in the middle, the department killed fewer wolves than it thought desirable from the standpoint of easing pressures on moose and caribou, but more than wolf protectionists thought tolerable. By the end of 1977 there were definite signs that all ungulate populations were beginning to recover, but whether mild winters or wolf reductions could be credited probably will never be known.

As Alaska's population grows and big game populations struggle to maintain themselves, wolves and hunters will come into sharper competition. At the same time wolf protection interests will continue objecting to wolf trapping for fur and to wolf-reduction programs. The logical course of management, based on an attempt to please everybody, is to identify some areas where wolves are protected even when their prey gets scarce and hunting is poor, some areas where wolves will be killed when hunting and ungulates otherwise would be threatened. The problem is communication and acceptance. Outside animal protection people can't believe that wolves aren't as scarce in Alaska as they are in the other 49 states; even the news in 1973–74 that wolves killed at least 30 pet dogs in and around Fairbanks made no impression. Gaining their acceptance of this fact and the unique role of hunting in Alaska is an absolute essential if "the wolf problem" is ever to be diminished. On the other side, hunters and the department have to accept the fact that wolves, alive and unmolested, have unique symbolic value to an urbanized nation longing to retain some evidence of lost wild America.

Diversity and Quality

To biologist and concerned citizen many elements of Alaskan wildlife stewardship cry out for attention. For example, the ten-year struggle for ownership of the vast federal public domain has built an argumentative, self-assertive, often parochial and sometimes hostile attitude among contenders and their followers. Owners and prospective owners (and of course the root problem arises from the American concept of "ownership" itself) reject any suggestion of giving up an iota of sovereignty for the sake of unified wildlife conservation. Meanwhile, wild things live their lives in total disregard for the invisible squared boundaries that preoccupy people. Never has there been such a need for moods and mechanisms of cooperative management of wildlife and the land sustaining it.

Another need is to raise the influence of wildlife spokesmen in all land-use decisions. Very real improvements have come   225 about since Alaska became a state, partly through improvements of the federal side (Fish and Wildlife Coordination Act, National Environmental Policy Act, Water Pollution Control Act, Coastal Zone Management Act) and partly through such Alaskan laws as the Critical Habitats Act and Anadromous Fish Act, both of which require explicit wildlife considerations in certain instances of state land use. More are needed. One reserving to aquatic wildlife a certain minimum volume of stream flow and another setting standards for timber harvests on state and private lands are two of many critical improvements.

However, two elements stand out among all the rest in terms of their intimate connections to the most basic issue of all, reforming the man–nature attitudinal relationship. One is the need to change the source of state wildlife-management funding; the other is the search for quality of experience.

I have mentioned already that many of the conflicts over Alaskan wildlife result from the widespread belief that state management favors sport hunters because sportsmen pay the bills. And sportsmen do; since statehood they have funded over 90 percent of all sport fish-and-game programs of the Alaska Department of Fish and Game. There will be no permanent relief from these conflicts until all constituencies know they pay a fair share and can expect — as well as demand — fair treatment for their interests. As new sources of money are tapped there will be new directions in programs, new personnel to make them work, and a revitalization and diversification of the state wildlife agencies.

Congress is now seriously considering legislation to establish a so-called "non-game" funding program for states. Under one proposal, general tax revenues would go into this fund. Under another, new excise taxes would be levied on birdseed, binoculars, cameras, and other equipment used by wildlife photographers, birdwatchers, and wilderness buffs. In either case, the money would go to states meeting certain requirements for continued programs benefiting wildlife not shot or caught.

Alaska, unlike most states, should have the wealth to broaden and strengthen its wildlife and fisheries programs from general-fund monies. Whether from federal or state sources, general funds seem more logical sources than special taxes. General funds, for example, do not single out any wildlife interest group as either contributor or special beneficiary. Also, because every person imposes costs on wildlife and wildlife-management agencies and because everyone benefits from effective wildlife conservation, it seems an elegant symmetry to have every taxpayer contribute to management. General funds do have the disadvantage of having to be sought and justified in every budget request; whereas dedicated funds — once established — are more certain. Perhaps the best of all worlds from a security standpoint would be a dedicated share of general funds. Security may not be the only consideration, however, and there may be real long-term advantages in toeing the mark with each legislature.

In any case, if the Alaska Department of Fish and Game is to recognize all wildlife constituencies, to meet the full diversity of their needs, and to begin to move toward management founded on the understanding of ecosystems instead of stocks or species, both more and more diverse funds are essential.

The Alaska State Constitution commands that wildlife and fish be managed on a sustained-yield basis. The phrase "sustained yield" is a fascinating one. It rings with conservation principle and rests on utilitarianism. What could be more modern than to insist that all harvests of renewable sources be within the bounds of what the stocks can sustain indefinitely? Yet what could be more Bentham-like than to stress that nature must yield up its goods to man? Furthermore, wildlife and fisheries people interpreted the constitution to mean *maximum* sustained yield, although it nowhere says so. Considering the pervasive frontier thinking of Alaska at the time the constitution was drafted in 1955, that interpretation undoubtedly was accurate.

Nevertheless, the acceptance of maximum sustained yield as management's goal inevitably led to an overriding focus on quantity. Bring more big-antlered moose to the gun, let hunters shoot 20 ptarmigan a day, ask federal regulators to allow a few more ducks and geese in the bag, declare emergency openings on caribou when their migrating herds come close to roads after the normal hunting season is over — all these are evidence of the central focus on maximum harvest. Game biologists often envied commercial fishery managers because ethics scarcely entered the man–fish relationship and quality was something to worry about after the fish was in the net, while quality and ethics were sometimes nagging barriers to full utilization of game crops. (Ironically, it was a piece of federal commercial-fisheries legislation, the Fishery Conservation and Management Act of 1976, in which a new mandate for *optimum* sustained yield replaced the old touchstone. Although no one really knows what "optimum" is, it obviously is meant to be a smaller number than maximum and builds in a safer margin of unharvested fish.)

The focus on quantity often led to brinkmanship and, at least a few times, to near disasters to big game stocks when hunting pressure built up faster than managers realized. But in a much more fundamental way, quantity is absolutely the wrong objective in Alaska today with ecosystems of low productivity strained by increasing harvests and undermined by environmental disturbances. The solution, it seems to me, is to emphasize quality. Sport hunting and fishing are human experiences, not solely or primarily meat-gathering or economic activities. One way out of the overexploitation syndrome, then, is to make harvestable surpluses of wildlife go further by decreasing the amount of game or fish required to give the hunter satisfaction.[2]

What this entails is a far better understanding of the angling and hunting experience. What share of hunting and fishing satisfaction comes between expeditions through anticipation and memory and curiosity about nature? How can those satisfactions be heightened? What is there about particular settings for hunting and fishing that increase or detract from the field experience? What does this mean to land and water management? What is the interplay of solitude-seeking and company-seeking for particular types of sportspersons, and what implications are there for the channeling and dispersing of recreationists? If we knew as much about the human recreationists' setting as we do about wildlife habitats, management might be far more successful.

Philosophers debate the concept of quality and I pretend to no answers. It does seem, however, that sportsmen know quality of experience when it comes to them. With equal certainty they can recognize its absence. Therefore, if managers can't turn to theory they can at least turn to recreationists and, through trial and error, respond to their best instincts and highest sense of fitness.

If Alaska's population keeps growing and tourists keep coming north in greater numbers, the total pressure on freshwater fisheries and on wild birds and mammals will force greater limitations on numbers of sportsmen and nonconsumer recreationists afield in more and more situations. Many techniques for restricting participation are practiced in other states and a few have been used in Alaska. Quota hunts on lottery or first-come–first-served bases and the opening of streams to fly fishermen and certain lands to walking and horseback hunts only are examples. These are valuable but may not go far enough. We may have reached a time when the privilege of recreational fishing and hunting is given only to those who meet certain standards of understanding and ethics. Perhaps a testing system would be as valuable in Alaska as it seems to be in Scandinavian countries, where it has been in use for many decades. The tests would reduce the rate of growth in numbers

of anglers and hunters and improve the level of interest, understanding, and ability of those who get licenses.

Wildlife agencies also need to re-evaluate hunting and fishing regulations to curb abuses of the harvest privilege and to
evolve new standards of hunting and fishing ethics. Hunting
and angling are far more than curious relics of mankind's
million years as pursuers of game. They are — or should
be — expressions of a venerable and authentic relationship
between man and nature that are both relevant and important in
contemporary society. Making the modern practice of hunting
and fishing consistent with this truth is one of conservation's
greatest challenges.

An overall strategy for wildlife stewardship in Alaska, then,
has to center on changing the terms on which people interact
with nature. Nature cannot sustain itself under thoughtless and
intensive attacks by the machines and chemicals of human
technology. The protective side of stewardship has to be
armed with better laws and bigger field forces. From subsistence to science and from art to angling, beneficial uses in all
their diversity have to be balanced and encouraged so as to
strengthen wildlife's political prominence but restrained to
leave a broad margin of safety. Beyond protection and beyond
use, the search for quality of experience must be a constant
reference point for the public and the steward alike.

CHAPTER IX

Prospects and Promises

A rough-limbed apple tree once shouldered a stone wall in the back yard of my boyhood home. I would run across the lawn through the embrace of forsythias, jump onto the gray puddingstones, and pull myself from knot to limb until I reached the outer rim of leaves. From there the yard and hedges, the two-storied white house, and the scattered toys and tools became an understandable whole, the medium and message of my youth. From this perch I could look across to the western horizon and upward to the immediate sky. The possibilities of the future were visibly connected to the facts of the present.

What prospect opens through the leaves of this book? Is there a nearby whole to be understood, any future perceived?

Alaska today combines the shards of a vast and ancient sweep of history, the ample litter of more recent events, and the shadowy images of the future. A child of Point Hope, running from the Chukchi beach to meet the daily plane, skips across the playgrounds of a hundred generations of Eskimo children before her. She passes church, store, and school — God, Mammon, and the BIA — the spiritual, economic, and intellectual battalions of the white frontier. Two strangers, an oil man and a park planner, step out of the plane, each plotting a future for her and her village by the cold gray sea.

Time is supposed to be nature's way of preventing every-   231 thing from happening at once. In the North, time has failed. An old way of life that gathered things created yearly by the sun was overrun in two long lifetimes by another way that exploits accumulated treasures. That way, in turn, has been eroded in two decades by self-doubt, anxiety, and new global realities.

Time's compression has confused our values and made a shambles of our traditions. No village is so far, no family so secluded, as to have escaped the overwhelming change. Once land was self; now it is for sale. Now that survival depends less on knowledge of land than of machinery where is the need for respect of wind, water, ice, and rock? Who now dares to leave a well-stocked wilderness cabin? Was it only ten years ago that Fairbanks and Anchorage listened smugly to tales of nighttime fear in Los Angeles and Washington, D.C.?

The view from the apple tree also reveals a growing congestion of landscape, community, and spirit. Alaska's countryside, like the features of an aging actress, looks best from a distance. Vehicle tracks indelibly craze tundra and scrub. Rubbish pocks the emerald Aleutians. Gravel pits yawn beside roads and pipelines. Taffeta patterns of oil shimmer in harbors. In towns there is the feeling of elbows, a crowdedness having less to do with the number of people than with the cumulated chaos of myopic self-interest. Worst of all, our spirits are becoming imprisoned by a progressive narrowing and ossifying of interests, a denial of our full true measure of generosity, tolerance, and diversity. We are beginning to be strident, mean, greedy, and mulishly parochial in the face we show to the world.

The heart of the matter is *change*. Change is time, and time is inevitable. But is change malleable? Some people feel powerless, and fear change. Others think they are in control, and welcome change. In Alaskan politics these attitudes are central. Some voices, like Jay Hammond's, call for decelerated and selective change, and are belittled as blind battlers against progress. Other voices, like Wally Hickel's, speak boldly of progress when they merely want more of the same.

I believe in society's capacity to create futures. I think we can protect good things already achieved, encourage improvements in the human condition, and soften the blows unleashed on us from afar. What general kind of future should we strive toward? The one I prefer is a future emphasizing and protecting organic diversity of town and country, encouraging awareness and unity with natural processes, maintaining the freedoms of a small society, testing and evolving new relationships among different traditions and styles of living, striving toward individuality while rejecting provincialism.

The greatest challenge to our ability to create our own future is national and world demand for oil, gas, coal, and mineral resources that we have underground. Someday, perhaps, mankind's wants will be diverted from physical goods to spiritual goods, from wants that are environmentally destructive and socially disruptive, to those that are not. Until then the scramble is on and we have to cope with it.

One by one Alaskan oil fields and mines will be opened, used up, and shut down. We can compress or stretch out this era of exploitation, and the choice we make is absolutely crucial to the kind of future possible for the state (see Figure 2). I am convinced that Alaska's goals should be to keep the state's population as low as possible and to build the minimum number of new permanent communities, roads, and other fixed structures during the exploitation period. In choosing this course we reduce the loss of irreplaceable wilderness assets and dampen pressures on landscapes, seascapes, and wildlife. We also lessen the erosion of the renewable-resource base and maintain the relative political power of fishing, farming, logging, and tourism at maximum levels. We string out the time for specific resource-use decisions and, by decreasing the general rate of social change, increase every individual's ability to adjust to and cope with change. In the long run we reduce the   233

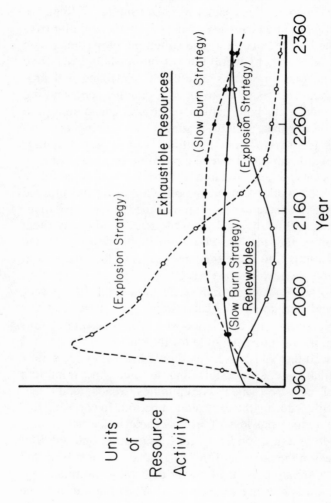

FIGURE 2. A perspective on three centuries of Alaskan resource activities with two styles of mineral exploitation. The total amount of petroleum, coal, and minerals extracted is the same in both cases. Production of renewable resources suffers under the accelerated mining approach, and state populations rise faster and decline more dramatically.

impacts of the inevitable collapse of each ore body and petro-leum province.

The points of leverage to accomplish those goals are the rate of exploitation of state-owned resources, the extent of local processing of raw resources, and the use of nonrenewable resource revenues. My answers to these issues are unequivo-cal: Extract as slowly as possible, ship resources south with a minimum of processing, and bank the biggest possible slice of nonrecurring revenues. We need to keep a speeding train from becoming a runaway.

Land-use and resource-exploitation strategies have to be in harmony. For example, it is essential to build a minimum number of interconnected highways to remote mines and oil fields. Today's massive government subsidy of highways should be diverted to systems with more flexibility and far less disruptive influence on rural living and wild country, like boats and airplanes. Whenever possible, mineral development projects should use work camps and temporary towns instead of permanent communities. Public land should not be home-steaded in patterns peppering the countryside with shacks, shantytowns, and "NO TRESPASSING" signs.

We need to treat the land as though it had standing in full equality with humanity. Land-use decisions must spring from the heart of the land as well as the people. What does the land tell us? The countryside and inland waters, lovely as they are, are relatively unproductive: "Don't expect too much of me," says the land. Northern plants and soils bruise and erode easily and recover slowly: "Treat me gently," says the earth. Cold northern waters and still northern airs pollute quickly and cleanse slowly: The land says "Don't dump on me." The North is an expensive place to live in southern comfort: "Ex-pect to pay a premium," says the land, "and beware of shortchangers."

Probably one of the hardest lessons we have yet to learn is how to judge the capacities of northern environments to absorb

235

use and how to guide actions to stay well within those bounds. Optimum must replace maximum, quality must replace quantity, and recreative experiences must replace recreation activities.

It is obvious that my choice of approaches to Alaskan development grows out of the assumption that nonrenewable resources are also exhaustible, and that our society in the long run will depend largely on nature's renewable bounty. Possibly I am wrong. Perhaps, as some economists think, resource hungers lead to the "creation" of new resources in a never-ending spiral of technological cleverness, indefinitely sustaining population and economic expansion. To me it would be much worse not to "run out" of resources soon, or at least come close enough to be frightened into sanity, than to postpone and infinitely exacerbate the day of reckoning. The population our cleverness "sustains" could learn to live crowded, but not without the loss of essentially everything unique about our way of life. Our style and depth of democracy, our personal mobility of social status and geography, our natural landscapes, would all have to go. The best we could hope for would be Simon and Garfunkel's Big Bright Green Pleasure Machine which, plugged into our mind, could recall our tribal memories of a vanished wilderness.

That isn't the kind of fate I want for Alaska. Nor, I gather from their unequivocal messages to me, is it what my wife and our children want. We want another kind of place:

A place where visitors from vast cities catch their breath at the frosted wine of alplands in autumn.

A place where the richest oceans in the world lap the salt-marsh and mussel-studded shingle.

A place where you know your neighbor.

A place where you matter.

A place where a young businessman can get a seat at the table, not merely a scramble on the floor for crumbs of a gargantuan feast.

A place where wolves speak to each other of fat moose and storms and dennings; where the sea spray rises to dapple the nests of eagles.

> *The woods are lovely, dark and deep,*
> *But I have promises to keep,*
> *And miles to go before I sleep,*
> *And miles to go before I sleep.*[1]

Notes
Index

Notes

Chapter I

[1] Don Dumond, *The Eskimos and Aleuts* (London: Thames and Hudson, Ltd., 1977).

[2] George Rogers, "Alaska Native Population Trends and Vital Statistics, 1950–1985," *Research Note* (Fairbanks: Institute of Social, Economic, and Government Research, University of Alaska, November 1971).

[3] Federal Field Committee for Development Planning in Alaska, Chapter 5, "The Land Issue," in *Alaska Natives and the Land* (Washington, D.C.: U.S. Government Printing Office, 1968).

[4] An informative summary of Alaskan mining history is in Chapter 8 of Ernest Wolff's *Handbook for the Alaskan Prospector,* 2nd ed. (Fairbanks: University of Alaska, 1969).

[5] Ernest Gruening, *The Battle for Alaska Statehood* (Fairbanks: University of Alaska, 1967).

Chapter II

[1] Jack Kruze, "Urban Impacts of Oil Development: The Fairbanks Experience," *Alaska Review of Business and Economic Conditions,* Vol. XIII, No. 3 (Fairbanks: University of Alaska, Institute of Social and Economic Research, 1976).

[2] Yupiktak Bista, *Does One Way of Life Have to Die So Another Can Live?* (Bethel, Alaska: Yupiktak Bista, 1974), see Introduction, pp. 4–7.

[3] Fairbanks *Daily News-Miner,* p. A-8, September 23, 1969.

Chapter III

[1] John Gulland, "Natural Factors Determining Potential Productivity of Northeast Pacific Fisheries," in *Alaska Fisheries Policy* (Fairbanks: University of Alaska, Institute of Social, Economic, and Government Research, 1972), pp. 117–129.

[2] Vera Alexander, "Phytoplankton Primary Productivity as an Indicator of Biological Status in Alaskan Freshwater Environments," in *Alaska Fisheries Policy* (Fairbanks: University of Alaska, Institute of Social, Economic, and Government Research, 1972), pp. 131–136.

[3] Division of Sport Fish, "Reports to the Board of Fish and Game" (Juneau: Alaska Department of Fish and Game), December 1970, p. 3.

[4] James King and Calvin Lensink, "An Evaluation of Alaskan Habitat for Migratory Birds," mimeographed (Washington, D.C.: Bureau of Sport Fisheries and Wildlife, November 1971).

[5] R.F. Taylor, "Yield of Second-Growth Western Hemlock-Sitka Spruce Stands in Southeast Alaska," *Technical Bulletin* No. 412 (Washington, D.C.: U.S. Department of Agriculture, 1934).

[6] J. Warren Wilson, "Arctic Plant Growth," *Advances in Science* (1957), 53:383–387.

[7] Robert Pegau, "Growth Rates of Important Reindeer Forage Lichens on the Seward Peninsula, Alaska," *Arctic* (1968), 21:255–259.

[8] Robert Pegau, "Succession in Two Enclosures Near Unalakleet, Alaska," *Canadian Field-Naturalist* (1970), 84:175–177.

[9] Arnold Schultz, "A Study of an Ecosystem: The Arctic Tundra," in *The Ecosystem Concept in Natural Resources Management* (New York: Academic Press, 1969), pp. 77–93.

[10] Ron Gordon, "Winter Survival of Fecal Indicator Bacteria in a Subarctic Alaskan River" (Fairbanks: U.S. Environmental Protection Agency, Arctic Environmental Research Laboratory, 1972).

[11] Oscar Ferrians, Jr., Reuben Katchadoorian, and Gordon Greene, "Permafrost and Related Engineering Problems in Alaska," *U.S. Geological Survey Professional Paper* 678 (Washington, D.C.: U.S. Government Printing Office, 1969).

Chapter IV

[1] Terence Armstrong, "The Northlands: The Scale of Development," mimeographed (Anchorage: American Society of Planning Officials, February 1975).

[2] David Kresge, "Alaska's Growth to 1990: Economic Modeling and Policy Analysis for a Rapidly Changing Northern Frontier Region," *Alaska Review of Business and Economic Conditions,* Vol. XIII, No. 1 (Fairbanks: University of Alaska, Institute of Social and Economic Research, 1976).

[3] *Proceedings of a Seminar on the Continental Use of Arctic-Flowing Rivers* (Wenatchee, Washington: Wenatchee *Daily World,* December 20, 1968).

[4] Hugh A. Johnson and Harold T. Jorgenson, *The Land Resources of Alaska* (New York: University Publishers, 1963); George Rogers, *Alaska in Transition: The Southeast Region* (Baltimore: The Johns Hopkins University Press, 1960); and Richard A. Cooley, *Alaska: A Challenge in Conservation* (Madison: University of Wisconsin Press, 1966).

Chapter V

[1] Adlai Stevenson, *The New America* (New York: Harper and Row, 1957), p. 260.

[2] John Gulland and Arlon Tussing, "Fish Stocks and Fisheries of Alaska and the Northeast Pacific Ocean," *Alaska Fisheries Policy* (Fairbanks: University of Alaska, Institute of Social, Economic, and Government Research, 1972), pp. 75–116.

[3] Summarized from George Gray, Jr., Robert Roys, Robert Simon, and Dexter Lall, "Development of the King Crab Fishery Off Kodiak Island," Alaska Department of Fish and Game, *Information Leaflet* No. 52 (April 1965), and from a letter of February 28, 1973, from Guy Powell, Division of Commercial Fisheries, ADFG (Kodiak).

[4] For example: E.O. Salo, "Study of the Effects of Logging on Pink Salmon in Alaska," Proceedings of the Society of American Foresters, Reprint A. No. 861, 1966, pp. 59–62; William Sheridan and William McNeil, "Some Effects of Logging on Two Salmon

Streams in Alaska," *Journal of Forestry,* February 1968, pp. 128–133.

[5] Richard Cooley, *Politics and Conservation: The Decline of the Pacific Salmon* (New York: Harper and Row, 1963).

[6] George Rogers, *Alaska in Transition: The Southeast Region* (Baltimore: Johns Hopkins University Press, 1960), pp. 287–290.

[7] A.S. Leopold and Reginald Barrett, *Implications for Wildlife of the 1968 Juneau Unit Timber Sale,* Report to U.S. Plywood-Champion Papers, Inc. (Berkeley: University of California, November 1972).

[8] Richard Behan, "The Myth of the Omnipotent Forester," *Journal of Forestry,* June 1966, pp. 398–401.

[9] Nunam Kitlutsisti, "Tourism's Ugly Head," *Newsletter,* Vol. 2, No. 4 (Bethel, Alaska: April 1976).

Chapter VI

[1] Thomas Morehouse, "Petroleum Development in Alaska: A Look at the Past, Present, and Future Potentials," *Alaska Review of Business and Economic Conditions,* Vol. XIV, No. 1 (Fairbanks: University of Alaska, Institute of Social and Economic Research, March 1977).

[2] David Kresge, "Alaska's Growth to 1990," *Alaska Review of Business and Economic Conditions,* Vol. XIII, No. 1 (Fairbanks: University of Alaska, Institute of Social and Economic Research, January 1976).

[3] T.S. Eliot, *Four Quartets,* Little Gidding, V.

[4] Arlon Tussing, "Opportunities for Cooperative Resource Management in Alaska," mimeographed (Anchorage: Joint Federal-State Land Use Planning Commission for Alaska, April 1976).

[5] Ernest Wolff, Nils Johansen, Chris Lambert, Jr., Edwin Rhoads, and Richard Solie, "Optimum Transportation Systems to Serve the Mineral Industry North of the Yukon Basin in Alaska," *Mineral Industries Research Lab Report No. 29* (Fairbanks: University of Alaska, 1973).

Chapter VII

[1] William Alonso and Edgar Rust, *The Evolving Pattern of Village Alaska* (Anchorage: Joint Federal-State Land Use Planning Commission for Alaska, March 1976).

[2] Harold Sparck, "The Other Village" (ms. sent to author by Sparck on March 17, 1977). Sparck is a member of the staff of the Association of Village Council Presidents, Bethel, Alaska.

[3] Judith Kleinfeld, *A Long Way from Home* (Fairbanks: University of Alaska Center for Northern Educational Research *and* Institute of Social, Economic, and Government Research, 1973).

[4] Transportation Planning Division, Alaska Department of Transportation and Public Facilities, *Work Program TQX–HPR–PR–1 (15), October 1, 1977, to June 30, 1978, Part 1* (Juneau).

Chapter VIII

[1] A 1974 report of the Federal-State Land Use Planning Commission for Alaska concluded that about 8000 people in Western Alaska harvested 700–900 pounds of red meat and fowl per person annually. Applying this to an estimated 20,000 rural subsistence people (but reducing the per capita consumption to 400 pounds to account for higher percentages of fish or lower total harvests in other regions) yields an annual harvest of 8,000,000 pounds. This is equivalent to the game consumption of about 16 million non-Alaskan Americans. I assumed further that the other 400,000 Alaskans ate at least 10 times as much game as the average American, making them equivalent in wildlife demand to 4 million non-Alaskans. These estimates are extremely rough but do not exaggerate the difference between northerners and other Americans.

[2] A growing number of articles by professional wildlife resource managers indicates that this perception is taking hold. A good example is "Quality Fishing: A Concept for Alaska Sport Fish Management," by Rupert Andrews, Director of Alaska's Sport Fish Division. This short article appeared in the Department of Fish and Game's *Fish Tales and Game Trails,* Vol. X, No. 2, March–April 1977. Another example is Robert LeResche's "Social and Ethical Considerations in Conservation," published in the Transactions of the 38th North American Wildlife and Natural Resources Conference (Washington, D.C.: March 1974).

Chapter IX

[1] Robert Frost, "Stopping by Woods on a Snowy Evening," *The Road Not Taken* (New York: Holt, Rinehart and Winston, Inc., 1951), p. 183.

Index